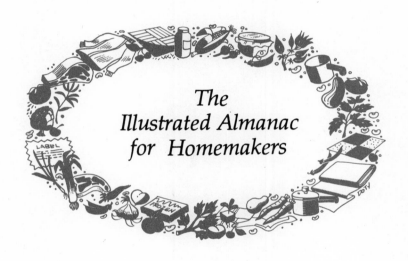

The
*Illustrated Almanac*
for Homemakers

# THE ILLUSTRATED ALMANAC for Homemakers

by Vera Kemp Stevenson and Robert P. Stevenson

Illustrated by Roy Doty

A Ridge Press Book / Grosset & Dunlap / Publishers / New York

Editor-in-Chief: Jerry Mason
Editor: Adolph Suehsdorf
Art Director: Albert Squillace
Associate Art Director: Harry Brocke
Managing Editor: Moira Duggan
Associate Editor: Mimi Gold
Associate Editor: Barbara Hoffbeck
Associate Editor: Kathleen Murray
Art Associate: Nancy Louie
Art Associate: David Namias
Art Production: Doris Mullane

For our sons:

John Kemp Stevenson
Who joined us first—
Whose gentleness of manner and
Joyous liking for others
Makes him
Beloved by all;

and

Peter Day Stevenson
Whose arrival made us complete—
And who now,
We are happy to see,
Dares to be different
From the crowd.

---

*"Home's not merely four square walls,*
*Though with pictures hung and gilded;*
*Home is where Affection calls–*
*Filled with shrines the Heart hath builded."*
—Charles Swain

---

*"Stay, stay at home, my heart, and rest;*
*Home-keeping hearts are happiest."*
—Henry W. Longfellow

---

# The Worth of Homemaking

Many books will help you be a better homemaker. This one will, too, but it is unique in that it organizes homemaking into a seasonal succession of activities. It brings together, in an orderly day-by-day sequence, practical and sometimes amusing information about the activities and duties that occupy a homemaker's time. It also proposes to make the homemaker herself a better person than she already is. In the fashion of old-time almanacs after which ours is patterned, we have spiced the flow of practical information with occasional surprising and interesting facts and historical notes solely for your reading amusement. That way, we think, most of us are more likely to remain in a happy mood as we accomplish today all of the necessary homemaking chores we really ought to complete today.

You can, if you wish, refer to this Almanac every day—or pick it up from time to time and browse through the appropriate weeks. Although this is by no means a cookbook, we have included occasional recipes that we think you may find timely, timesaving, or just plain interesting. All in all, our aim has been to lighten your work in as entertaining a manner as we can.

In number of persons involved (at least part time), homemaking is the world's leading occupation. A homemaker, the dictionary says, is one who manages a household. In our Almanac, we carry that definition further; we believe that every member of the family may be in part a homemaker, for each at times contributes to the joint effort of making a home out of living quarters. Our major concern, of course, is with the activities of the wife and (usually) mother.

The woman who makes the home is a prime asset of the family. Her role is extremely diversified. It embraces cooking, housecleaning, doing the laundry, rearing children, making household purchases, undertaking minor household repairs, working in the yard, gardening, and taking care of countless other details needed to keep the house in good running order. The wife/mother homemaker always shoulders the greater part of this load of managing the home whether or not she has an outside job.

The cash value of a homemaker's activities is often overlooked. Too often, in our opinion. Arriving at a fair and logical figure for such services admittedly is complicated. How can you equate dollars and cents with the love and patience that most homemakers contribute to all of their many duties? Putting this important factor aside, however, it is possible to develop cash values for the varied activities of a homemaker and place her on a theoretical salary basis.

A research team at Cornell University has evaluated household work on that basis. In making the study, Kathryn E. Walker and William H. Gauger observed that when household services are turned over to someone else "they have money value—the value of the time spent by the worker. The same services are just as valuable when provided by a family member."

The researchers first studied the hours that all family members devote to household activities. They then multiplied these total hours by prevailing wage rates for comparable work—domestic cleaning, dishwashing, cooking, laundry work, yard care, etc. In a typical family with three children (one of them less than a year old), the mother was found to contribute annual services worth $8,400. This was on 1971 wage rates. Since then inflation may very well have raised the total to $10,000 or more a year.

In the study, the housewife's daily time spent in home activities varied from a low of about four hours a day when she had no children and worked outside the home to a high of 12 hours daily—seven days a week—when she supposedly was "unemployed" and remained at home to take care of the household and seven or more children.

On the average, wives employed outside the home were found to devote two hours less time to household activities each day than wives who work only at home. The researchers concluded that "the causes of this reduction in time may be more efficient use of time, leaving some of the work undone, buying the services of industry (as in ready-prepared food), or hiring the services of a helper."

The researchers concluded that their figures show very clearly that it is the wife who contributes the giant share to household work, both in time and dollars. They decided:

"This is true whether or not she is employed.

The figures do not show that husbands increase their work contribution if their wives are employed. This points to an interesting conclusion. While one social convention—that against mothers working—has broken down, another social convention—one that labels most household tasks 'women's work'—leaves her with a disproportionate share of the household tasks. One can only speculate about how long it will take society to change its perception of household work responsibilities in order that there might be a more equitable sharing of household tasks."

How much help does the typical husband give? Not much. The report said that the husband's time in homemaking duties for all families averaged about one and a half hours daily, but the figure "tended to be somewhat greater in large families with babies."

We hear much nowadays about "modern conveniences" as great timesavers, but your modern housewife with small children who labors some 12 hours a day for seven days a week, as the Cornell study showed, certainly must be tempted to shout "Oh, yeah! Who says so?" The study supports this housewife's indignant shout even though there has been something of a reduction from the before-dawn to after-dusk household routine of our grandmothers.

Homemaking indeed may at times seem to be a hopeless succession of the same old thing, and you may begin to feel as Dame Partington must have felt the day she and her mop fought the whole

Atlantic Ocean. English essayist Sydney Smith told about the good dame's plight in a speech at Taunton, England, in 1813. In the midst of a terrible storm, Smith told his audience, "Dame Partington, who lived upon the beach, was seen at the door of her house with mop and pattens [an early form of wet-weather boots], trundling her mop, squeezing out the sea-water, and vigorously pushing away the Atlantic Ocean. The Atlantic was roused; Mrs. Partington's spirit was up. But I need not tell you the contest was unequal; the Atlantic Ocean beat Mrs. Partington."

Yes, there is still lots of apparently fruitless, repetitious drudgery in homemaking. We have tried to minimize this. Among other things, our Almanac passes along some of the shortcuts we have learned, often the hard way, in three decades of making our house a home for our sons and ourselves.

We are old enough to remember well-run homes in the days when life was made of a simpler fabric. Many good things from those olden days are now on the way to being forgotten. In our book we have tried to give these new life. In our opinion, it's sometimes best to look backward to make progress forward.

In putting this book together, we have had the help of many people. Not the least of these are the thousands of unnamed government workers, in Washington, D.C., and elsewhere, who—unknown to many of us—are constantly striving to guard us from those greedy persons and companies who would profit illegally from all of us if not constrained by laws. We herewith express our thanks to all governmental friends of the American consumer.

Some of those who have helped us we want to thank by name. Scattered through the book at the end of certain daily items you will find initials in parentheses like this: (JSD).

JSD stands for one of our major helpers—Jean Slaughter Doty, charming wife of Roy Doty, illustrious illustrator of our book. Jean has contributed all of our daily entries about pets. You may already know of Jean as the author of two long-time classics, *Horsemanship for Beginners* and *Pony Care*, both written under her maiden name, Jean Slaughter. In recent years, JSD has been writing fact and fiction in magazines and books about dogs and cats, as well as horses and ponies. While not writing or taking care of her family, Jean finds time to breed Siamese cats and a loveable race of Dutch dogs, keeshonden.

We also gratefully acknowledge the contributions made by several friends and relatives. Their initials follow the entries they supplied from their own experience in homemaking: (M de G) Mary de Gaugue, (HD) Helen Dill, (DH) Dorothy Halsey, (PK) Piper Krause, (PSL) Priscilla Stevenson Lockard, (JOP) James O. Peale, (RP) Ria Peale, (MLR) Mabel Lockard Ruse, (JKS) John Kemp Stevenson, (LSS) Louise Sandusky Stevenson, (ADS) Adele D. Straehl, and (EFW) Edith F. Webber.

Vera Kemp Stevenson   Robert P. Stevenson
*February, 1974*

# January 1

## New Year—Clean Slate— Clean House?

Easy to "wipe the slate clean," but what about the house? One way to make it easier to "wipe clean" is to keep dirt out. It's that easy. Just keep dirt out.

You don't have to scrub the outside steps as Baltimore homemakers do every day, but do sweep walkways, steps, and porches that lead to house entrances which are used daily. This takes only a few minutes, but can save hours of cleaning time inside the house.

An ancient Japanese custom requires family members to remove their shoes when they enter the house. Inside, they go barefoot or wear stockings or a *tabi*, a sock with a separate compartment for the large toe. Adapting this custom to your home will keep a lot of dirt out. If you have a "mud room," make a rule that the family enter and exit through it. Provide a plastic tray on which wet boots and rubbers, as well as dirty shoes, can be placed. Provide members of the family with something to put on their feet after they deposit shoes in the tray. The "something" might be slippers, the leather-soled socks skiers wear after they remove their boots, or a clean pair of shoes.

Objections from the family? Tell them it's a Japanese custom. Tell them about the cleaning time it will save you—time to spend baking their favorite goodies and time to spend with them doing the things they want to do. Or just tell them.

Use doormats. Use them not only outside doors, but also inside. Inside mats resemble carpeting and are available in a variety of colors and patterns. Select those that blend with your floor coverings. Don't forget a mat for the top step of the cellar stairs.

When you've done what you can to keep the dirt outside, eliminate the clutter inside. Insist that personal belongings (fishing poles, tennis rackets, toys, etc.) be kept in bedrooms (you can close the doors). Then arrange magazines and the rest of the clutter neatly. A neat house will look clean even if it isn't. Conversely, a cluttered house will appear dirty no matter what its condition of cleanliness.

---

**WHEN YOU REPAINT a room, clean out a nail-polish bottle and save some of the leftover paint in it. Use the brush when small touch-ups are needed.**

---

"For a man's house is his castle . . ."
—Sir Edward Coke

# January 2

## Poor Richard's Advice for Homemakers

On this second day of the new year, we probably couldn't do anything better than to recall a few of the sayings "Poor Richard" coined more than two centuries ago. Some of them seem especially suited for homemakers:

Glass, china, and reputation are easily crack'd, and never well mended.

An egg today is better than a hen tomorrow.

Keep your eyes wide open before marriage, half shut afterwards.

Pray don't burn my house to roast your eggs.

Three may keep a secret if two of them are dead.

Fish and visitors stink after three days.

Light heel'd mothers make leaden heel'd daughters.

Great talkers should be cropped, for they have no need of ears.

Mine is better than ours. [Let's rewrite that one by reversing it.]

Let thy maidservant be faithful, strong, and homely.

And these in verse:

> What is a butterfly? At best
> He's but a caterpillar dressed.

> If you would have guests merry with cheer,
> Be so yourself—
> Or at least so appear.

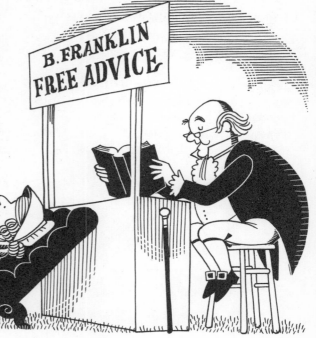

11

# January 3

## Games You Can Play with Soda Straws

The packages of drinking straws you keep on your kitchen shelves have more uses than just sipping sodas and other drinks. You can also make use of them in various party games. Some of the games obviously are folk games that date far back in history when natural straws from grains and grasses were used instead of artificial ones.

One game that will intrigue guests of all ages makes use of beans as well as straws. It is called a bean and straw race. Any number can play.

Put the beans in a dish in the center of a table. (Make sure the beans are too large to pass through the straws. Small ones could be pulled up the straws, and possibly—and dangerously—be inhaled.) Give each contestant a drinking straw and a cup. Explain that the object of the game is to transfer beans from dish to cup by picking up one bean at a time by sucking through the straw. Winner is the player who transfers the most beans in a set time.

The game may be varied by putting the same number of beans in the players' cups and having them transfer the beans to the dish. Winner is the first person to empty his cup. Another variation: Divide the guests into two teams and have a relay race. The first person on each team has the beans in his cup. He transfers them to the cup of the second person on the team, who transfers them to the third person, and so forth. Young children will be more successful using puffed rice.

A different game may be played by having the contestants throw straws at a target (perhaps a wastebasket). The player who hits the target or comes closest wins.

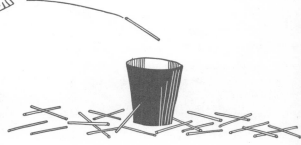

# January 4

## This Year: Enrich Your Family Traditions

The family is an important vehicle for passing along our cultural heritage. Family traditions help do this. You probably have more traditions than you realize. The early days of a new year are a fine time to review them—and consider if you wouldn't like to establish a few additional ones.

Do you top birthday cakes with candles to represent each year? Do you add an extra "to grow on"? Will good luck come to the family member who successfully blows out all the candles with one huge gasp of air? Some families employ a "Birthday Fairy" who deposits the gifts in a special spot each year, perhaps at the foot of the bed. Do the rest of the family sing "Happy Birthday to You" to the birthday celebrant? Does the celebrant choose some of his favorite foods for the birthday menu?

What about a cherry pie for Washington's Birthday, now celebrated as President's Day?

Do you dye eggs at Eastertime? How about an "egg tree," a tree branch decorated with colored and decorated egg shells from which you have blown the contents? Does the "Easter Bunny" arrive at your home with baskets filled with candy and toys? Does he hide the baskets?

The "Tooth Fairy" has visited countless children for many years, substituting a coin for the tooth left under the pillow. Does she visit your home? On Thanksgiving Day some families take a traditional family walk or go to local football games while the traditional turkey roasts.

Christmas, of course, is the time for many family traditions. Does each member of the family hang his stocking by the chimney? Do the children leave carrots for Santa's reindeer? Does everyone participate in the tree trimming?

Other holidays and family occasions will suggest other traditions, and you may learn of ideas

for unusual regional or ethnic customs from friends and neighbors. For instance, the illustrator of this book, Roy Doty, and his family told us of a couple of interesting ones. In their family, the night before Easter each child takes all of the clothing he wore during the day and makes a nest with it at the foot of his bed as a place for the Easter Bunny to leave his gifts. And, instead of simply finding a coin for a lost tooth under his pillow, the child finds a riddle, which leads him to another riddle—and eventually to the reward. The more traditions you have, the happier will be the memories your children have of their growing-up years.

do them all in one year, but make a list and try to get a few of them into the big budget!

Most family budgets cover only the big and obvious categories, with no allowances for the little household changes that mean so much to the homemaker, but a small improvement every year can make a big difference in the end. (JOP)

## January 5

**REFRIGERATE BANANAS? If green when bought, let them ripen at room temperature. Then refrigerate. The skin will darken, but no matter. The bananas will remain flavorful and firm.**

### Get Your Homemaking Needs into the Family Budget

Before you sit down with the others involved on the family budget, it might be a good idea to rough out your own homemaker's budget first. Then see that your ideas get incorporated into the whole.

Any homemaker has a mental list of the things she would love to see added to the house, or improved, or replaced. You may find it impossible to

**SCALE INSECTS on indoor plants? Control them by dipping the plants in a solution of Malathion. Or spray if you can't dip them. Make the solution by putting two teaspoons of 57 percent Malathion liquid concentrate (available at garden stores) plus one-half teaspoon of a mild household detergent in a gallon of water. Repeat treatment every two or three weeks if necessary.**

## January 6

**TODAY IN HISTORY:** *A six-day bicycle race for women participants began on Jan. 6, 1896, in Madison Square Garden in New York.*

## Do Your Children Know Bicycle Safety?

Bicycles are important to all of us these days, young and old alike. We ride for many reasons—for pleasure, for exercise, for sport, or just to get from place to place.

As you might expect, car-bike accidents have increased with the increase in the number of bikes. The bike riders, the record keepers tell us, are at fault far more than 50 percent of the time.

Bicycle safety should begin at home. If you have a bicycle, ride along with your children. You can set the example of adhering to the rules and have some good exercise at the same time. Allow them to ride without you only when you are convinced they will practice the following safety rules:

1. Ride *with* the traffic. There's a widely held belief that you should ride against traffic for the same safety reasons that you walk against traffic. Don't do it. Ride *with* traffic.

2. Keep to the right side of the road.

3. Ride single file only.

4. Be alert at all times. Look ahead, and listen for vehicles approaching from the rear. (Beginning riders should dismount when they hear vehicles in the rear and wait until they pass.) A rear-view mirror on bicycles is a good idea.

5. Obey all traffic signs and signals—stop signs, red lights, one-way streets, and railroad crossings. Use caution at intersections even if there is no stop sign or light. Walk bicycles across busy intersections.

6. Use hand signals to indicate turns and stops to riders or vehicles in the rear.

7. Do not allow anyone to ride on handlebars or fenders.

8. Remember, pedestrians always have the right-of-way.

9. Do not carry anything that obstructs vision or endangers balance.

10. Only ride at night if your bike is equipped with a white light in the front of the bike and a red

light or reflector in the rear.

Also, suit your child's bike to his age. The small 20-inch wheel usually is safest for the five- to seven-year age group and the 24-inch for youngsters eight to ten, with the full-size bike limited to children 11 and older. Beginners should not take chances on high-speed bikes for the sake of vanity or pride. Coaster brakes are safest for young children.

Insist that a child wear light-colored clothing if he rides after dark. Inspect your children's bikes every few days to be sure they remain in safe operating condition.

## *January* 7

### A Calendar—for a More Efficient You

Your engagement calendar can be used for more than social affairs and doctor, dentist, and hair appointments. Note on it items which will make you a more efficient homemaker and a more responsible person. If you don't have an engagement calendar, save one of the calendars that you receive at this time of year—one that provides enough space for several notes each day.

A week in advance, note a possible main dish for each day's dinner. You then will find it relatively simple to build the rest of the meal around the main dish—even at the last minute. Use each day's note to remind you to take from the freezer foods that must be thawed. Use the note, too, as a help in compiling your shopping list.

Note school openings, closings, and holidays.

Note the day each week that the laundry is to be picked up and delivered.

Note times to pick up shoes from the shoemaker, clothes being altered or dry-cleaned, car-servicing appointments, etc.

Note important phone calls you should make.

Note dates when recycling centers will take your bottles, cans, and paper.

Note dates and times of elections.

Note dates important bills are due—taxes, insurance, mortgage, etc.

Note dates house guests will arrive.

Note birthdays, not only on the actual date, but also a few days in advance so you have time to mail a card or buy a gift.

Note the date your dog is due at the rabies clinic.

Write yourself a reminder on the dates to do those chores that are not done on a regular basis —defrosting the freezer, shampooing a rug, washing slipcovers, etc.

Note gardening chores—times to plant or spray, for instance.

Note anything else you might forget, such as watering house plants.

The notes themselves will not make you more efficient. You have to make good use of them. Check your calendar first thing every morning. Make that a habit—and you'll remember everything else.

# January **8**

## Removing Stains from Resilient Floors

To prevent permanent damage, stains and spots should be removed as quickly as possible from any kind of floor or flooring. When your particular problem concerns a resilient flooring, remember to refer to the helpful table that you will find in the Appendix at the back of this book. It was compiled especially to solve stain problems on asphalt and vinyl asbestos tile floors.

# January **9**

**TODAY IN HISTORY:** *Carrie Chapman Catt was born on Jan. 9, 1859, in Ripon, Wis. She became one of the leading advocates of woman suffrage. A schoolteacher, she was superintendent of schools in Mason City, Iowa.*

## To Cast an Intelligent Ballot, Be Informed

The homemaker, in addition to her many household duties, should accept civic responsibilities. The most important, perhaps, is to participate in local, state, and national elections. Intelligent participation is achieved through information about issues and candidates. The League of Women Voters, founded by Carrie Chapman Catt (born on this date), is one important source of this information.

The League is a nonpartisan organization open to all citizens—women and men—of voting

age. You might like to join the local chapter and participate in its meetings and other activities.

Discuss the information you gather from the League and other sources during family conversations, perhaps at the dinner table. It will serve a dual purpose. You'll contribute something more elevating to the conversations than what did or did not go wrong in the house or what junior did or did not do. You'll also contribute to the political education of your children in showing them that a responsible voter does much more than put a ballot in the box or turn down keys on election days.

## *January* **10**

### How to Prepare Citrus Fruits for Fruit Cocktail

While grapefruit and navel oranges are in good supply at this time of year, use them as the base for a vitamin-rich fruit cocktail.

There is a trick to cutting citrus fruit that every homemaker ought to know. The object is to cut out the tough membrane that surrounds the fruit sections. The cutting procedure divides into three stages.

With a sharp butcher knife, first cut off a slice from the end of the fruit. Make this cut deep enough so that you go through the skin and slightly into the pulp.

Then, starting at the edge of this cut, peel the fruit as you would an apple. Rotate the fruit with your left hand as you make a continuous encircling peel from top to bottom. Cut deep enough so that you remove not only the rind but also the membrane next to the pulp.

The final step removes the luscious pulp whole from the membrane that surrounds each fruit section. Position your knife from end to end of the fruit, parallel to the uncut sections. Choose one section and cut into it immediately to the right of the membrane on its left side. Cut toward the center of the fruit just to the depth of the section.

Then, holding the knife at that depth, twist the knife edge toward the right—against the membrane on the right side of the fruit section. A sweeping movement of the knife will drop the section of pulp into a bowl below your hands.

Move the knife to the section just to the right, again cut down inside the membrane, and once more twist the knife to remove the section of pulp. Continue around the fruit in this manner. When all pulp sections are removed, squeeze juice out of the remaining mass of membranes.

A good proportion for fruit cocktail is four grapefruits to six oranges. Sweeten as desired with sugar or grenadine syrup. You may store the mixture in jars in the refrigerator for several days, adding diced bananas, apples, or other fruit just before serving.

# January 11

TODAY IN HISTORY: *Ben Franklin really knew a tasty dish when he encountered one. Historians tell us that on Jan. 11, 1770, he shipped rhubarb roots from London to his good friend John Bartram, renowned American botanist. Presumably, Bartram planted the roots in his garden at his home (which still stands) along the Schuylkill River near Philadelphia.*

**FIRST WOMAN TO FLY SOLO from the Hawaiian Islands to the Pacific Coast was Amelia Earhart Putnam, who left Honolulu at 10:15 P.M. on Jan. 11, 1935, and landed at Oakland, Calif., 18 hours and 16 minutes later. The distance is 2,408 miles.**

## A Favorite Rhubarb Recipe: Stew It in the Oven

People had been eating the stalks of rhubarb as a sauce and in pies or preserves a long time before Benjamin Franklin helped introduce the plant to America. Rhubarb apparently originated in China and Tibet and was gradually carried westward into Europe. In the Orient, a purgative was derived from its roots. Only the stalk of rhubarb is edible. The leaves are poisonous. Eating large amounts of them can cause convulsions and death.

You may expect to find rhubarb stalks in your local markets today, or soon.

Here is an easy way to prepare rhubarb so that it holds its shape and does not become watery: Cut the washed stalks into one-inch lengths. Make a layer in the bottom of a buttered casserole and cover with sugar. Alternate layers of rhubarb and sugar with sugar as the top layer. Use about half as much sugar as rhubarb.

Let stand a few hours or overnight. The sugar will "draw" the juice. Bake at 300 degrees only until tender—about 20 minutes—when a paring knife will easily pierce the stalks.

When cool, add a few drops of almond extract and more sugar, if desired.

# January 12

TODAY IN HISTORY: *An act of Congress dated Jan. 12, 1895, authorized the Superintendent of Documents under the Government Printing Office to distribute and sell government publications to the public.*

## Help for Homemakers Available from U.S. Government

You can benefit directly from the act of January 12, 1895, mentioned above. The Superintendent of Documents offers a great variety of inexpensive publications, giving advice that you can use to advantage in running your home more efficiently. Your Congressman sometimes will provide a few of these without cost.

Write the Superintendent and ask for the latest list of publications of special interest to homemakers and home owners. Address the Superintendent of Documents, Government Printing Office, Washington, D.C. 20402. Note this address. Elsewhere in the Almanac you will find references to particular publications that you may wish to order.

## *January* 13

**TODAY IN HISTORY:** *A patent was issued on Jan. 13, 1863, to William Canter, New York City, for a machine to make a woolly or hairy yarn called chenille. This yarn may be made of cotton, wool, silk, or rayon.*

## Chenille Is French for Caterpillar

What do you think of when you hear the word "chenille"? A rug, carpet, bedspread, or bathrobe? You might apply the term to any of those household items, as well as to tassels and fringes. The yarn is fuzzy—like a caterpillar. Hence, the origin of the word from French. Chenille rugs usually are of high quality.

## *January* 14

## If Your Car Hits a Dog

On wintry roads, it is often difficult to avoid hitting a dog that chases your car. In many states it is mandatory that you stop, assist the injured dog if possible, and report the accident to the police. You ought to do so in any case.

Do not touch the injured dog without taking precautions. Any hurt animal, even your own pet, may bite. Protect yourself by wrapping the dog's head gently in a blanket, coat, or jacket. If the dog is quiet enough, an emergency muzzle can be made from a soft belt, a man's tie, a woman's stocking. Tie the cloth gently but snugly around the dog's muzzle—keep in mind the jaw may be broken. Then tie the ends in a knot behind the animal's ears.

Even if the dog is unconscious, muzzle it before you pick it up. Put it on the car floor, cover the animal with a coat or blanket to keep it warm, and get help.

More dogs die of shock after being hit by a car than from their injuries. Get the hurt dog to a veterinarian as quickly as you can. If you don't know of one nearby, stop at the nearest telephone and call the local humane society or the police. (JSD)

---

**TO GIVE A DOG A PILL, put the pill inside a lump of cream cheese —and it will go down easily. (PK)**

---

## *January* 15

### Ten Ways to Save Money When You Grocery Shop

First, refer to the notes you made on your calendar for the main dish for the week's dinners as an aid to compiling your shopping list (see entry for January 7). Include on your list any ingredients you need to prepare the main dishes you plan to have, as well as foods needed to build a complete meal around the main dishes.

Second, keep a list of the food staples and housecleaning items that you always want to have on hand. Check your supply of these before you go to the store and add any that are in low supply to your shopping list.

Third, take advantage of any special prices on items you always want to have in the house even if they are not needed at the moment.

Fourth, avoid "compulsive buying." Stick to your shopping list unless you see a real purpose for something else—a main dish that you hadn't

thought of perhaps.

Fifth, don't "supermarket hop" (go from store to store to buy only a few items) unless lower prices make it really worthwhile. Decide whether it is on the basis of the mileage involved. Figure ten cents a mile wear and tear on the car plus gasoline consumed.

Sixth, check price and quantity of each item. Is the "giant economy size" really a bargain? In some areas, stores are required to post the unit cost of items. If this is the case where you live, make a habit of checking the unit prices.

Seventh, make sure the price is legible on items you load into your shopping cart. If not, make your own notations on them. Carry a pen, pencil, or grease pencil with you for this purpose.

Eighth, while vegetables or other per-pound products are being weighed, note what the scales say—and that the correct figure is marked on the package.

Ninth, before you get in line at the check-out counter, estimate the cost of your cart's contents. Or use a pocket computer or adding machine to arrive at the exact cost.

Tenth, position yourself at the check-out counter so you can see each item being rung up on the cash register. Did you select an item that is sale priced? Watch carefully that you are not charged the regular price, either for sale-priced groceries or day-old baked goods. The clerk usually is working at top speed; therefore, honest mistakes can sometimes happen.

## January 16

---

**TODAY IN HISTORY:** *A patent for a power loom to weave Axminster carpets was granted on Jan. 16, 1877, to Halycon Skinner and Alexander Smith, both of Yonkers, N.Y.*

---

### What's an Axminster Carpet?

Axminster carpets and rugs got their name from the community in England where they were woven in the eighteenth century. Axminsters are one of the four types of woven carpets and rugs. The others are Wilton, chenille, and velvet.

In the days of our grandmothers, Axminsters were the most commonly used kind of floor covering. In recent years their popularity has declined.

Axminsters can be woven in a great variety of colors from man-made fibers or wool. Pile tufts are knotted to the backing one at a time. Axminsters can be produced in a wide range of qualities, but most come in a low-price range.

Before buying a rug or carpet you may want information about quality, prices, and advantages and disadvantages of different types. A 32-page U.S. government publication, ''Carpets and Rugs,'' will help you. It discusses common carpet fibers, texture variations, paddings, and installation. See January 12 for how to get your copy.

## January 17

### Can You Replace a Fuse, Shut Off the Water?

Unless you can answer ''yes'' to both of these questions, learn how—as quickly as you can, preferably from someone who knows, and read the following carefully.

A blown fuse or tripped circuit breaker indicates that an electrical overload has occurred in the circuit that the fuse or circuit breaker protects. First try to find out if faulty electrical equipment—a lamp or appliance, perhaps—caused the problem. Unplug the suspected equipment before you replace the fuse or return the circuit breaker switch to its operating position. Put faulty equipment aside to be repaired before putting it back into use.

At the fuse or circuit-breaker box every fuse or switch should be labeled to show the circuit each one protects. Knowing in what rooms there is no

## January **18**

### Hickory Smoked Barbecued Lamb Riblets

Feeling housebound during these cold January days? Bring an atmosphere of happy summer indoors by preparing a dinner that can compare very favorably with an outdoor barbecue.

> **1 cup chili sauce**
> **¼ cup vinegar**
> **Juice of 1 lemon**
> **1 clove garlic, crushed**
> **1 tsp. grated lemon peel**
> **1 tsp. hickory smoked salt**
> **3 lbs. lamb riblets**

Combine chili sauce, vinegar, lemon juice, garlic, lemon peel, and hickory salt. Place lamb in a plastic bag, add marinade mixture, and marinate several hours. Remove riblets, reserving marinade. Place riblets in large shallow baking pan and bake at 325 degrees for 1½ to 2 hours. Turn occasionally to brown lamb evenly. Brush frequently with marinade during last 45 minutes of baking. (Four servings.)

power will then lead you to the blown fuse or tripped breaker. A blown fuse also can usually be determined by its appearance (the glass cover will appear cloudy). Before replacing the fuse with another (of the same amperage), turn off the house master switch—near the fuse box. Then unscrew the old fuse and screw in the new one. If you have a circuit breaker, simply push the switch to the "on" position.

You will want to know the location of water shut-off valves and how to work them, to forestall flood damage if a faucet or washing machine refuses to turn off. In modern houses with up-to-date plumbing, you usually will find shut-off valves under or near lavatories or bathtubs. But also find the shut-off where the water line enters the house from the water main or pump. Check to be sure you can work it.

---

**"Tell me what you eat, and I will tell you what you are."**
**—Anthelme Brillat-Savarin**

---

# *January* 19

## How to Shop for Home Improvement and Repair Ideas

Have you ever strolled through one of those huge modern stores that used to sell nothing but lumber and building supplies? They are now likely to call themselves home improvement centers. They offer all sorts of things for sprucing up a home.

A leisurely shopping trip through the acre or

The tour will also give you ideas for house improvements. Lazy Susans and drawers are available for installation in kitchen cabinet spaces that are hard to reach. Louvered shutters could be just the way to treat that problem window. How about strings of beads to divide room space in a novel way? Stained glass, press-on tiles, shelves, and brackets are only a few of the other items stocked that will give you ideas for home improvements.

so of merchandise displayed in such a store can be a fun thing to do on a winter day like this. If there is no store of this type in your area, go to a large hardware store.

As you shop, you'll be reminded of little repair jobs that need to be done around the house and at the same time you can prepare to do them.

Buy a tube of bathtub seal for the tub that has needed to be caulked for some time. Get a bottle of porcelain repair to fill in the chip inside the refrigerator door. Add the drapery cord for that traverse that does not traverse. A look at the many products on the shelves will suggest other needed purchases.

# *January* 20

## An Old Rule for Choosing Lubricants and Polishes

January is an ideal time for cleaning out closets and sorting the contents. One thing that may come to light is an accumulation of assorted oils and greases, bought for lubrication, preservation, or polishing. However, it's amazing how many of them may actually be harmful, rather than beneficial, for the surfaces they may be used on.

An old English saying is: "Use animal on animal, vegetable on vegetable, and mineral on mineral"—a pretty good rule, although there are rare exceptions. For instance: Beeswax, which is animal in origin, makes an excellent furniture polish, although wood furniture is obviously vegetable.

However, never put any mineral-based oil or grease on any wood (vegetable) or leather (animal). It will usually cause damage. Likewise never use an animal oil such as neat's-foot oil or suet on metals or wood, and never use vegetable derivatives such as turpentine on leather. (If used to clean leather, alcohol evaporates quickly and causes no harm.) You're pretty safe if you stick to the old rule. (JOP)

**DO YOU COMPOST your garbage? Check books in your local library on how to make good use of all organic leftovers. Use the compost on flower or vegetable gardens.**

## Use Outdoor Equipment to Sleep More Guests

How many sleeping bags are there in your household? What about air mattresses? Is all of this fine equipment stored out of sight—and out of mind—until next camping season?

If so, you're missing a good bet. When friends or relatives descend upon you, and there just are not enough beds to go around, haul out the sleeping bags. The kids will love it; to them it will seem like a party. In fact, why not let your kids invite their friends—all of them—some night for a slumber party? Each guest can bring a bag. Great!

When you're buying outdoor lounge chairs, keep in mind your year-round need for suddenly increased sleeping accommodations. Buy the kind

of chair that folds completely flat so you can lie on your stomach in comfort while sunning yourself. Indoors, such a chair can do double duty as a cot.

## January 22

### Keep Your Staples Fresher by Storing in Jars

Are your kitchen shelves filled with supplies still in original boxes or bags? They would stay fresh longer if you kept them in a set of airtight glass jars. The jars also keep food products safe from insects, and you can see quickly what you need from the market.

Suitable containers will cost you nothing. Use the wide-mouthed jars with screw tops that so many food products come in—mayonnaise, peanut butter, etc. Start saving the jars now. Transfer some of the packaged products each time you empty a jar. Wash the jar well first and apply an adhesive label.

## January 23

### First Aid for Your Wood Furniture

When wood furniture accumulates scratches and other blemishes, only complete refinishing can restore the original appearance. Before going to the expense of a professional job, or starting this task yourself, try some first aid.

**Nut meats, linseed oil.** The oil from a Brazil nut, black walnut, or butternut may provide enough color to hide a minor scratch. Break the nut meat in half and rub well into the blemish. Rubbing the mark with linseed oil may help, also, but don't use crude oil—this could soften the finish on the wood.

**Coloring crayon, wax sticks.** Try coloring the blemish with brown crayon. Or use wax sticks —these are made especially for furniture in wood tones. They are softer than ordinary crayon and easier to work with. Fill the scratch with wax and rub in well with your finger. Wipe with a soft, dry cloth.

**Shoe polish.** Use a paste shoe polish in the brown shade for walnut, the cordovan shade for mahogany, and the tan shade for light finishes. Apply with a cotton-tipped swab, rubbing carefully on the blemish; then buff dry. If the color is darker than the wood tone, erase with naphtha. Black paste shoe polish can be used to touch up scratches on black lacquered wood. Remember that the polish will provide a shine when it is buffed, so the repaired area may be noticeable if the furniture has a dull finish.

**Iodine.** To conceal scratches on red-finished mahogany, use new iodine; for brown or cherry mahogany, iodine that has turned dark brown with age. For maple, dilute iodine about 50 percent with denatured alcohol.

**Rottenstone and oil.** Get an ounce of rotten-

# January 24

**TODAY IN HISTORY:** *A patent was granted on Jan. 24, 1922, to Christian K. Nelson, of Onawa, Iowa, for the Eskimo pie.*

## The Joys of Making Your Own Ice Cream

Many older Americans remember with delight the ice cream that was made at home in hand-turned freezers during their childhood days. Wouldn't your own children have fun doing the same thing?

The freezers you buy these days are sometimes motor-driven, so, if you wish, you can escape the old-time chore of hand-turning.

In many parts of the U.S., the ice you need is available free for the gathering at this time of the year—from streams, ponds, or lakes. You might even use a huge icicle that has formed somewhere in the neighborhood. If there is an ice machine in the vicinity, you can of course get what you need at low cost. Wrap the ice in a piece of canvas and crack it fine with an ax or heavy hammer.

Prepare the milk or cream according to your

stone from a paint or hardware store and keep it in an old salt shaker. Put a few drops of lubricating or salad oil on the blemish and shake on some rottenstone—enough to make a paste. Rub briskly with the grain of the wood, using a clean, soft cloth. Wipe frequently in order to compare and match the gloss of the damaged area with the original finish.

(NOTE: The foregoing information was supplied by Johnson Wax. If you would like additional information about furniture care and finishing, write to Johnson Wax, Consumer Education Center, 1525 Howe St., Racine, Wis. 53403.)

## How to Make a
## Kitchen Pan Rack

A satisfying chore for a miserable January day is to make yourself a handsome kitchen rack for hanging pots and pans. It's easy!

Drill a series of ½" holes at a slight upward angle in a length of 1" x 2" clear pine, placing the holes far enough apart so that the pots will hang clear of each other. To accept the handle rings, drive in 3" lengths of ½" doweling, secured by a few drops of white glue.

Sand the surfaces and edges and give the rack a coat of wax, stain, or paint to match your kitchen décor, and you'll have a practical addition to your kitchen that you can be proud of. (JOP)

own favorite recipe and pour it into the metal freezing container. Pack ice around the container, sprinkling it well with rock salt. Turn the freezer until the mixture is well frozen.

The following recipe will yield 1½ quarts of vanilla ice cream, which is good as is or which may be topped with your favorite sauce or fruit:

> **1 qt. half-and-half**
> **¾ cup sugar**
> **Pinch of salt**
> **1½ Tbs. vanilla extract**

Warm the half-and-half in a saucepan over low heat. Add the sugar and salt, and stir until sugar is dissolved. Cool, then add the vanilla.

**NEED MORE LIVING SPACE?** Because of high mortgage rates you may be smarter if you add on to your present home and forget about buying or building a larger one. But be careful not to spend so much for improvements that your total investment exceeds the price tags for other homes in your neighborhood.

**WANT TO HIDE VALUABLES** in your home in a spot where few burglars would think to look? Put them above a suspended ceiling, if you have one in your home. Hang a shelf to the original ceiling for a small strongbox. Gain access through one of the removable ceiling squares.

# January 26

## Keep Road Salts Washed from Your Car

CAR WASH

Ice- and snow-melting salts and chemicals splashed up underneath your car and on its finish can quickly create rust conditions. Make it a practice at this time of year to wash the car often.

But make sure you get the right kind of wash job. Many of the drive-through car-wash centers take care only of the top surfaces—from fender edge to fender edge. They remove road slush from the upper finish, but probably do not touch all of the accumulated gunk in the wheel wells, behind the bumpers, and on the car's underbelly. To get this off, you need an old-fashioned washing with a hose.

# January 27

**TODAY IN HISTORY:** *Lewis Carroll was born in England on Jan. 27, 1832. Have you recently read his* Alice's Adventures in Wonderland? *It was published in 1865. The sequel,* Through the Looking Glass, *appeared in 1871.*

## The Importance of Reading to Your Children

Educators agree that most children who are good readers are those who have had early exposure to reading. They are read to by parents; they see magazines, newspapers, and books in the home; and they acquire a value for reading by seeing their parents read.

The listening vocabulary of children (and adults) is appreciably larger than their reading, writing, and speaking vocabularies. All can listen with understanding to material that is more difficult than they can handle on their own.

Begin reading to your children as soon as they are able to sit and listen. Even if a child doesn't understand all the words you read, he may be content to listen to the word rhythm and the expression in your voice. The length of time you read should be governed by his span of attention. Each child's attention span differs. When he becomes restless, it is the signal to stop.

*Alice in Wonderland* and *Through the Looking Glass* by Lewis Carroll, born on this date, are books that young children will enjoy listening to and you will enjoy re-reading, this time aloud. The *Winnie-the-Pooh* books by A. A. Milne are among many, many other fun books to read aloud.

Older children like to be read to also, and they

may want to take turns doing the reading. Consider adding a family read-aloud session to your family traditions (see entry for January 4). The content of the books is important, of course, but not as important as the fact that you spend time reading to (or with) your children.

**PLACE A SHEET** of heavy aluminum foil between the pad and cover of your ironing board. The foil will reflect heat back to the article you're ironing, making the iron more efficient. The foil also will keep steam from dampening the pad.

## Menus for This Month

A January "Dinner for 8 Persons" suggested in 1861 by Mrs. Isabella Beeton in her *Book of Household Management* published that year was:

"First Course. Mulligatawny Soup. Brill and Shrimp Sauce. Fried Whitings. Entrees. Fricasseed Chicken. Port Cutlets, with Tomato Sauce. Second Course. Haunch of Mutton. Boiled Turkey and Celery Sauce. Boiled Tongue, garnished with Brussels Sprouts. Third Course. Roast Pheasants. Meringues à la Crème. Compôte of Apples. Orange Jelly. Cheesecakes. Soufflé of Rice. Dessert and Ices."

A "Plain Family Sunday Dinner for January," suggested by Mrs. Beeton, included "Codfish and oyster sauce, potatoes. 2. Joint of roast mutton, either leg, haunch, or saddle; brocoli [sic] and potatoes, red-currant jelly. 3. Apple tart and custards, cheese."

Even if the foods listed above were available, diet-consciousness and high prices would keep us from duplicating the menus. Instead, we present in the following two entries dishes which are seasonal, simple to prepare, and nutritious. Accompanied by a salad, each can constitute the evening meal.

For more information about Mrs. Beeton's charming and useful book, see the entry for November 22.

# January 29

## Finnan Haddie

This is dried, smoked haddock available from fish stores and in season during the winter months. It was originally known as "Finnan Haddock." In the book mentioned in yesterday's entry, Mrs. Beeton describes its origins as follows:

"This is the common haddock cured and dried, and takes its name from the fishing-village of Findhorn, near Aberdeen, in Scotland, where the art has long attained to perfection. The haddocks are there hung up for a day or two in the smoke of peat, when they are ready for cooking, and are esteemed, by the Scotch, a great delicacy."

To prepare, barely cover the fish with milk. Bring to the boiling point and simmer until tender. Drain, then flake the meat, discarding skin and bones. Add the flakes to a white sauce and pour over toast. Top with chopped parsley and a little lemon juice.

# January 30

## Scotch Woodcock—Two Recipes

From Mrs. Beeton's nineteenth-century homemaking guide: Spread hot buttered toast thinly with anchovy paste. Pour over a sauce made by stirring three beaten egg yolks into ¼ pint cream—bring to boiling point, but do not allow to boil or the sauce will curdle.

From a modern cooking guide: Add finely chopped hard-cooked eggs to a white sauce that has been seasoned with anchovy sauce and paprika—pour over toast.

---

**ANTIQUING OLD FURNITURE is one way to furnish your home quite inexpensively, yet colorfully. Look for appropriate pieces in used furniture stores or buy unfinished pieces. Antiquing kits are widely available.**

## January Potpourri
## for Homemakers

When it snows in your area, join the children in sculpting an owl, rabbit, or other animal instead of the traditional snowman. Ice the surface by covering with a fine spray of water.

To avoid laundry losses, keep a list as you send items to the laundry and dry cleaner. Check off the items when they are returned.

Stains in the kitchen sink? When scouring powders won't remove them, leave the dishwater in and add one cup of bleach. Let stand for at least 15 minutes and then try again.

To dust under low pieces of furniture, wrap dust cloth around the end of a yardstick.

An old metal breadbox placed in the cabinet under the sink is a fine pest-proof storage place for sugar and flour still in the original packaging.

Allergic to gold? Paint the side of jewelry that touches the skin with clear nail polish.

**Your Own Reminders:**

_____

_____

_____

_____

_____

_____

_____

# February 1

## Name Your Baby with Webster's Help

The festival of Ste. Bridget, today, reminds us that Bridget has long been a favorite name for Irish girls. This brings to mind the help Webster's gives in choosing given names for babies. Many college dictionaries have a section in the back listing alphabetically names for men and women, together with information as to the origins and meanings of the names.

If you're stumped as to what to name your baby, skim the section in Webster's for ideas. If your surname (last name) is one syllable, look for given names that contain two or more syllables. These combinations will have a more pleasing sound to the ear. Conversely, a one-syllable given name sounds best with a surname of two or more syllables.

Ponder carefully the effect on the child of carrying through life an offbeat name inspired by current happenings. The child may resent, rightfully, having been named Apollo, Mars, or Saturn, for instance. Consider, too, the nicknames that might evolve from the name you select. Looney from Luna, for example. And, also bear in mind the initials. Your child may be teased if his initials spell RAT or TUB.

A young child is often called Dickie, Johnny, Petey, or other affectionate version of his given name. This is fine for family and friends, but do make sure you switch to Richard, John, or Peter when the child reaches school age. Children can be cruel, and names often give them the ammunition they need to "take it out" on their peers.

Many names have had cycles of popularity. The Prudences and Ezras of yesteryear are the Deborahs and Kevins of today. Names that endure through the centuries, however, are the Biblical Ruths, Davids, Johns, and Marys.

Eudora···Eugenia·Eulalia···Eunice

ADMITTING →

UNPAINTED PLASTER quickly picks up dirt and becomes difficult to clean. Yet new plaster should not be painted with oil-based paint until cured—which takes about two months. To protect it, apply one coat of a water-based paint, which is not affected by alkali in the walls and lets moisture from the plaster escape through the drying paint.

# February 2

## Ground-hog Day

Folklore in many countries has long stated that the weather on February 2 forecasts weather for the following six weeks. In the United States, the ground hog, or woodchuck, is supposed to break its winter sleep on this day to take a look at weather conditions. An old English rhyme expresses the weather-forecasting tradition this way:

If Candlemas Day be dry and fair,
The half o' winter's to come and mair;
If Candlemas Day be wet and foul,
The half o' winter's gone at Yule.

**BUYING A NEW REFRIGERATOR?** For energy conservation and economy of operation, a frost-free model is not a good choice. It has been estimated that these machines use 50 percent more power than those you must defrost.

**WERE THEY UNDERPAID?** An act of Congress of Feb. 2, 1901, set up the Army Nurse Corps (female) as a permanent branch of the U.S. Army. The act provided $1,800 annual salary for the corps superintendent, and $40 a month for nurses serving in the U.S., $50 a month for foreign service.

# February 3

## Running Gingerbread Man Cookie Cutter

Run, run, as fast as you can.
You can't catch me.
I'm the Gingerbread Man.

Most of us know this rhyme from the ancient childhood folk tale. Today's cookie bakers still like to create luscious ginger cookies. But most cutters produce a symmetrical likeness of the man, facing you head on. Here is the outline for a cutter that has him in his most typical pose—running.

To make it, buy or beg a piece of sheet aluminum. Roof-flashing aluminum is fine. Cut a strip, ¾" to 1" wide, using heavy shears or tin snips. Shape it to the outline shown here. Crimp the ends together by bending them flat in opposite directions and hooking them together. Secure the crimped joint by resting the interlocked folded ends on a piece of wood and dimpling (driving a couple of holes through) the metal with a metal punch, an awl, or an ice pick.

# February 4

## How to Get Baby-Sitters and What to Tell Them

The recommendation of a friend or neighbor is the best way to find a baby-sitter. Schools recognize that sitting is one of the few ways teen-agers can earn money and sometimes offer child-care courses or include information concerning care of children in home economics courses. Contact the school office for the names of sitters in your area. Some newspapers run free ads for young people seeking such jobs.

Women who are housebound with small children of their own, senior citizens who must augment fixed incomes, and college students on vacation often insert ads in Help Wanted columns of newspapers. If you answer an ad, however, insist on references. Bonded agencies which supply sitters exist in some communities. These sitters can take over care of the house or apartment, as well as the children, of vacationing parents. Look for such agencies in the Yellow Pages. Be sure to insist on interviews.

Sitting is done today not only for babies and young children but also for elderly family members, pets, and the house or apartment itself. Going rates differ from area to area. In any case, look for a sitter who is mature, responsible, and firm, yet kind.

Before you leave the house, make sure the sitter has a telephone number where she (or he) can reach you. Tell her, too, the time you expect to be home (and stick to this). Next, give her the phone number of a responsible neighbor whom she can contact if unable to reach you. Also, make sure she knows what to do in case of fire or other emergency. Call the sitter's attention to your list of emergency numbers at or near the telephone —your doctor, the fire department, and the police.

Write down the routine you wish the sitter to follow: meal content and time, preparations for bed and time, and permitted indoor and outdoor play activities and television viewing.

Do not expect the sitter to do housework. But do expect that she will: prepare simple meals and wash the dishes afterward, keep the home tidy (pick up toys and clothes), dress the child for outdoors and bed, and (in the case of infants) diaper and give bottles.

# February 5

## Store Poinsettia Soon

If you received a poinsettia for Christmas, no doubt it has stopped blooming and lost some of its leaves by now. If it has a rest period, it may blossom again or provide cuttings for other plants.

Gradually withhold water until the potting mixture is completely dry. Then store at about 50 degrees until all danger of frost is past. See May 16 for how to revive it.

## Housekeeping without Power: Refrigeration

Modern housekeeping depends heavily upon power, usually electricity or gas or both. Unfortunately, the flow of these energy sources into our homes is now subject to possible interruptions, a situation that may continue for years. So what do we do?

Housekeepers, we think, ought to consider a general return to greater self-sufficiency. All of us should examine once again the housekeeping procedures that our grandmothers followed and see what we can borrow from them. We ought to review possible advantages of "the simple life."

The latter idea already has attracted the attention of many young people. Smart kids! Self-sufficiency was given a good boost by the widely sold *Whole Earth Catalog* and similar publications that have followed it.

At appropriate times in this book we intend to suggest how homemakers can plan to be more self-sufficient in the absence of power. Today, for instance, we want to talk about the problem you face if a blackout occurs while you have a refrigerator/freezer fully stocked with food.

A return to the old household icebox holds little promise, for you would have great difficulty stocking it with ice. Reducing food costs by buying in quantity and storing in a freezer no longer makes sense if there's a chance of losing it all in a prolonged blackout.

A standby electrical generator is good insurance. But one large enough to operate a freezer costs considerable money. Moreover, a gasoline engine usually powers such a generator—and you just might be short of gasoline.

When power loss shuts down a refrigerator/freezer during cold weather, you may be able to conserve your food by moving it outdoors. Even if it's only 40 degrees or thereabouts outdoors, you can approximate the usual refrigerator environment. If the temperature is below 32 degrees, you will have to protect refrigerator food from freezing, possibly by wrapping it in newspapers.

An insulated picnic hamper or plastic cooler would be ideal for this. You might want to keep one on hand just for such use. Apartment dwellers could place food containers on windowsills or balconies.

If you know or suspect that power will be off, set the freezer control at its coldest setting right away. The lower temperature of freezer and food will delay thawing. A fully loaded freezer usually will stay cold enough to keep foods frozen for one or two days; in one with half a load, food may not stay frozen for more than a day.

If normal operation will not be resumed before the food will thaw, use dry ice (if you can get it) to keep the food cold or transfer the food in insulated boxes to a locker plant or other low-temperature storage space outside the blackout area. If the blackout is local, friends in another area may have enough freezer space to solve your problem.

If dry ice is put in the freezer soon after it goes off, 50 pounds should keep the temperature of food in a 20-cubic-foot cabinet below freezing for three to four days; in a cabinet with half a load or less, for two or three days.

Do not open the freezer door while the freezer is not operating except as a part of a food-saving procedure.

---

**FEBRUARY AND AUGUST are the best times to root geranium cuttings —in water or in vermiculite.**

---

## February 7

### Lilies of the Valley Bloom Indoors

Garden shops sometimes offer a few potted pips of lilies of the valley for forcing into bloom indoors at this time of year. If you have a well-established bed of these lovely flowers, you can get a similar jump on the blooming season by using your own pips as soon as the ground thaws. Plunge an old knife into the midst of the bed area and cut out a small section just large enough to fit into a flowerpot. Or dig up a larger section, cut off the bottom half of the roots, and pack into a shallow container with growing medium. Water well and place the pips in a warm area. You should get fragrant blooms well ahead of those outdoors.

Caution: Our gardening friends point out that you may not get blooms unless the pips have undergone prolonged freezing temperatures in the ground during the winter. Like certain other plants, they need this winter rest. If you have had a mild winter, better bag the pips after digging and keep in a freezer for a few weeks before planting.

## February 8

### How to Make Perfect Pie Crust

The frozen pie shells and graham-cracker crusts available in grocery stores are good and worth keeping on hand. But nothing beats a pie you have made yourself, including the crust. A cold winter day when you're housebound is a good time to try your hand; the warmth from the oven will increase the coziness of the kitchen.

Our recipe makes three covered pies or six pie shells. Both baked and unbaked pies and shells freeze well.

Sift into a large bowl 3 cups flour, 1 rounded teaspoon baking powder, and ½ teaspoon salt. Work in ½ pound lard with your fingers. Then continue to work in small additional amounts of lard until mixture resembles coarse crumbs and tends to stick together. Gradually add ice water, and mix it in with your fingers until dough will stay in one large ball when pressed together.

Roll out about ⅔ cup of the dough at a time on a floured pastry cloth. The excess may be re-rolled.

To make pie shells which will hold their shape, prick the pastry in several places with a fork before baking. Then press a square of aluminum foil into the bottom and against the sides. Remove the foil immediately after baking. To bake the shells, place in a 400-degree oven for 10 minutes.

# February 9

## Keep Tab on Local Rainfall With a Rain Gauge

Everybody talks about the weather, but you *can* do something about one phase of it. You can record rainfall by putting up an inexpensive rain gauge in your yard and making regular reports to your local weather station, newspaper, or other interested organizations. It's a lot of fun to keep an accurate record of actual rainfall for future reference or to settle arguments. Just check the gauge once a day and jot the figure down on a calendar. Suspend operations and bring in the gauge during the months when ice may damage it.

A source of gauges is Tru-Chek Division, Ed-

wards Manufacturing Company, Albert Lea, Minn. 56007. (JOP)

# *February* 10

## Recycle Bacon Fat to the Winter Birds

What happens to the bacon fat produced in your household? Does it all go into the garbage? You can make good use of it in feeding winter birds.

Store a one-pound coffee can and its plastic lid near the range. Each time you fry bacon, pour off the fat from the pan into this container and let it congeal. During the summer, after each can is full,

you might put it into the home freezer to await bird-feeding time.

Perhaps you have a backyard feeder on a wooden post. If so, bore holes ¾- or 1-inch in diameter and an inch deep into the post. Every day or so, knife the hardened fat into the holes—and watch all types of birds enjoy it. Wooden pegs driven into small holes below each feeding hole will help some to perch and eat better. One draw-

back: On warm days, the fat will become liquid and run down the post, making it messy.

You might make a special feeder for this sort of fat (the salt in bacon fat is good for the birds) by drilling 1-inch holes at a downward slant into a 2" x 4" a couple of feet long. Again put perching pegs below the feeding holes.

# *February* 11

## Will Power Tools Make You More Creative?

Perhaps we ought to take what Dean Peel says with a grain of salt—even though he is a good friend of ours. But we believe him when he says that women have become important as buyers—and users—of the tools for which he is national sales manager. What do women do with these tools—the hand-held Moto Tool (which looks somewhat like a miniature electric drill) and the table-top jigsaw? Listen to Dean:

"Women are using them increasingly to find an outlet for their creative energies and, in these times of high and rising prices, to decorate their homes or to create unusual display pieces—decorated eggs, gems, jewelry, carvings of all kinds, and similar items that might otherwise strain the budget.

"Women have been operating powered equipment for decades. So it's no big deal to switch on a table-top jigsaw or pick up a powered hand tool and shape silver, copper, wood, plastic, or ceramics."

If such activity interests you, why not stop in at a hardware store and get the details about creative tools of this kind?

## February 12

### Weights and Measures for Homemakers

An old axiom, "A pint's a pound the world around," is a practical reminder of liquid weights. Since there are two cups in a pint, each cup weighs half a pound—or eight ounces. It is helpful to know also that one tablespoon equals three teaspoons, that a cup equals 16 tablespoons.

Homemakers may also like to know that:

Thread, silk, and yarn are measured in skeins. One skein equals 360 feet.

Cloth is measured in bolts. A bolt equals 120 feet.

Butter and lard are measured in firkins. One firkin weighs about 56 pounds.

The line (equal to 1/40 inch) is used to measure buttons.

**SNAILS AND SLUGS** are hermaphrodites. Each individual has both male and female reproductive systems and mutual fertilization usually takes place. Each individual may lay eggs, or in some species, individuals may alternate between being males and females. Lucky creatures!

**TRANSLUCENT PAPER CAPS** are sometimes used over early season garden plants as a frost guard. But perhaps you should not use them. "The prevailing body of professional opinion has little regard for this method," say two Weather Bureau meteorologists, writing in a pamphlet on the subject of frost. "Many authors point out that plants get progressively less hardy under the caps."

**ALWAYS TURN PAN HANDLES** toward the back of the range. You'll then be less likely to upset one, and youngsters will be unable to reach up and spill the contents on themselves.

**SOUP IN A CUP?** Youngsters prefer drinking it from a mug to spooning it from a dish.

## Tattoo Your Dog for Certain Identification

The loss of the family dog can be a heartbreaking experience. Even a properly cared for dog can sometimes escape through an open door or unlatched gate. Identification can be difficult. A collar with a license and a tag with your address and telephone number can be a help, but collars are easily lost or removed.

Dog thefts increase every year. In many suburbs across the country, dog thieves have been known to steal family pets even from fenced yards. Another favorite source of supply for the thief is the dog left alone in a parked car, especially in a busy shopping center.

Tattooing your dog provides permanent, unalterable identification. This is extremely useful if your dog has merely strayed. Humane societies and dog wardens look for tattoo identification.

And it makes the owner feel less desperate to know that proof of ownership cannot be argued, and that the dog can easily be traced and returned.

Call or write The National Dog Registry, 227 Stebbins Road, Carmel, N. Y. 10512. Telephone (914) 277-4485.

The Registry will tell you how and where you can have your dog tattooed. One fee will cover every dog you will ever own. Your identification number, name, address, and telephone number will be put into a central file (changed immediately if you move) and your dog can then be traced to you, anywhere in the country, any hour of the day or night.

Dog thieves do not want to be involved with tattooed dogs. It is common practice to abandon these dogs when tattoos are discovered. The dogs may then be found, identified, and reported.

There are other registries. One accepts tattooing on the ear as identification. This is not adequate; many a pet has lost his life in a laboratory having "accidentally" lost an ear while in the hands of dog thieves. Most unidentifiable stolen dogs are sold to labs. (JSD)

**LOOK FOR NEW-CROP** asparagus in food markets about this time.

# February 14

## St. Valentine's Day

How did this holiday become associated with lovers? There are various theories and traditions, but the one we like best is that an early form of our word "gallant"—meaning "attractive to ladies"—became confused with the names of the two Christian saints—Valentine—who are said to have been martyred on this date in early Rome. When the Normans thronged into England after the Conquest, they brought along their word "galantin." The initial letter "g" may at times have been pronounced as "v." Thus, in the popular mind, the original saint's day could have gradually shifted to one when it is also proper to court the ladies—or vice versa. But anyway you look at it, it's a lovely day for lots of hearts and flowers.

**WEAR YOUR HEART on your sleeve? This expression may have come from an old English custom whereby young men did just this on Valentine's Day and for several days thereafter. Each young man pinned to his sleeve a piece of paper with the name of his lady love written on it.**

# February 15

**TODAY IN HISTORY:** *On Feb. 15, 1768, one Benjamin Jackson advertised in a Philadelphia newspaper that he was "the only mustard manufacturer on the continent. I brought the art with me into the country." He sold his product in labeled glass bottles.*

## The History of Mustard

The delights of mustard as a food accompaniment apparently had been known only a few years before the appearance of the advertisement described in today's historical note. In fact, Benjamin Jackson may very well have learned his trade directly from the woman who is believed to have introduced mixed mustard into England about 40 years before the 1768 advertisement. Mrs. Isabella Beeton (see November 22) told about mustard's introduction in the first (1861) edition of her book, the *Book of Household Management.*

"Before the year 1729, mustard was not known at English tables," Mrs. Beeton wrote. "About that time an old woman, of the name of Clements, residing in Durham, began to grind the seed in a mill, and to pass the flour through several processes necessary to free the seed from its husks. She kept the secret for many years to herself, during which she sold large quantities of mustard throughout the country, but especially in London. Here, it was introduced to the royal table, when it received the approval of George I. From the circumstances of Mrs. Clements being a resident of Durham, it obtained the name of Durham mustard."

(For a recipe for mixing your own fresh mustard, see the label on a box of Coleman Mustard).

# February 16

## Nylon—the "Granddaddy" of Man-Made Fibers

Ten years of research had preceded the granting of a patent for nylon to Dr. Wallace Carothers. The first truly synthetic fiber, nylon is made from such basic materials as coal, air, and water.

Today nylon is a word synonymous with hosiery. The original was the "granddaddy" to new kinds of nylon fibers developed to fill specific needs in the fields of apparel, home furnishings, and industry. Nylon and its descendants —Cantrece, Antron III, Qiana, Du Pont 420, and others—have great resistance to wear and tear. Nylon has the ability to spring back to its original shape after stretching or crushing and has no attraction for moths, silverfish, and other insects destructive to many fibers. It is also immune to damage from mildew and is not weakened by perspiration. Its extra-wear life means economy in clothing and home furnishings.

Descendants of the original nylon include the following:

Cantrece nylon used in stretch hosiery and panty hose provides improved fit, comfort, and appearance.

Antron III provides substantial anti-cling, anti-static protection and has the ability to disperse moisture from the body.

Products made of Qiana have the elegance of silk fabrics; a soft, delicate touch; graceful, supple drape; deep, rich luster; and vivid, clear colorations. First used in luxury fabrics, it has now moved into medium-priced fashion items.

Du Pont 420 nylon was especially engineered

to be a good "working partner" with rayon and cotton. Tests have shown that when fortified with at least 15 percent of this type of nylon, cotton work clothes and men's and boys' rayon suits, slacks, and jackets can give up to 70 percent longer wear than all-cotton or all-rayon garments of similar construction.

Du Pont produces only nylon fibers. Various manufacturers make the finished products and attach care instructions. These instructions for apparel care are explained in detail in the Appendix.

Specific care information for bedding, upholstery, curtains, carpets, and other products made of Du Pont textile fibers are found in later entries. Before you refer to these entries, however, read the following general instructions which apply to all of them:

Before hand or machine washing, pretreat badly soiled areas and spots. For heavily soiled areas, pretreat by rubbing with a heavy-duty liquid detergent or a paste of a detergent and water. For spot or stain removal, follow normal procedures for other washable fabrics. For best results, wash white garments with white articles only. Hand wash if garment has delicate trim or construction. Remove articles of trim such as ribbons and bows which you suspect are probably not washable. If, after washing, touch-up ironing is required, use a steam iron or a dry iron at moderate or synthetic setting.

---

**REMOVE CLOTHES** from a dryer while they still feel a little damp to the touch. Actually, they aren't damp. The moisture within the dryer just makes them seem so. Washed items removed at this stage will feel much softer.

---

## All about Flapjacks

The word flapjack is associated with an old custom of making and eating this delicacy on Shrove Tuesday, a movable celebration that is fixed each year by the date of Easter. The ancients always had a final fling on Shrove Tuesday, for the following day—Ash Wednesday—begins the Lenten season of fasting. Pancakes were eaten in great quantities, and the day was often known as Pancake Day. When one side was cooked, the pancake maker flipped the pancake into the air so its uncooked side would come down—flap. Hence: flapjacks.

Old-time cooks and chefs took pride in this exercise and practiced it until they could flip the cake without a miss. No spatula was used. A single

large cake was baked in a pan. Then, according to an old English cookbook, "the way is to hold the pan very steady and toss the pancake with a sudden jerk" while keeping the pan in the correct position to catch the descending cake.

Any kind of pancake can be called a flapjack, but we like a recipe that mixes ½ cup corn meal with 1½ cups of prepared pancake flour. Stir into the flour mixture 2 cups milk to which you have added 1 beaten egg and 2 tablespoons of melted shortening. Bake on a hot greased griddle—or in a pan if you want to try your hand at flipping a flapjack.

## February 18

### Recipe for Fastnachts

Among Germans, the day preceding Ash Wednesday is known as *Fastnacht*. (See yesterday's entry.) Like the English, the Germans long ago made a practice of using up all fats in the house before the beginning of the Lenten season, when no meats were to be eaten. In the Pennsylvania German (or "Dutch") regions, the fats were used for deep-frying doughnuts—and the doughnuts themselves became known as "fastnachts."

Here's how to make them:

 2 cups fresh milk
 6 cups flour, sifted
 1 cake yeast (softened in 1 cup
  lukewarm water)
 1 cup sugar
 3 eggs
 ¼ cup melted butter
 ½ tsp. nutmeg
 ¼ tsp. salt

Scald the milk and set it aside to cool. Add ½ cup of the flour to the softened yeast, and mix to a batter. When scalded milk has become lukewarm, add it to the batter. Then stir in 1 teaspoon of the sugar and about 3 cups of flour. Set batter in a warm place overnight to rise.

Next morning beat the eggs well. Add eggs, butter, nutmeg, salt, and the remaining sugar to batter, and mix thoroughly. Stir in flour until the batter can no longer be stirred with a spoon. Again set aside to rise until light.

Roll out dough on a well-floured board and cut fastnachts with a doughnut cutter. Let the dough rise again. Then fry in hot deep fat (370 degrees) until brown. Yield is about 50 fastnachts.

---

STIR VARNISH , NEVER SHAKE IT. Shaking entraps tiny bubbles that the brush picks up and deposits on the surface being varnished. When the varnish dries, the bubbles disappear but leave imperfections in the coating.

---

# February 19

## Today's SERvants Are SERvices

Your ancestors may have had a valet, butler, cook, gardener, and several maids among their servants. Today, however, only the wealthy can afford servants—when they are available, which they often are not.

If you're lucky, and can afford it, you may get some part-time help with cleaning and other chores. Watch help-available ads in the local newspaper or phone the nearest high school. You may get helpers for ironing, child care, or other jobs through such sources.

Actually, you wouldn't want all of the hired help your grandmother may have had. Instead, such work is now done by a variety of special services.

Consult the Yellow Pages of your telephone book for any number of available services, among them janitorial services (window and wall washing, floor waxing), rug cleaning (done in your home or out), child-care centers or nursery schools, caterers, lawn and garden services, and dry cleaners especially set up to do draperies and slipcovers. Also seek recommendations from your friends.

**PARSNIPS IN PRODUCE SECTIONS** of supermarkets now have been wintered over in the ground and freshly dug. They're at their best.

**SMALL ROOMS?** Use mirrors to create the illusion of more space.

**START FLOWER AND VEGETABLE** seedlings indoors now if your area is normally free of frost about the middle of April.

**SAVE WORN AND TORN** bed sheets to use as drop cloths when painting.

## February 20

### Removing Lipstick from Napkins

Women who really ought to know better invariably wipe their lips and their lipstick on the monogramming of your best napkins.

To remove the lipstick stains, dip the napkins in full-strength household ammonia before washing. This cuts the grease, and the stain then comes out in an ordinary washing. The treatment is especially good for colored napkins when one doesn't want to use bleach. (PK)

## February 21

### Getting Rid of Odors in the Kitchen

If an onion odor clings to dishes and pans after use, even after you have washed and dried them in the usual way, scour them well with table salt. Leave salt within the pan or dish and set the receptacle on the range until the salt browns, shaking frequently. Then wash the container again with soapy water.

Dry mustard will drive an unwelcome odor out of jars. Make a solution, using a teaspoon of mustard to each quart of water. Fill the jar and let it sit overnight. Wash thoroughly in the morning.

---

A SMALL STAPLING GUN is a tool more homes should have. You can often use it—more conveniently—in spots where you usually would use a tack hammer.

---

## February 22

### Kippered Cherries for Washington's Birthday

They want us to celebrate George Washington's birthday as part of a long weekend. Nevertheless, February 22 remains the anniversary of his birth. If you tend to think of cherries on this day because of the cherry-tree chopping legend, we have a great substitute for the usual cherry pie—kippered cherries. This is a fine accompaniment to meat and poultry—and simply great in Manhattans. Here's the recipe:

Pit sour red cherries, place in a crock or glass jar, and cover with cider vinegar. Marinate for two days. Drain vinegar and add a cup of sugar for each cup of cherries. Stir occasionally until the sugar is all dissolved. Put in sterile glass jars and seal.

When fresh cherries are not available, use canned pitted, water-packed red tart cherries. Drain off the water and proceed as above. (M. de G.)

---

FOUNDATION GARMENTS made of nylon were introduced on Feb. 22, 1941.

---

# February 23

## Taking Care
## of Formica Surfaces

So many homes have Formica laminates on kitchen counters and other surfaces that we want to pass along some good care information from a booklet put out by the Formica Corporation.

The tough, durable laminate resists scratches and hard knocks. But slicing can damage the finish. So confine sharp knife edges to a chopping board. And be careful not to hammer or bump edges and corners, for this can cause cracks and chips.

Heat up to 275 degrees, which includes boiling water, is unlikely to cause any harm to the surface. But remember that pots and pans, straight from the range or oven, are blistering hot. Always set them on a trivet or asbestos-lined hot pad. Also keep irons on your ironing board and lighted cigarettes on ashtrays.

For ordinary cleaning, simply wipe with a damp cloth. Avoid use of abrasives, scouring powders, peroxide, or strong bleaches. These can dull the surface and make it stain-prone. If a stain should appear, wipe with a mild soap and a damp cloth. If the stain still persists, use a very *light* touch with Bon Ami or Lava soap.

Indelible inks may stain a countertop. Since this type of ink is sometimes used on food packages, be careful when unpacking groceries on a damp countertop.

---

**FORCE BLOSSOMS of forsythia, flowering quince, and fruit trees this month by placing cut branches in a container of water. Put the container in a warm place.**

---

# February 24

## Check Quality Grades of
## Vegetables You Buy

Many canned and frozen vegetables are sold under quality grades established and maintained by consumer and marketing experts of the United States Department of Agriculture. Grade A is top quality and generally costs more. For economy you may want to choose a lower grade.

If a vegetable is packed under continuous USDA inspection, individual cans and frozen packages may be labeled with any one of the following grade names, sometimes within a shield.

"U.S. Grade A or Fancy." These vegetables are carefully selected for color, tenderness, and freedom from blemishes. They are the most tender, succulent, and flavorful vegetables that it's possible to buy, canned or frozen.

"U.S. Grade B or Extra Standard." These are of

excellent quality, but not quite so carefully selected for color and tenderness as the top grade. They usually are more mature and therefore may have a slightly different taste from top-grade vegetables.

"U.S. Grade C or Standard." These are not so uniform in color and flavor as vegetables in the upper grades and they usually are more mature. They are a thrifty buy when appearance is not too important—for instance, if you're using the vegetables as ingredients in soups or soufflés.

"Packed under continuous inspection of the U.S. Department of Agriculture." This statement provides assurance of a product of at least minimum quality.

Most canned and frozen vegetables are packed and priced according to quality even though a grade is not shown on the label. Sometimes a grade name is indicated without the "U.S." By law, such vegetables must be of the quality indicated even though they were not officially inspected.

Brand names also are often a measure of quality. Producers of nationally advertised products spend considerable effort to maintain the same quality year after year in order to keep their customers. Unadvertised brands may also offer an assurance of quality, often at a slightly lower price. And many stores, particularly chain stores, carry two or more qualities under their own labels.

## Try These Breakfast Surprises

Most people like a change now and then from conventional breakfasts. Here are a few ways to get variety—and maybe surprises—into breakfast on these wintry mornings.

Cut slices of leftover oatmeal, corn-meal mush, or other cooked cereal and brown in a little fat. To slice and brown well, the cereal must be thick and cold.

Split leftover rolls, biscuits, muffins, or corn bread and toast in the oven. Or put crisp bacon between halves of toasted rolls.

Use stale bread to make an old favorite: French toast. Dip bread in a mixture of egg and milk or egg and tomato juice. Brown carefully in a little fat.

Sauté chicken livers and serve on toast. Crisp bacon can be used as a garnish.

Mix fruits when you do not have enough of one kind to go around. This gives a nice change of flavor. You might use berries with sliced peaches, for instance, or sliced bananas with oranges.

To add interest to cereals, top with your favorite fruits—fresh in season, or frozen, canned, or dried. Fruits go well with both hot and ready-to-eat cereals.

Sprinkle grated cheese over eggs to be baked, or combine with scrambled eggs for a different flavor treat.

Scramble eggs with tomatoes. To serve six: Beat together 6 eggs and 1 cup of cooked or canned tomatoes. Season, and cook in a little fat over low heat, stirring constantly, until the eggs are done as desired.

Broil or fry tomatoes—red or green—seasoned with salt and pepper, and serve with bacon.

Take a tip from New England and have Saturday night's baked beans on Sunday morning—perhaps with codfish cakes and brown bread.

Chop cold, cooked potatoes and heat in a little fat. Then scramble them with eggs.

## February 26

### Do Your Children Say "Please" and "Thank You"?

The question above reminds us of a story: Dr. Spock, the famous pediatrician, concluded a speech to a woman's club and opened the floor to questions. One woman stated that her son was six years old and asked how soon she could start teaching him table manners. The reply from Dr. Spock was to hurry home, as she had already missed the best six years.

Children's manners, as well as morals and values, are established in the preschool years, according to child educators. They learn from example—your example. If you make requests saying "please" and follow with "thank you," so will they.

That's why, when you encounter a youngster who strikes you as being exceptionally polite, you can be absolutely sure he learned it at home. When parents always remember the niceties of human relationships, children naturally will do likewise. In such homes, "please" and "thank you" are common expressions.

Honesty is another characteristic that children learn by example. Its opposite likewise is quickly picked up—a fact that all parents ought to keep in mind when their children see them doing something questionable. The same holds true for honesty's first cousin—truthfulness.

What does this all add up to? It can be stated very simply:

Be what you want your children to be.

# February 27

## The Children's Hour

Between the dark and the daylight,
    When the night is beginning to lower,
Comes a pause in the day's occupations,
    That is known as the Children's Hour.

I hear in the chamber above me
    The patter of little feet,
The sound of a door that is opened,
    And voices soft and sweet.

From my study I see in the lamplight,
    Descending the broad hall stair,
Grave Alice, and laughing Allegra,
    And Edith with golden hair.

A whisper, and then a silence:
    Yet I know by their merry eyes
They are plotting and planning together
    To take me by surprise.

A sudden rush from the stairway,
    A sudden raid from the hall!
By three doors left unguarded
    They enter my castle wall!

They climb up into my turret
    O'er the arms and back of my chair;
If I try to escape, they surround me;
    They seem to be everywhere.

They almost devour me with kisses,
    Their arms about me entwine,
Till I think of the Bishop of Bingen
    In his Mouse-Tower on the Rhine!

Do you think, O blue-eyed banditti,
    Because you have scaled the wall,
Such an old mustache as I am
    Is not a match for you all!

I have you fast in my fortress,
    And will not let you depart,
But put you down into the dungeon
    In the round-tower of my heart.

And there will I keep you forever,
    Yes, forever and a day,
Till the walls shall crumble to ruin,
    And moulder in dust away!

—Henry Wadsworth Longfellow

## February Potpourri for Homemakers

Use paper towels under milk containers in the refrigerator. They will catch any drips and you won't have to wash the refrigerator shelves so often. Use paper towels, too, under the can in which you store waste fat.

---

Clean pictures and mirrors as well as windows by using paper towels and a liquid window cleaner.

---

Absorb excess fat by placing bacon, sausage, and other fatty foods on paper toweling after cooking. Pour the fat from the pan into the waste-fat can and wipe the pan well with paper towels. Congealed fat is the number-one drain clogger.

---

Blot up liquid spills on rugs and carpets with paper towels, then proceed to clean the area in the manner recommended to remove the particular spill.

---

Use pieces of waxed paper to spread the fat when greasing casseroles and oiling molds.

## February 29

### Lemon Meringue Pie:
### Leap Year Overture

Today comes only once every four years. We call it Leap Year Day. It's the traditional time for gals to take the initiative and make overtures to guys. There's no better overture than a lemon meringue pie. What man doesn't rank this among his favorite desserts?

Take one of the baked pie shells you froze (see February 8) from the freezer, unwrap it, let thaw, then put it in a 400-degree oven for 6 or 7 minutes. Cool on a wire rack.

Filling: Separate 3 eggs. In a saucepan mix 1½ cups sugar, 6 tablespoons cornstarch, and ¼ teaspoon salt. Add 1½ cups boiling water and cook over high heat, stirring constantly until mixture is thick and transparent. Remove from heat. Stir some of the mixture into 3 well-beaten egg yolks, return it to the rest of the mixture, and cook over low heat 6 minutes, stirring constantly. Remove from heat and add 2 tablespoons butter and ½ cup fresh lemon juice. Cool. Put into pie shell and top with meringue.

Meringue: Beat 3 egg whites with ¼ teaspoon cream of tartar until foamy. Gradually add 6 tablespoons sugar and continue beating until the whites will hold peaks when the beater is removed. Spread over lemon filling, making sure the meringue touches the edge of the crust. Bake at 400 degrees until the meringue is browned. Cool several hours before cutting.

### Your Own Reminders:

_____

_____

_____

_____

_____

_____

_____

_____

# March 1

## New Resilient-Tile Floor? Put It Down Yourself

Public relations people for some of the resilient-tile manufacturers are getting smarter. They're producing literature showing housewives putting down the tiles. And why not, indeed!

Perhaps you'd like to have a new floor as part of your renovations this spring. If so, you may want to undertake the task yourself. Invite the man of the house to help, if you wish. But you won't really need him.

For how to go about the job, check several of the local outlets for names of major flooring manufacturers—companies such as Armstrong Cork, Kentile, and Azrock. Or write directly to those companies whose addresses you can find in magazine or newspaper advertising. In some cases a new floor can be put down over an old one.

# March 2

TODAY IN HISTORY: *March 2, 1866, was an important date in the development of sewing needles. The Excelsior Needle Company was organized on that date in Wolcottville, Conn. Until then, needles had been made by hand. Machines in the Excelsior plant began turning them out inexpensively in uniform sizes and shapes.*

## Necessary Supplies for Your Sewing Basket

The machine-made needles developed in 1866 are the heart of all hand sewing. An assortment of various-sized needles should be kept in your sewing basket. You will also want to equip the basket with a thimble and spools of Size 50 or 60 cotton and silk thread in a range of colors. Extra strong button thread is needed to sew buttons back on heavy garments. Buttons kept in a small see-through plastic bag in the basket will help you find quick replacements for lost buttons.

Include a tape measure and papers of common (straight) pins, hooks and eyes, and snaps. And don't forget a pair of scissors.

Stretch socks containing man-made fibers are so long-lasting that the art of darning has pretty much passed out of existence. If you still darn socks, however, you will want to include in your basket assorted shades of darning cotton and a darning egg.

**A HOTEL FOR WOMEN ONLY was opened in New York City on March 2, 1903—the Martha Washington.**

# March 3

**TODAY IN HISTORY:** *On March 3, 1879, Belva Ann Bennett Lockwood became the first woman lawyer admitted to practice before the U.S. Supreme Court. An act permitting admission of women had been signed only a few days before by President Rutherford B. Hayes.*

## "Where There's a Will There's a Way"

Belva Ann Bennett Lockwood, the first woman lawyer admitted to practice before the U.S. Supreme Court in 1879, undoubtedly knew all the answers about wills and estate planning. But the rest of us need help.

Good financial planning should meet the needs of the family both currently and after the death of those upon whom the family depends for its livelihood. It should be adaptable to changing situations.

As a first step toward a financial plan which meets the above criteria, we suggest you inventory your assets and liabilities. Assets include personal property, real estate, investments, insurance, and equity in pension or profit-sharing plans. Liabilities embrace not only outstanding debts such as mortgages, but also taxes which would be due in the event of your death.

A good second step is to get an overview of the more than a dozen options open to you in planning your estate. There are excellent books published on the subject which can help you. Refer to the card catalog in your library under "Wills."

Last, and most important, consult a competent lawyer who is an expert in tax laws and laws having to do with wills and who is well versed in the variations in the laws of your state.

# March 4

**TODAY IN HISTORY:** *The Government Printing Office began operation on March 4, 1861, in a printing plant purchased from Joseph T. Crowell, of Washington, D.C.*

## Government Pamphlets about Seafood

We have already told you about the many useful Government Printing Office publications you can order through the Superintendent of Documents (see January 12). We want to return to that topic today—on the anniversary of the Printing Office—to tell you about the great wealth of useful material that's currently available to help homemakers make the best use of seafood, a fine source of protein for the family at any time of the year.

Several dozens of valuable seafood publications have been issued in recent years through the efforts of two major branches of the U.S. Government—the Department of the Interior and the Department of Commerce. Some publications were subsidized by commercial fishing interests. Several are printed in both English and Spanish, an example being "Common Sense Fish Cookery."

Other titles you may like to know about include the following:

"Fish for Compliments on a Budget"
"Portraits with Pollock"
"Take a Can of Salmon"
"Flavor of Maine (Sardine Secrets)"
"Let's Cook Fish"
"Time for Seafood"

and many more.

---

**FIRST WOMAN MEMBER of a President's cabinet was Frances Perkins, who took office on March 4, 1933, as Secretary of Labor after appointment by President Franklin Roosevelt. She served 12 years, until June 30, 1945.**

---

## *March 5*

### How to Squeeze More Cents Out of a Dollar

All of us know certain homemakers who always seem to make their money do more and buy more than some of the rest of us. What's their secret? More than likely, it's not any one thing or practice.

Rather, it's probably a constant awareness of choices to be made or rules to be followed. Some of them:

Buy seconds or irregulars in sheets, shirts, towels, socks, and underwear.

Wait and take advantage of annual or semiannual "white" sales.

When certain items are used in quantity, it makes sense to buy them in quantity if you can get a lower rate per item.

If you will need a tool or other item only once or twice, rent it instead of buying it. Check the

Yellow Pages for companies that rent all sorts of things.

Shine your own shoes instead of paying to have it done.

Buy for cash whenever you can. It costs you money to buy "on time."

Take a freeway instead of a toll road.

Do your grocery shopping with a list of what you actually need. Impulse shopping can really cost you money—for things that you find you do not really want or need.

When you discover that you need an item for your home, put it down on your Wanted List—and then, if possible, wait to see if you read or hear of it being on sale at a bargain price.

Do your own telephone dialing instead of asking an operator to do it. The services of an operator usually cost money.

## *March* **6**

### Uses for Ammonia Water

Ammonia water will accomplish many jobs. It's a "must" among your housecleaning supplies. An alkaline, it will cut oil and grease, as well as neutralize the acids in urine and perspiration.

Follow directions on the label as to the amounts to add to tap water for various jobs, increasing the amounts if needed. Always add the ammonia water to the tap water (not the other way around) to decrease its pungency. The solution may be used to wash windows, woodwork, and floors. Use it to wash nylon hosiery, combs and brushes, and jewelry. Add a little to the water you rinse socks in to "sweeten" them. After removing baby or dog "mistakes," go over the area with the

solution to remove any odor, then rinse with clear water.

An ammonia-water solution will make your kitchen counters, appliance surfaces, and range top sparkle.

If you have a self-cleaning oven but must remove the racks before starting the self-cleaning action, soak them in a wash tub or bathtub in a strong ammonia-water solution. The baked-on grease will then be easily removed with a metal sponge.

If your oven is not self-cleaning, the next time you decide to clean it, set a pan of full-strength ammonia water on an oven rack the night before

and close the door to the oven. It will loosen the baked-on grease so that it can be removed with a steel-wool soap pad. Then rinse with an ammonia-water solution.

When doing any of the jobs mentioned above, take care that the solution does not come into contact with the eyes or prolonged contact with the skin. And, keep it out of the reach of children!

## March 7

### Raise Shasta Daisies, Burbank's Pride

This is the birthday of Luther Burbank, the almost legendary plant breeder and hybridizer, born in 1849 on a farm at Lancaster, Massachusetts.

One of his finer products was the Shasta daisy, which you should include in your garden if you haven't already done so. Burbank crossed the English daisy, the wild American variety, and a Japanese type to produce the Shasta, whose glistening white flowers are actually summer-blooming chrysanthemums.

Burbank did most of his experiments with plants in California, which celebrates his birthday as Arbor Day.

## March 8

### Feeding the Sick Family Member

The "cure" suggested by doctors for so many of the strange viruses that beset us is bed rest and lots of fluids, including juices, broths and bouillons, and eggnogs. Keep cans of juices and packets of instant bouillon on your pantry shelf in readiness for the time the "bug" hits the family.

When the sick member of the family begins to feel better, but still is not up to eating his usual fare, he will probably be able to tackle such soft foods as cooked cereal, soft-cooked eggs, and milk toast. To make milk toast, pour a cup of scalded milk over two pieces of toast which have been buttered and seasoned lightly with salt and pepper.

When the ill family member has recuperated to the point that he is able to eat table food, don't overwhelm him—make the portions small. He can always ask for more.

When food must be served in bed, make the tray as attractive as you can. A small vase of flowers, or a toy for a child, will work wonders.

---

**USE ALL OF ORANGES or grapefruit. Candy the rind. See a cookbook recipe for how to do it.**

---

60

## March 9

### Gather Your Own Escargots? Maybe You Can

Depending on where you live in the U.S., you may be able to gather enough edible snails in your backyard to try one of the gourmet recipes found in most cookbooks.

A report from the agricultural extension service at the University of California says the brown garden snail (*Helix aspersa Muller*) is the most common snail pest in that state, chiefly in coastal or semicoastal regions where cool, humid conditions exist. The report adds: "It was introduced from France during the 1850s for use as food, but is eaten here only by an occasional European immigrant."

The snails are active at night or on dark, cloudy, or foggy days. Under dry conditions they either seal themselves to various surfaces, such as walls, curbs, or tree trunks, or close the opening of their shell with a white, parchmentlike membrane. They resume activity when conditions become moist.

The brown snail lays its eggs in a nest in damp soil. The eggs are white, spherical, and about one-eighth inch in diameter. The egg mass contains an average of 86 eggs. The young snails remain in the nest from two to four days and then work their way to the surface. They mature in two to three years.

Want to raise your own? Maybe you could. Gather a few, let them multiply.

# March **10**

## How to Buy Fish and How Much to Buy

Fish are sold in various ways. Some forms are ready to cook. Others need cleaning. How much you should buy for your family depends on the form in which you buy it.

Fish is sold in the following ways:

**Whole or round.** This is fish just as they were caught. They must be cleaned (by removing the insides) and the scales must be taken off before they can be cooked. The head, tail, and fins may be cut off before cooking. For each person that you want to serve, buy from three-fourths to one pound of whole fish.

**Drawn.** A drawn fish has been cleaned. It must be scaled, however, and have the fins cut off before it is cooked. Buy three-fourths of a pound per serving.

**Dressed.** A dressed fish has been both cleaned and scaled. The head, tail, and fins usually have been cut off also. A pound of dressed fish serves two.

**Fillets.** These are the sides of a fish. They have been cut away from the backbone. They are ready to cook.

**Steaks.** These are slices of fish ¾- to 1-inch thick. They have been cut across the fish. A part of the backbone is the only bone in a fish steak. Fish steaks are ready to cook.

**Chunks.** These are pieces cut across the fish also, but chunks are larger than steaks. They are ready to cook.

**Portions.** These are pieces of fish cut from blocks of frozen fillets and usually covered with batter. All in a package are the same size. Some are sold raw, some are cooked a little before being frozen. Both types must be cooked. Read the package label for cooking instructions.

A pound of fish fillets, steaks, chunks, or portions will serve three people.

**Sticks.** These are made the same way as portions. All sticks are cooked somewhat before being frozen. You must finish the cooking before serving. A pound of sticks serves four.

**Canned.** Tuna, salmon, mackerel, and Maine sardines are cooked and then canned. Canned fish are good in cooked dishes, sandwiches, and salads. They are ready to use when taken from the can. A pound of canned fish when combined with other ingredients will serve six.

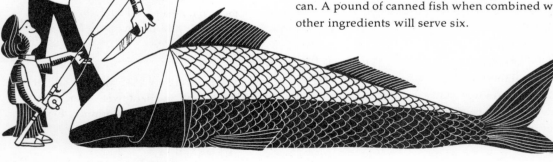

# March 11

## Good Rules for Storing Food

Put meats and poultry in a refrigerator only if you plan to use them within a few days. For refrigerator storage maintain temperatures of between 35 and 40 degrees Fahrenheit. Keep meats and poultry in the coldest part of the refrigerator, usually near the ice cube compartment or in a special meat keeper. See the storage table in the Appendix for the safe length of time you can usually refrigerate various items.

Wrap meat loosely to allow air to circulate around the meat. Sometimes you can loosen the store wrapping. The special wrap on prepackaged poultry is designed to control moisture loss in the refrigerator. Wrapped raw poultry should be unwrapped, placed on a platter, and covered for refrigeration. Wrap and store giblets separately.

Refrigerate ready-to-serve meats, such as luncheon meats, in their original wrappings until you use them.

Store canned products in a cool, dry place—not in a cabinet above the stove. Any unused product may be left in the can, covered, and refrigerated. Refrigerate canned products marked "perishable" or "keep under refrigeration."

Cover leftovers tightly and refrigerate or freeze immediately. Whenever possible put large quantities in several small containers rather than one large one to speed cooling.

Separate the meat or poultry, stuffing, and broth or gravy, and store in the refrigerator in different containers.

Use leftovers promptly.

---

"In love of home, the love of country has its rise."
—Charles Dickens

---

# March 12

## How Does Your Kitchen Rate in Efficiency?

In a kitchen the sequence of work moves from storage to preparation, to cooking and serving. The logical arrangement has the refrigerator and its associated storage areas for foodstuffs near the service entrance, followed by the sink (or mixing center), then the cook-and-serve area as convenient as possible to the eating area. For fastest after-meal cleanup, the eating area also should be convenient to the sink and food disposal equipment.

Kitchen planners long ago agreed that for greatest efficiency you should have the three work centers—the sink, refrigerator, and range—each at the point of a work triangle.

Hotpoint's Kitchen and Laundry Planning Service points out that each work center should have sufficient counter space. The refrigerator should have a minimum of 15 inches of counter at the opening side for loading and unloading. Ideally, the range should have space on each side, as should the sink, the latter enough to accommodate a dishwasher.

Placing unrelated appliances side by side —refrigerator and oven, for instance—overlooks the need for functional counter space. The open door of the highest built-in oven should be lower than the user's elbow. Mounting too high can make it difficult to remove roasting and baking pans.

Appliance doors should open so as not to block kitchen traffic.

## March 13

## Help Children Form Good Health Habits

Parental guidance and supervision are necessary if children are to develop good health habits. The time to begin is in the early years.

Baby teeth, important to gum and bone structure, should be brushed twice a day. Provide a stool that the young child can use to reach the basin and the correct size toothbrush for his mouth. Place your hand over his to guide him in brushing the correct way—down on the upper teeth and up on the lowers.

A stool will also enable the child to reach the basin for hand washing before meals and after toileting and for face, neck, and ear washing before going to bed. Bathing on a regular schedule is important, too. (Caution: Never let a young child bathe unless you are in the bathroom with him.)

Toothbrushing, washing, and bathing habits are usually pleasant for the child to acquire as almost all children enjoy "playing" with water.

Your guidance and supervision are also necessary if the child is to develop good eye habits. Make sure the room in which the television set is located is properly lighted and avoid prolonged viewing. Long before the child can read words, he will "picture read" magazines and books. Help him to position these correctly.

# March 14

## Facts about Cotton for Homemakers

Cotton is strong, absorbent, and washable. Mercerized cotton has been treated with caustic soda to make it even stronger. Most cotton sewing thread has been strengthened in this way.

Look at the labels when buying cloth or garments to see if shrinkage has been minimized by a patented process such as Sanforization. If not, allow for shrinkage when purchasing such items.

Cotton is subject to attack by mildew and silverfish, therefore cotton articles should be stored in a clean, dry condition. Soiled cotton items should not be put in the clothes hamper if they are damp or wet and they should be washed as soon as possible. Cotton is resistant to moths.

There are two basic types of cotton sheets and pillowcases—muslin and percale. Muslin wears better and is less expensive. Fine sheets are made of percale. Its lighter weight makes it easier to handle.

No ironing is necessary for bedding and clothing when fiber content labels state polyester and cotton in certain percentages. These products are increasingly popular as they offer advantages for travel and home laundering.

> "Love me, love my dog."
> —John Heywood

# March 15

## How to Be a Smart Meat Shopper

Meat costs put a big dent in our budgets nowadays. So you ought to buy all meats and poultry carefully and take care of them properly until you are ready to cook them.

Try to shop only in stores with well-kept stor-

age and display cases. If a store is sloppy in that respect, it may be sloppy in other ways you cannot see. Buy frozen items only if they are kept hard-frozen in the store.

Select frozen meats and poultry, as well as other frozen foods, just before leaving the store. Ask the clerk to package them together. Get the frozen package home as soon as possible—and into the freezer. If you have other errands, shop for groceries last. Don't leave frozen or fresh meat and poultry sitting in a hot car.

Use U.S. Department of Agriculture shields as

a guide in buying better meats. USDA grades for beef, veal, and lamb are an indication of the tenderness, juiciness, and flavor of the meat. USDA Choice is the grade most commonly sold. Highest grade is USDA Prime. Lower grades include USDA Good, Standard, and Commercial. There are no consumer marks for pork.

USDA grades for poultry are guides to meatiness and appearance. Tenderness depends on the age of the poultry, indicated by words such as "young" or "broiler-fryer." USDA Grade A is the only grade you are likely to find on a poultry label. Lower grades are seldom indicated.

## *March* **16**

### How to Make Your Own House Numbers

Is your house number displayed prominently somewhere on your property? You can buy suitable numbers and put them up. But perhaps a tool-using member of your household would like to make them—as part of the spring spruce-up of your home.

We have seen homemade numbers we think you'd like. They were made from redwood, a material that's long lasting in any weather, that has a handsome natural grain, and that's easy to work. Your local building-supply center can sell you the small amount of redwood you'll need.

For full information about completing the project, send a dime to Redwood House Numbers, Lousiana-Pacific Corporation, 1300 S.W. Fifth Ave., Portland, Ore. 97201. The plan set includes sample numbers on graph paper so you can enlarge them to the size you want.

One should know that four-inch letters are readable from 140 feet away, six-inchers from 210 feet, and eight-inchers from as far as 280 feet.

You cut out the number patterns with a coping, saber, or jig saw. You then give the numbers a rugged three-dimensional surface with a gouge, wood rasp, or power tool. This texturing provides a dramatic surface, making the numbers easier to read. The plans include finishing suggestions.

---

**WASH ALUMINUM window and door screens at least once a year, using water, a mild detergent, and a stiff brush. This will remove any build-up of airborne dirt.**

---

**REMOVE SNAPS and buttons when you discard old garments. Save them in your sewing basket for future use.**

---

# March 17

## An Irish Fruitcake, Begorra!

It's St. Patrick's Day. So let's think Irish. For instance, how about an Irish whiskey fruitcake? Never heard of one? Neither did we, but we note you can get an imported one by mail order—in a green tin (sometimes), with Molly O'Rourke's label. For the facts, write to Country Store, Pine Mountain, Ga. 31822.

# March 18

## Tips on Taking Care of Aluminum Cookware

Aluminum cookware designed for service and display is almost always made of polished bare aluminum or porcelain-finished aluminum. The porcelain-finished pots may be washed by hand or in the dishwasher. Almost any type of powder and soap, even steel wool, may safely be used on porcelain because it is so hard.

Polished aluminum pots can be washed in the dishwasher and by hand with mild soap or detergent or some fine polishes. Some dishwasher detergents may etch the polished surface. Mirror-bright aluminum pots can only be washed with soaps and detergents; polishes and nylon pads usually dull the finish.

When an aluminum pot is used to cook eggs and certain other foods (or exposed to some tap water) the inside may become blackish. This will harm neither the pot nor the food. However, if the color is disturbing, try cooking some tomatoes or sauerkraut in the pot. If you do not care for these foods, add one to two tablespoons of cream of tartar to every quart of water the pot holds and boil.

Pots lined with Teflon and similar non-stick materials should be washed clean, dried, and then rubbed with a little cooking oil before using. Some of the newer Teflon coatings are abrasion resistant. If not advertised as scratch resistant, it is best to use a rubber or plastic kitchen cooking tool when working with these pots. Forks, for example, tend

to make holes in the non-stick coatings, reducing their effectiveness.

This information and tips on care for other popular aluminum items are included in a booklet "Care of Aluminum," available for 25 cents from The Aluminum Association, 750 Third Ave., New York, N.Y. 10017.

> **"That worldly principle, Charity begins at home."**
> **—Sir Thomas Browne**

## March 19

### Try Putting Up Wallboard? Why Not?

In the spring one tends to think about sprucing up the home. In that mood, many of us get out painting supplies or buy wallpaper—and set to work. But there's really no reason a homemaker should set such limits to her abilities. She can do many other home improvement tasks, too—for instance, putting up wallboard.

If that prospect interests you, we'd like you to know about one good source of instructions. You can write for a free four-page illustrated brochure entitled "Do-It-Yourself . . . Gypsum Wallboard Application." It shows and tells you everything you need to know about the job. Write to C. T. Martin, Georgia-Pacific Corporation, 900 S.W. Fifth Ave., Portland, Ore. 97204.

## March 20

### How to Make Your Own Furniture Polish

You can make a wonderful, time-tested furniture polish, very easily and very cheaply. The formula has been used, both in England and America, for a couple of centuries. Here it is:

Melt 1 pound pure beeswax in 1 quart of pure spirits of turpentine (do *not* use a substitute or compound!) in a double boiler over a low flame. Precise proportions are not important; if you want the polish harder, add more wax; if softer, add more turpentine. This quantity will give you enough to share with a friend, and you'll like what it does to your antique furniture. Both ingredients are great for the wood and the finish.

You can put it in any available wide-mouthed jars, but avoid those with rubber sealing rings —the turpentine tends to dissolve the rubber. (JOP)

---

"We may live without poetry, music
   and art;
We may live without conscience
   and live without heart;
We may live without friends; we
   may live without books;
But civilized man can not live
   without cooks."
   —Edward Robert Bulwer Lytton

---

"No legacy is so rich as honesty."
   —William Shakespeare

---

## March 21

### Wringer Washer? Maybe You Could Use One

Automatic washing machines have driven wringer and spinner washers from the majority of modern homes. But the older machines still are put to good use in some homes—especially where the man-of-the-house engages in a daily occupation that results in grimy clothing (miners and mechanics, for instance). Use of the older washer conserves the automatic.

If the idea interests you, perhaps you can locate one of the antiques in a second-hand store—if nowhere else. Mail-order catalogs offer repair parts.

## March 22

### When Does Easter Come?

Easter is a Christian holiday whose date varies each year. In A.D. 325, a church council agreed that Easter should be determined by the time of the first full moon after March 21, falling on the first Sunday thereafter. This means, therefore, that Easter never can come earlier than this date—March 22. Nor can it be later than April 25.

The holiday, in fact, comes most often during the month of April. During the quarter century from 1975 to 2000, Easter will come in March only six times—March 30 in 1975, 1986, and 1997; March 26 in 1978 and 1989; and March 31 in 1991. In the year 2000, Easter will fall on April 23—the only time in the quarter of a century it will be that late.

**CUT BRANCHES** of pussy-willow trees now to force for indoor blooms.

**DON'T BE GYPPED!** A pamphlet with that title is available from the Federal Trade Commission, 6th St. & Pennsylvania Ave. N.W., Washington, D.C. 20580. Ask for FTC Buyer's Guide No. 8.

"And hie him home, at evening's close,
To sweet repast and calm repose."
—Thomas Gray

# *March* **23**

## Serve Breakfast for Less

Breakfast can be inexpensive and still provide its share of the day's food requirements. Nutritionists advocate that breakfast make up at least one-fourth of the day's needs. If every penny counts in your household, consider the following:

Evaporated milk, skim milk, and buttermilk may be less expensive than fluid whole milk. Non-fat dry milk is an especially good buy because of its low cost.

Whole-grain and enriched cereals—particularly the kinds you cook yourself—are bargains in food value. Make them the main part of breakfast often.

Shell color doesn't affect the food value you get from eggs. So buy the less expensive ones. Another way to save is to choose lower grade eggs when they are satisfactory for the use you want to make of them. Grade A eggs, for instance, are best for cooking in the shell, frying, and poaching. Grade B eggs are all right for scrambling, for omelets, and other cooking or baking.

Fresh fruits usually are good buys when they are in season locally. At other times of the year, check cost of a serving of fruit prepared in different ways—fresh, frozen, canned, dried, or as juice.

Ready-to-eat foods and those partially prepared when you buy them often cost more than the same items made at home.

---

**DINNER SUGGESTION: Warm slices of leftover beef or pork roast in barbecue sauce to which you've added a little lemon juice, Tabasco sauce, Worcestershire sauce, and brown sugar. (The amounts depend on your taste.) Serve on hamburger rolls.**

---

## Important Facts about Fluorescent Lamps

Most households use fluorescent lighting in some form. In choosing tubes, you should keep in mind that white fluorescent tubes are labeled either "standard" or "deluxe." The whiteness of a standard tube is indicated by letters, WW for warm white; CW for cool white. The addition of an X to these letters indicates a deluxe tube.

A deluxe warm white (WWX) gives a flattering light, can be used with incandescent light, and does not distort colors any more than incandescent light does. A deluxe cool white (CWX) tube simulates daylight and goes nicely with cool color schemes of blue and green. Deluxe tubes are the only fluorescent tubes that government experts recommend for home use. Ask your dealer to order them if he doesn't have them on hand.

---

*"I in mine own house am an emperor and will defend what's mine."*
—**Philip Massinger**

---

# *March* **24**

## Children Have Two Eyes, Two Ears, and Two Feet

They will never have more, nor will they be able to replace what they have. As a parent it is your responsibility to help them safeguard these precious body parts.

If you suspect any eye or ear ailment or deficiency, take the child to your doctor promptly. Only he is equipped to diagnose and recommend treatment. Follow his recommendations to the letter, including suggestions for follow-up visits.

School nurses and school doctors screen children for vision and auditory perception, both essential for normal reading development. They will notify you of any deviations from norms. Check these out with your doctor as soon as possible. If eyeglasses or exercises or hearing aids are prescribed, make sure your child follows the prescription. If you move and the child changes schools, eye or ear problems are normally included in the transcript forwarded to the new school, but oversights can occur so it is wise to notify the new school by note, telephone call, or in person.

Handing down clothing from older to younger children in the family is an economic necessity for most of us. Hand-me-down shoes should be an exception, however, unless you are assured that they fit properly. A shoe salesman in whom you have confidence may be willing to give you this assurance. Otherwise, don't take a chance—discard the shoes.

---

**WANT MORE FACTS about "the Pill"? Write to the Government Printing Office, Washington, D.C. 20402, and ask for a copy of an article entitled "The Pill" reprinted from the Food and Drug Administration's Publication, "The FDS Consumer."**

---

**"Set thine house in order!"**
        **—2 Kings XX, 1**

# March 25

## Hand Tools Homemakers Should Have

In every home, the man of the house ought to have the hand and power tools necessary to make household repairs. But in our opinion the homemaker should have her own basic collection of tools that only she uses—when she decides to undertake a job without waiting for the M.O.H. to get around to it.

Take a hammer, for instance. There always seems to be a need to pound *something*. Make it a lightweight claw hammer. Then you can pull out nuisance nails and tacks, too.

Next, let's have a couple of screwdrivers—a medium-sized one and a very small one; maybe also a Phillips-head screwdriver for those pesky Phillips-head screws you occasionally find.

For making holes to start screws, get a small twist drill—the kind with a wood handle placed crosswise at the top of the drill.

A pair of pliers? Yes, a pair with a wire-cutting slot. Also a small adjustable open-end wrench. Use the wrench instead of pliers to turn the nuts that need turning.

Add a handsaw if you wish, but that's a tool you might better depend on scrounging from the M.O.H. when need arises.

Keep *your* tools in a kitchen drawer.

# March 26

## Stuffed Lamb Cushion for Easter

Lamb is a traditional food for Easter. The lamb is a symbol of Jesus. In John 1:29 Jesus is referred to as "the Lamb of God, who takes away the sin of the world." Historians tell us the symbol was derived from the ancient Jewish practice of sacrificing the paschal lamb in the Temple in Jerusalem during the traditional Passover ceremony.

The following recipe yields from six to eight servings:

4 oz. stuffing mix
½ cup chopped walnuts
1 cup mixed candied fruit
1 vegetable bouillon cube
2 Tbs. melted butter
1 lamb shoulder (3½ to 4 lbs.)
Salt & pepper
3 Tbs. flour

Combine in mixing bowl the stuffing mix, walnuts, and half the candied fruit. Dissolve bouillon cube in 1 cup hot water and lightly stir half the bouillon and the butter into stuffing mixture. Fill a pocket cut into the lamb shoulder with the stuffing and sew or skewer the edges to hold them tightly.

Sprinkle the shoulder with salt and pepper. Bake at 325 degrees about 2 hours, or until meat thermometer reads 165 to 170 degrees for medium doneness. Baste occasionally with remaining bouillon and pan drippings. To prepare gravy, blend flour and ½ teaspoon salt into pan drippings and brown over low heat, stirring constantly. Add 1¼ cups cold water; cook and stir until gravy is thickened. Add the remainder of the candied fruit and serve with holiday lamb.

**WHY NOT TRY HYDROPONICS?** **Growing plants in a water solution, without soil, was done successfully on several Pacific islands during World War II to produce green vegetables for the armed forces. The plant roots are placed in water to which chemical nutrients have been added. Check the library for books on how to try hydroponics in your home on a limited basis this winter.**

## Make Sure Your Family Gets Enough Milk

Milk is an excellent source of calcium, protein, and riboflavin. It also supplies fat and sugar, and contains many other vitamins and minerals. Because of this, dieticians urge that we be sure to get enough milk each day—in one form or another.

They recommend that children under nine have the equivalent of two or three eight-ounce glasses each day, that children from nine to 12 and pregnant women have three or more, that teenagers and nursing mothers have four or more, and adults at least two.

This intake need not always be fresh whole milk. On the basis of the calcium provided, you can substitute any of the following for each eight-ounce glass of whole milk:

1 cup (8 ounces) custard

1⅓ ounces natural cheddar cheese

1½ ounces processed cheddar cheese

1⅓ cups creamed cottage cheese

1 cup cocoa made with milk

1⅓ cups ice cream

¾ cup homemade macaroni and cheese
   (see March 28)

1 milkshake made from ⅔ cup milk
   and ½ cup ice cream

1 cup oyster stew

1/5 of 15-inch-diameter round pizza,
   made with cheese topping

1 cup pudding, made with milk
   and cornstarch

1 cup yogurt

## Thoughts on Child Rearing

Everyone has opinions about the art of raising children. Here are a few quotes on the subject that we find particularly appropriate.

"Give a little love to a child, and you get a great deal back." —John Ruskin

"The hand that rocks the cradle is the hand that rules the world." —William Ross Wallace

Women know the way to rear up children (to be just),
They know a simple, merry, tender knack of tying sashes, fitting baby-shoes,
And stringing pretty words that make no sense.
                —Elizabeth Barrett Browning

## March 28

### Macaroni and Cheese

The next time you make this "All American" favorite for the family's main dish or for a company casserole to accompany meat, try our version. It's sure to elicit raves from family and guests. The recipe, which follows, will fill a four-quart casserole. You may divide it to fill two two-quart casseroles and freeze one for later use.

Cook 1 pound elbow macaroni according to package directions. Drain and place in buttered casserole.

In the top of a double boiler, make a thin white sauce by gradually adding 1 quart milk to a mixture of ¼ cup melted butter, ¼ cup flour, 1 teaspoon salt, and pepper to taste. Add 1 pound of grated *sharp* cheddar cheese and stir until the cheese melts. Pour over the macaroni. Top with croutons made by tossing very small cubes of fresh bread (a good way to use bread heels) in melted butter. Sprinkle lavishly with grated Parmesan cheese. Bake at 325 degrees until bubbly and brown on top.

# March 29

## Buy Food, Not Packaging

When you set out to shop for food or home supplies, resolve to bring home as little packaging as possible. By doing so, you'll save yourself money, and help reduce the packaging wastes that are becoming more and more of an ecological problem.

Potato chips, for example, are usually cheaper when packaged in a bag. Don't pay for a box or can unless you need the protection that one will provide. Check unit prices of everything for the best buy. Cheese spread is packaged in a variety of ways. If it's in an aerosol can, you're getting mostly can and paying mostly for convenience. Be sure it's worth the price to you.

Whatever you buy, keep in mind the national need to reduce wastes. It's a paying practice—for you and everyone else.

# March 30

**TODAY IN HISTORY:** *Today is the anniversary of "Seward's Folly"—the term many applied for years to Secretary of State William H. Seward's purchase of Alaska from Russia for $7,200,000. On March 30, 1867, he signed the treaty by which it was ceded to the U.S.*

## Recipe for Baked Alaska

This dessert, usually available only in the "best" restaurants, is actually no more than cake and ice cream covered with meringue and browned quickly in a hot oven. You may make one large Alaska or several small ones for individual servings.

Cover a bread or cutting board with kraft or other heavy paper. Nothing else will do as the paper, along with the meringue, insulates the ice cream and prevents it from melting. Place ½-inch slices of sponge, angel, or other cake on the paper and top with ice cream (brick or brick slices are easiest). Make sure the cake extends ½ inch beyond the ice cream on all four sides. Cover completely with meringue made as follows:

Beat egg whites with a pinch of salt and ¼ teaspoon cream of tartar until foamy. Gradually add 2 tablespoons sugar for each white and continue beating until the whites stand in peaks when the beater is removed.

Bake the Alaska in a 450-degree oven until browned. Slide from paper onto serving dish.

> **"A man of worth in his own household will appear upright in the state also."**
> **—Sophocles**

# March 31

## March Potpourri for Homemakers

Toddlers love to empty cabinet contents onto the floor. Your defense: Store all breakables in above-counter cabinets.

After washing a shower curtain or liner, rinse in a strong vinegar solution to remove soap scum. Then rinse in clear water and spread to dry.

Keep your old vacuum cleaner when you buy a new one. The old has little trade-in value. Store and use it upstairs to avoid carrying one up and down the stairs. Use it, too, to vacuum cars, workshop, furnace, and fireplace.

Wax drippings can be easily removed from candlesticks by pouring boiling water over them.

## Your Own Reminders:

## April 1

### Get Fishing Worms
### the Easy Way

You may not give much credence to the old saying that you can catch a bird by putting salt on its tail, but have you heard that you can catch fishing worms by using another staple from your kitchen shelves—dry mustard? Here's a bit of old-time lore to pass along to the fishermen of your family for use in the fishing season now opening in many parts of the U.S. The tip has nothing to do, either, with the fact that today is April Fool's Day.

Stir a tablespoon of dry mustard into a pitcher containing about two cups of water. Go into the yard and get down on your hands and knees or sit down. Feel under the grass for earthworm castings—they are tiny balls of soil cast above the surface of the ground by the worms. Gently push the castings aside to expose the worm hole. Pour about a teaspoon of mustard water into the hole. In just a few seconds the earthworm will emerge to escape the burning by the mustard. If not, try another teaspoonful. When the worm emerges, grab it (not too soon though or it will escape) and pull it out. Put it immediately into a container or bait box with a little soil.

If no worms emerge from the holes, try another area of the lawn.

Children are so fascinated with this method of acquiring fishing worms (and you may be, too) that they may take more than are needed. Restrain them. Earthworms have a purpose far more important than getting fish to bite. They are one of nature's cultivators, bringing nutriments from the subsoil to the surface to aid the growing process.

---

"Not many sounds in life, and I include all urban and all rural sounds, exceed in interest a knock at the door."
—Charles Lamb

---

# April 2

## Eggs for an Easter Tree

A symbol of spring's new life to the ancients, eggs were first associated with Easter by early Christians. Today they are dyed and used in egg hunts—or decorated to hang on a tree branch for house ornamentation at Eastertime.

The branch of any tree will do—select one that

has a number of twigs. Insert it in a flower holder to steady it and place in a decorative container.

To prepare eggs for the "tree," pierce both ends with a sharp needle and blow the contents into a bowl for later use in omelets or scrambled eggs. It takes a lot of energy to accomplish this; you may have to enlarge the holes.

The shells may be dyed or painted, then decorated as you wish by gluing on ribbon, sequins, glitter, small artificial fruits and vegetables, or pic-

tures which are symbolic of the season. You may create tiny scenes in the eggs after using a sharp pair of cuticle scissors to cut windows. Glue ribbon or tape around the cut edge of the window.

To hang an egg, tie sewing thread around a small piece of toothpick. Insert the piece into the hole you made at the top of the egg. Make a loop with the other end of the thread and secure with a knot. Use the loop to suspend the egg from a branch twig.

# April 3

**TODAY IN HISTORY:** *A patent was granted on April 3, 1829, to James Carrington, of Wallingford, Conn., for a revolving hand mill for grinding coffee. Thus was born countless numbers of lamp bases in modern homes.*

## Uses for Leftovers, Including Coffee

Leftover foods accumulate despite the most careful meal planning. You should use them as promptly as possible to avoid spoilage. But what to do with them?

If you have a blender, its recipe book may contain suggestions for creating absolutely "new" dishes—mousses from leftover meat, fish, and poultry, for instance.

Get ideas from the indexes of your cookbooks. One book, *The Joy of Cooking*, contains a "Left-Over Food Suggestions" section. This cookbook is

Leftover raw fruits can be added to gelatin salads or desserts. (Do not add fresh or frozen raw pineapple to gelatin, however. Fresh pineapple contains an enzyme that prevents gelling.)

Frozen fruits lose quality rapidly after thawing. Leftover thawed peaches, for example, soon change flavor and darken. Cook and refrigerate these leftovers.

Frozen berries should be eaten soon after thawing. Leftover frozen berries can be cooked as a sauce for ice cream or pudding, or added to a gelatin salad.

Leftover canned or cooked fruits are good in fruit cups, salads, gelatin desserts, and puddings, or over ice cream or cake. Use leftover syrups in gelatin or beverages.

## *April* 4

---

---

now available in a paperback edition.

One of our favorite ways to use leftover coffee is in pot roast. After browning the meat, simmer it in two cups of strong coffee and two cups of water for up to six hours. The gravy will be a rich brown and will not have a coffee taste.

A bit of imagination can transform leftover vegetables into new, interesting dishes. Try cold leftover vegetables in egg, meat, gelatin, or tossed green salads. Add them to soups, stews, or casseroles. Or combine them—yesterday's corn with today's lima beans, for instance. Tomatoes add extra juiciness and flavor to meat loaf and ground meat patties.

Actually, you can use leftover vegetables in any recipe that calls for cooked vegetables. Cream, scallop, glaze, or fry them as you would freshly cooked vegetables, or purée them to make cream soups.

## Be Kind to the Easter Bunny: No Pets

Baby rabbits, ducklings, and chicks are traditionally associated with Easter, but it is not a good idea to give one as a pet. If it survives—which is seldom—you will be faced with the problem of how to care for it as it grows.

Rabbits need strong and sturdy cages if they

are kept in a garage or outdoors. They have many natural enemies, including the neighborhood dogs and cats; the cage must be strong enough to keep the rabbit inside and to keep all other animals out. It is a shattering experience for a child to find his pet torn and dying, or vanished altogether from a broken cage—and this isn't much fun for the defenseless rabbit either.

Young chickens and ducklings are not easy to raise. Like all young things, they must be kept warm and protected, and be fed and watered with thoughtful care, then safely penned as they grow.

Stuffed toy animals are just as appealing in a youngster's Easter basket without the potential problems and sorrows which so often accompany the gift of an unsuitable live pet. (JSD)

## Pest Control Begins with Good Housekeeping

Systematic housekeeping helps control household pests. You can rid your home of practically all pests, and keep it free of them, by a combination of continuous good housekeeping and the proper use of the right pesticide at the right time.

Here are basic rules to follow:

**Practice sanitation.** Many household pests live on spilled food and organic matter that has not been completely cleaned up. They breed, multiply, and hide in small areas where food is left available to them—in cracks and crevices in cupboards, walls, and floors; around baseboards; and behind kitchen drawers. They hide in seldom-used storage cabinets, behind washtubs, and around water pipes and toilets.

Keep these places clean. Frequent scrubbings with hot water and soap or detergent will do the job. (Scrub surfaces *before* treating them with pesticides; do not scrub newly treated surfaces.)

**Promptly dispose of garbage**, bits of food, crumbs, scraps of fabrics, lint, and other waste materials that pests may eat or in which they may breed.

**Keep all foods in tightly closed containers**, and keep the containers clean outside as well as inside. Before purchasing dry foods, examine the packages carefully for evidence of breaks and resultant insect infestation.

**Don't permit insect pests to hitchhike into your home.** Cockroaches and silverfish often enter in crevices of cardboard cartons used in transporting groceries or other materials. Don't leave these containers in the kitchen or basement where the pests may escape to infest your home.

**Permanently seal up openings** where pests may enter. (See September 9.)

**Practice pest-prevention measures** at all times. Pesticide may be needed to supplement good housekeeping.

The foregoing advice comes from U.S. Department of Agriculture Home and Garden Bulletin No. 96, "Controlling Household Pests." We suggest you get a copy. In it you'll find what you need to know about controlling termites, wasps, rodents, pantry pests (weevils), bedbugs, and all the other pests that beset a homemaker.

---

**BROILED FRUIT served with the usual meat-potato-vegetable plate adds variety. Place drained canned peaches, pineapple, or other fruit in a buttered baking dish. Sprinkle brown sugar over and dot with butter. Broil until the fruit is thoroughly heated and the sugar is bubbly.**

---

## Guidelines for Buying Fresh Fruit

Fresh fruits are available in fairly good supply in our stores through most of the year, but quality is usually higher and prices more reasonable if you make it a point to buy a particular fruit in its most abundant season. Newspapers will often give you clues to what fruits are most plentiful at any time.

Be wary of low prices. Unless the low price is a result of overabundance of the fruit, you may end up discarding much of your purchase. Even with modern handling methods some products decline rapidly in quality while on display. Such off-quality fruit can often be bought at a reduced price, but waste may offset the price reduction.

Home refrigeration makes it possible to keep an adequate supply of most perishable fruits on hand, but never buy more than you can properly refrigerate and use without waste—even if the product is cheaper in quantity.

Don't buy by size alone. Large-sized fruits are not necessarily the best quality, nor are they always economical. They may appear to be bargains, but may be entirely unsuited to the purpose you have in mind.

Select fruit for best eating quality rather than outer appearance. Appearance and quality are associated in many respects, but fine appearance does not always denote fine quality. Often a fruit with a very attractive appearance may have relatively poor eating quality because of a varietal characteristic or because of some internal condition such as overmaturity. On the other hand, a fruit with poor appearance due to poor color or superficial blemishes may have excellent eating quality.

Don't pinch! Rough handling of fruits while you are selecting them causes spoilage and waste.

Such loss to the grocer usually is passed on to the consumer.

## *April* **7**

### Are They Carpet Beetles?

Adult carpet beetles are likely to show up on the inside of windows these warm spring days. They are about an eighth of an inch long and either all black or a mottled black or brownish with white markings. But look closely. Are the beetles mostly orange with black spots? If so, you are looking at ladybug beetles, beneficial insects, and you have nothing to worry about.

In themselves, adult carpet beetles are not harmful. But the presence of the beetles means that they have bred, and caused damage, somewhere in your home. Their presence reflects somewhat on you as a housekeeper. (See April 5.)

In your housecleaning, be sure to use the vacuum cleaner on all hard-to-reach cracks and crevices. Move heavy furniture occasionally and clean rugs and carpets well in the area where the furniture sits. If you suspect beetles have infested wall-to-wall carpet, pull it up around the edges and treat the underside and the pad with a pesticide recommended for the purpose, such as methoxychlor.

### Sealant Will Repair a Refrigerator Gasket

After a few years, the sealing gasket around the inside edge of a refrigerator or freezer sometimes cracks, causing the machine to run longer to maintain the proper temperature. You can buy a sealant at your hardware or home-improvement store to repair the gasket. Squeeze some of the sealant from the tube and mold it to the contour of the gasket. When you shop for it, check the other rubberlike products now available for a variety of household fixes.

---

**PERFUMED CARDS** encased in plastic which department stores sometimes include in their mailings to charge customers make excellent sachets. Remove the plastic from these samples of perfume scents and place them among your handkerchiefs or lingerie.

---

# April 9

## How to Clean and Dress Fish

Most fish sold in markets are cleaned and dressed. But sometimes you will have to do this yourself. Fishermen in the family will want to know what to do when they bring home a catch.

**Scaling.** After washing the fish, put it on a cutting board. Hold the fish firmly by the tail with one hand. In the other hand, hold a knife so the blade points away from you and the sharp edge is down. Hold the knife this way to scrape off the scales. Start at the tail and scrape toward the head. Scrape off all scales around the head and fins.

**Cleaning.** Cut the belly open from the vent to the head. (*Always use a sharp knife to cut fish.*) Take out the insides. Next, cut around the fins below

and just behind the head and cut them out.

**Filleting.** Cut along the back of the fish from the tail to head. Then cut down to the backbone just back of the collarbone. Turn the knife flat. Cut the flesh away from backbone and rib bones. Lift off the side of the fish in one piece. Turn the fish over and cut the fillet from the other side in the same way.

**Skinning a fillet.** Skin the fillet if you wish; they do not have to be skinned. Put the fillet on a cutting board with the skin side down. Hold the tail end with your fingers. Cut down through the flesh to the skin about half an inch from the end you are holding. Turn the knife flat against the skin. Slide the knife forward. This will cut the flesh away from the skin. Hold the tail end tightly so it won't slip out of your fingers.

**DEVELOP INTERESTS**—many of them—reading, hobbies, club and church activities, and civic responsibilities. Such interests help homemakers keep pace with husbands as they grow professionally and socially.

"Of all the days that's in the week
I dearly love but one day,
And that's the day that comes betwixt
A Saturday and Monday."
—Henry Carey

**NEED A GIFT FOR AN INVALID**—or any person of limited mobility? Buy a pair of barbecue tongs. They're fine for retrieving articles that are just out of reach.

# April 10

## Facts about Gingham for Homemakers

Gingham is made by dyeing the yarn rather than the cloth. Most gingham is woven from cotton yarn. The yarn is woven into solid colors, plaids, or checks. Plaids and checks of gingham should be constructed so design lines match perfectly. If you use gingham for sewing, select patterns which lend themselves to this matching. Look for the match when purchasing ready-to-wear gingham clothes.

A popular member of the gingham family is madras. Handwoven India madras is made from yarns dyed with native vegetable colorings. The handweaving and the tendency of the colors to bleed result in a fabric which is both desirable and interesting—no two pieces are ever alike. Labels on madras garments instruct the purchaser to wash them separately in warm water with mild soap or detergent.

**SEED CATALOGS are fun reading for children, too. One catalog (Burpee's) has a special section that includes a bean wigwam, pumpkin hideaway, performing beans, and gourds (bottle gourds can be made into birdhouses).**

# April 11

## Day Lilies—Cooked or in Salads

In some parts of the country clumps of day lilies grow wild along roadsides and provide bright spots of orange color in July. Right now their yellowish-green leaves have emerged and are easily distinguished from the darker greens of grasses. (When gathering wild plants for eating, it is

always wise to check one of the excellent guides to edible wild plants if you are not positive of identification.)

Cut the lilies just below the surface of the soil when they are two to three inches tall. Wash well, changing the water several times. They may be eaten raw in salads or cooked.

To cook, lay the leaves in a saucepan with ¼

cup water, bring to a boil, then simmer until just a little more than wilted. Drain, season with salt, pepper, butter, and lemon juice.

## *April* 12

### How to Save Money and Energy in Oven Use

Efficient use of the kitchen oven can save a lot of electricity or gas, and thereby reduce your utility bills. So today we would like to remind you of the following good practices:

Before turning on the oven, position the racks. When using one rack, position it to divide the oven in half. When using two racks, divide the oven in

thirds.

Use the recommended utensils. The size and shape of baking pans affect the volume and texture of baked foods. Cake pans, cookie sheets, and muffin pans made of lightweight aluminum with shiny interiors and slightly dulled bottoms conduct heat efficiently and aid in achieving delicate browning. Anodized aluminum pans that have a dull finish are best for pies. They transfer heat quickly to produce crisp, flaky pastry.

A practical demonstration of efficient conductivity of heat and energy saving with aluminum can be shown by driving an aluminum spike through the center of a potato. With the spike in place, the potato will bake in about half the usual time. Aluminum spikes or nails generally measure about four and one-half inches long and are available in hardware stores or in the kitchen section of department stores.

Gas and electric ovens are insulated to hold heat in. When used to capacity, they utilize energy more efficiently than cooking on top of the range. But heating an oven to bake a pie or a few potatoes is a waste of energy. Small baking tasks can be done quite successfully on top of the range in a sturdy aluminum skillet with a tight fitting cover. Be sure the skillet is not too full. The temperature should be set lower than for oven baking (low, medium-low, to medium). Potatoes, quick breads, and cakes can be baked in this way.

Oven energy is efficiently used when recipes are doubled or tripled, freezing the additional food overnight (when power demand is low) for later use. This saves on preparation time, too. Foods that can be cooked in quantity, saving considerable energy and time for homemakers, include chili con carne, meat stews, pot roast, barbecued meats, chicken and fish casseroles, yeast and quick breads, pies, cakes, and cookies.

## April 13

### Know the Forms of Canned and Frozen Vegetables

Both canned and frozen vegetables are sold in many styles. Beets, green beans, potatoes, and other vegetables may be found whole, cut, sliced, diced, and in other forms. Whole vegetables generally cost more than cut styles because it is hard to keep such fragile products as vegetables whole during processing, say consumer and marketing experts of the U.S. Department of Agriculture.

Some vegetables, such as beets, are sized when they are processed whole. This sizing also adds to the cost of the processed product, but whole vegetables of about the same size make an attractive serving, either hot or cold.

Fancy-cut vegetables, such as French-style green beans or julienne carrots (both French-style and julienne are sliced lengthwise) usually cost more than other cut styles and, because they are more attractive, are best used to dress up a dinner plate or cold salad.

Short-cut green beans, diced carrots, and tomato pieces are examples of the least expensive styles of processed vegetables, and the styles that are best used in soups and soufflés.

Many frozen vegetables are available in butter sauces, with mushrooms, or other garnishes or flavorings. Some canned vegetables are also available in butter sauces or with other garnishes, such as tomatoes with green peppers and onions. These vegetables, of course, cost more than the plain product, but let you serve something different without any extra work.

Grade A or Fancy vegetables (see February 24), in the whole or fancy-cut styles, are probably the most expensive vegetables. They are the most tender and flavorful and make the most attractive servings for a special luncheon or dinner, either hot or in a cold salad.

Grade B or Extra Standard vegetables, in sliced or plain-cut styles, are less expensive. They are good served hot or in casseroles or gelatin salads.

Grade C or Standard vegetables, diced or in pieces, are usually the least expensive vegetables. They are a good buy for use in soups, purées, or soufflés.

## April 14

### Think about Noise If You Must Move

Because of job transfers and other reasons, Americans move frequently to new homes. If you must do so, consider the problem of noise "pollution" in choosing your new house or apartment.

Science has recently determined that noise can seriously affect the physical well-being of you and your family. The decibel is used to measure sound intensity at its source. The decibel level starts at zero, the hearing threshold, and goes to 180, the level heard when a rocket is launched. Brief exposure to noise levels over 140 can rupture eardrums and result in permanent hearing loss. Prolonged exposure to noise at much lower levels can also impair your ability to hear.

Noise can be a serious problem in many new homes which have been hurriedly and inexpensively built. Modern construction sometimes relies on thin and light materials that actually transmit noise and vibration. The site also may add to noise problems.

In choosing your new home, the U.S. Environmental Protection Agency suggests that you

consider these points:

Stay away from major noise sources, such as airport flight paths, heavy truck routes, high-speed freeways. When buying a home, check the area zoning master plan for projected changes. (In some places, you can't get FHA loans for housing in noisy locations.)

Look for wall-to-wall carpeting, especially in the apartment above you and in the corridors.

Find out about the wall construction (staggered-stud interior walls are among the quietest). Can you hear a portable radio at normal volume in the adjoining apartment?

Check the electrical outlet boxes. If they are back-to-back, they will act as noise transmitters.

Ask about the door construction. Solid or core-filled doors with gaskets or weather-stripping are quieter than hollow core doors without weather-stripping.

Make sure sleeping areas are well away from rooms with noise-making equipment.

Check the heating and air-conditioning ducts. Inside insulation makes them quieter.

## *April* **15**

### Why Not Make Your Own Plastic Bags?

Plastic bags are a great convenience for the homemaker these days. You can freeze foods in them. You can use them to pack school or picnic lunches. You can use them to store winter clothes in a mothproof way. You can refrigerate leftover foods in them. You can make your own appliance covers or bag up the children's books on rainy days.

Some foods and other items now come in plastic bags that are reusable. But if these are insufficient for your needs, you might like to buy your own flat plastic and a bagmaker. Check your local stores to see if you can find one. If not, you may want to write to Bagmaker Corporation, Long Island City, N.Y. 11101, and ask where the company's product is available.

## How to Contract for a Painting Job

It's the time of year again when many of us think about redecorating, especially interior painting. This is an improvement that any woman can undertake herself—and lots do. But suppose you would rather pay a pro to do it?

If so, try to hire someone whose work you can check with a friend or neighbor. Find out what kind of job you are going to get. Painting contractors may offer three types of jobs—premium, standard, and minimum. The difference is in the quality and cost of the work.

It is always a good idea to get a signed agreement specifying:

The exact price for the job.

What areas or surfaces are to be included.

The types, brands, and quality of paints to be used and the number of coats, including primer coats, to be applied.

What will be done to protect floors, furnishings, and other parts of the house.

A cleanup satisfactory to you.

A completion date (allowing for possible delays).

Check to be sure the painter is fully insured—with workmen's compensation and employer's liability, public liability, and property damage insurance. Otherwise, you could be held liable for an accident that occurs on your property.

**DOES YOUR COMMUNITY** have clean air? If not, do something about it. For guidance on how to organize a local campaign, send a quarter to the Superintendent of Documents, Washington, D.C. 20402. Ask for Public Health Service Publication No. 1544, "Clean Air for Your Community."

# April 17

## Spanish Rice à la Queen Isabella

Because our recipe for Spanish rice is fit for a queen, we've named it for the queenly friend of the dashing young sea captain from Genoa.

The recipe offers both good eating and economy in your meal preparation. The basic recipe is delicious as it is, but it is also a fine way to extend small amounts of leftover meats.

> **2 onions, minced**
> **1 clove garlic, minced (optional)**
> **2 green peppers, minced**
> **3 cups cooked rice (follow directions on box)**
> **2 cups canned tomatoes**
> **1 tsp. salt**
> **1 tsp. paprika or chili powder**
> **2 Tbs. butter, bacon fat, olive or cooking oil**
> **Grated Parmesan cheese**

Sauté the onion, garlic, and green pepper in the fat until onion is soft. Add the other ingredients and pour into a buttered casserole. Top with grated Parmesan cheese. Bake at 350 degrees for 30 minutes. (Serves 6 as a main dish.)

You may add any amount of diced or chopped leftover meat—even only one pork chop or hamburger patty.

Broiled mushrooms are an excellent accompaniment to the meal.

---

**THE NATURAL GAS YOU USE in a kitchen range may once have been liquid. Various companies now buy natural gas in foreign countries, reduce it to a liquid, ship it back to the U.S. in tankers, and then convert it back to gas for distribution to homes and industry.**

# April 18

---

**TODAY IN HISTORY:** *Take clothes to a laundromat? A business called a "washateria" was opened on Apr. 18, 1934, in Fort Worth, Texas. It rented electric washing machines by the hour. You supplied your own soap.*

---

## Housekeeping without Power: Laundering by Hand

Sometimes you may not be able to wait until power is restored to wash clothes. Prepare for this by having on hand the following necessary and helpful items:

Bar of laundry soap, box of pre-soaking laundry formula, detergent suitable for hand washing, plumber's helper, washboard, clothesline, clothespins, wooden drying rack, and metal pants stretchers.

Sort soiled clothes as you are accustomed to do—separating pants and socks, colored and white articles, for instance. Greater attention to pretreatment of stains and heavily soiled articles, and pre-soaking will ease the hand-washing job. That's why you need a bar of laundry soap and a box of pre-soaking laundry formula.

If you don't have a washtub, use the bathtub to pre-soak and wash items too large for the sink, such as sheets. Be sure that the detergent you use is suitable for hand washing.

Squeeze suds through the load you are washing. For heavy items this can be accomplished with a plumber's helper. Washboards, some in sizes which will fit the sink, are still available. They'll save your hands as they help do the scrubbing of embedded soil. Work the soiled portion of the item up and down the washboard against its ripples.

After washing the white items, wring out as much water as possible and hold them in a container for rinsing—a scrub bucket will do nicely. If possible, save wash and rinse waters for the other loads.

A clothesline and clothespins are necessities if you do not have a dryer. Use the line outdoors if possible and hang clothes on a breezy day if you can. A breeze will dry clothes faster, minimize wrinkles, and make them softer to the touch. If you can't use the line outdoors, the basement, a porch, or even the attic will do. You might want to have on hand a wooden rack to dry clothes indoors. This can be placed in the bathtub or on the floor near a heat register with newspapers under it to catch dripping water.

Unless you have a flatiron and a means of heating it, ironing is not possible. Some "ironing" can be done with your hands by smoothing garments before they are completely dry. You might put wet pants on metal stretchers, which are still available, before hanging them on the clothesline. Otherwise, use ordinary clamp-type pants hangers. Skirts, dresses, blouses, and shirts will dry with a minimum of wrinkles if placed on hangers before hanging them up to dry.

**MRS. CALVIN COOLIDGE, wife of the President, officially opened the Woman's World Fair in Chicago on Apr. 18, 1925. The Fair exhibited work done by women in 70 industries. It continued for a week.**

## Child Development Books Help You "Keep Your Cool"

Although it's questionable whether you can follow any single book to the letter in raising your children, there are many which may help. We suggest you include in your home library at least one reference on child psychology and at least one other in the area of child rearing.

Even though each child develops physically, socially, and emotionally at his own rate, it will help you "keep your cool" by knowing that there are stages of child growth and development and by recognizing the norms (when changes occur and when certain behaviors are typical). For instance, you won't panic when your two-year-old exhibits anti-social behavior if you know that such behavior is to be expected at that age, that it isn't going to last forever, and that he will change to a "social animal" at about the age of three.

Knowing what to expect in growth and development will help you to understand your child. You will be able to provide play and other activities which the child is able to accomplish successfully and which encourage his normal growth patterns.

Consult your bookstore or librarian for recommended books in these areas of child psychology and child rearing.

"Now, good digestion wait on appetite, and health on both!"
—William Shakespeare

A CRACK OR CHIP in a slate floor can be repaired. Pulverize a spare piece of slate with a hammer. Mix the resulting powder with a clear cement recommended for use on ceramics. Press the mixture into the crack with a metal putty knife.

# April **20**

## Caring for and Using a Vacuum Cleaner

You can avoid many problems with a vacuum cleaner by knowing practical points about its care and building these points into your cleaning routine.

Each time before you use the cleaner do these things:

Pick up by hand any small, hard, or sharp objects like clips or pins that might damage the fan blades, the belt, or the hose, or puncture the dust bag.

Check the dust bag and empty or replace it if it is almost full. A clean dust bag will give you better efficiency and protect the motor. The motor is cooled by air flow. Unless a disposable bag is intended for re-use, don't use it again. Don't operate the cleaner unless the bag is in place.

Remove hair and thread from rotating brushes to improve their efficiency.

Adjust the nozzle height of an upright to the rug pile if the cleaner does not have an automatic adjustment.

While you are using the vacuum, switch the motor off at once if there is a sudden change in the sound of the cleaner. You might damage the motor if there's a problem with the air flow. Air flow may be limited because the bag needs changing. Check

also to see if the belt is broken or off the pulley.

After completing the cleaning, store the vacuum in a dry place, with the hose suspended over two hooks or dowels placed well apart.

Make it a practice to check agitator brushes in uprights for wear every month or so. Also check the belt. When a belt becomes stretched or wears thin, it will no longer drive properly. Also occasionally clean the tools, filters, and housing of the cleaner, following the directions in the owner's manual.

# April 21

**TODAY IN HISTORY:** *A patent was granted on Apr. 21, 1857, to Alexander Douglas, of New York, N.Y., for an "improvement in bustles."*

## 1853 Advice for Making a Home Happy

In 1853 the 216-page *Skillful Housewife's Book* by Mrs. L. G. Abell was published by R. T. Young, of New York, N.Y. It included many recipes and directed itself to such other topics as household duties, health care, gardening, flowers, birds, and education of children. It included the following good advice on how to make a home happy:

"It is not the imposing majesty of a sumptuous mansion, nor the hollow glare of gaudy furniture, nor the obsequious attention of servants, that make the blessedness of home. No, it is the steady exercise of those holy charities, that soothes our sorrows, and that builds the nest of peace, love, and true enjoyment in our bosoms. It is mutual respect and attention, a kind consideration of each others feelings, under all circumstances—a sympathy in our cares, a regard to our interests, the exercise of a patient and forbearing, and forgiving temper, that makes home the 'only Paradise that has survived the fall.' And let it never be forgotten, that even a smile or a frown may gild with brightness, or overcast with clouds, the whole horizon of that sacred spot—HOME."

That's still good advice. Very.

NOTE: Our copy of the *Skillful Housewife's Book*—its pages loose and yellowed with age—came to us from the attic of an old home. The publisher's preface attributes to Mrs. Abell "a highly gifted and disciplined mind" and notes that her book resulted from "fifteen years of careful and extended observation, while acting in the twofold character of a Christian mother, and an experi-

enced and practical housewife." To the best of our knowledge, the book is no longer in print. For that reason we are bringing you interesting and pertinent excerpts. You will find them scattered through the remainder of our own book.

## *April* 22

### Check Those Labels When You Buy Clothing

There should be a label on every garment you buy. You may find two or more labels—both important to you and both required by Federal Trade Commission regulations. Garments made of wool, fur, or textiles must have a label telling you exactly what they are made of.

In addition to this label, most ready-to-wear clothes should have care labels affixed in a permanent manner. Care labels specify washing, drying, and ironing instructions. Insist on this labeling. It is required for all garments except headwear, handwear, footwear, and a few other items. If garments are not labeled, report the matter to the store manager or write to the manufacturer.

In deciding between two garments, compare care labels. For full understanding of the care terms, see the Appendix. A garment which can be home laundered will be much less expensive in the long run than one which requires dry cleaning. Permanent press clothes will save the time and energy of ironing and pressing.

Other considerations in the selection of clothing are construction, becomingness, and accessories. Are the seams and hems full and the buttonholes properly finished? Has patterned fabric been well matched at the seams? Is the color and style becoming to you? Do you have shoes, hand-

bags, and other accessories which are suitable, or will you have to buy new ones?

## *April* 23

### Guard Your Family from Electric Shocks

Do you get a tingling sensation when you touch a lamp or other piece of electrical equipment? Have certain cords become frayed, perhaps even exposing the wires? Did a fuse blow or circuit-breaker trip when you plugged in a particular appliance? Are young children likely to thrust metal objects into a convenience outlet?

Be aware of such electrical hazards as you go about your daily work. Never take a chance, even the slightest, with electricity. Electricity is a fine servant. But give it the respect that's due it. Any of the situations suggested above could lead to the electrocution of a member of your family.

Remove all defective equipment from service until repairs are made—by a competent person. Equip convenience outlets with covers designed to protect young children.

## April 24

### Use Dandelion Greens for Salad

When you cut dandelions out of your lawn, make use of them as salad greens. Gather them before the flowers bud, cutting the plants at ground level with a sharp knife.

Separate the leaves and wash well, changing

the water several times. Blot dry and put into a salad bowl. Make the dressing as follows:

Fry bacon until crisp, leaving the fat in the pan. Crumble the bacon over the greens along with a chopped hard-cooked egg. Pour the heated bacon fat over the greens to wilt them. Add vinegar and salt and pepper to taste. Toss and serve.

---

**GOOD ADVICE from Shakespeare's** *Hamlet:* **"Neither a borrower nor a lender be."**

---

## April 25

### Reminder: It's Time to Dig the Vegetable Garden

As a housewife, you already know the cost of food. One way you can save, and usually have better quality too, is by raising some of your own in a vegetable garden.

If the idea interests you, and you have the space for a garden, better not wait too much longer to start. You probably have a friend or neighbor who can tell you how to go about it. If not, ask your county agent for some helpful booklets.

## April 26

### Pointers about Buying Asparagus

Fresh asparagus should be reaching the markets soon—if it isn't there already. Asparagus is more expensive than other vegetables because much of the harvesting and preparation during processing is done by hand.

The spear, or stalk, consists of the stem and head (tip). When buying fresh asparagus, choose crisp stalks with tips that are closed. The stalks should be a uniform size, so that they cook in the same amount of time.

There are two types of asparagus—green and white. White asparagus is a delicacy, produced by mounding earth around the plant so that the stalk develops entirely underground. Green asparagus may be canned or frozen; white asparagus is

---

**"He hath eaten me out of house and home."** **—William Shakespeare**

---

canned. Sometimes canned asparagus is packed in glass jars, with a note on the label that color preservative has been added.

## Spring Cleaning?
## It's "For the Birds"

If you shudder to think of spring and fall because they are housecleaning seasons, relax. It isn't necessary today to go through the trauma of tearing the house apart twice a year, or even once. There *was* a reason years ago. In the spring, the dirt and dust that had accumulated during the winter from space heaters had to be disposed of, the heaters dismantled, rugs beaten, curtains washed, and woodwork scrubbed. The same process was reversed in the fall to ready the house for winter.

Today's heating systems are cleaner and need only an annual servicing to keep them running in top condition. What dirt does accumulate is sucked into that modern marvel, the vacuum cleaner.

Today's housecleaning should be divided into daily, weekly, and seasonal jobs. Each day, such chores as bedmaking, dishwashing, and dusting are done. Each week do the vacuuming, starting in a different room each time. Vacuum that room thoroughly and wash any woodwork and windows that need it. Then whiz through the other rooms.

Intersperse the seasonal jobs throughout the year at times when you feel like doing them or when it costs less money to do them or when it makes sense to do them. For instance, shampoo rugs in the winter when furnace heat will speed the

---

"A mother's price, a father's joy."
—**Sir Walter Scott**

---

*April* **27**

## Add Flowers to Your
## Cooking Repertoire

Candied violets or the petals of roses make festive edible cake decorations or garnishes for meats and salads. Use a gentle touch in all steps of the candying process to avoid bruising.

Dip the flowers or petals in cool water and dry on paper towels. Dip them, one by one, into egg white that has been beaten until it is foamy. Place on a plate that has been covered with granulated sugar and sprinkle more sugar on the top. Roll them, if necessary, so that each is completely coated with the sugar. Place in a warm place until thoroughly dry.

drying, defrost the freezer at a time when frozen food supplies are lowest, clean closets prior to a church rummage sale, and have draperies and slip-covers cleaned when the dry cleaner announces special rates. (See tomorrow's article also.)

# *April* 29

## Cleaning Draperies and Blankets of Man-Made Fibers

There's a good reason for giving certain curtains, draperies, and blankets a thorough cleaning at this season. You can hang them on a clothesline outdoors on a warm and breezy day and let them drip dry.

Drip drying is included in instructions that Du Pont supplies for the care of its products made of Orlon and Dacron. Other pointers for Dacron curtains and draperies:

Shake out loose soil. Wash frequently. See general instructions (February 16), then proceed as follows.

For badly soiled spots, pour a little detergent directly on soiled area and pat gently. Wash by hand using warm water (100 degrees Fahrenheit) and a heavy-duty detergent. Fold the fabric into the wash water rather than gathering it into a bunch; this prevents unnecessary wrinkling. Wash white curtains only with white. Sodium perborate or chlorine bleaches may be used. Rinse in clear water, let drip dry—do not wring out.

If pressing is desired, use a steam iron or dry iron at synthetic setting.

For those curtains designed to be machine washable, use synthetic setting. After completion of the rinsing cycle, and before beginning the final spin-dry cycle, remove for drip dry, or tumble-dry in modern equipment on the "wash and wear" setting.

Suggestions for blankets of 100 percent Orlon or Dacron:

Prior to either hand or machine washing, pre-treat spots or soiled bindings with a heavy-duty liquid detergent. Wash only one blanket at a time. If after washing, pressing is desired on bindings, use a steam iron or a dry iron at moderate or synthetic setting and a press cloth. When dry, the blanket may be brushed with a soft brush to fluff up the nap.

Machine washing: Wash in warm suds (100 degrees F.) of a synthetic detergent for five minutes. Stop machine after two or three minutes of the final spin-dry cycle. Use the complete special fabric cycle if it is available. Remove blanket and air dry by hanging evenly over a clean clothesline. Straighten blanket and smooth bindings while damp. If desired, a home dryer may be used. Preheat dryer for ten minutes at 180 to 190 degrees F.—tumble blanket ten minutes. Blanket should be removed from dryer as soon as drying is complete.

Hand washing: Wash in warm (100 degrees F.) water using a synthetic detergent. Work blanket gently up and down in suds until soil is removed. Rinse in as many warm rinses as are necessary to remove the suds. Squeeze out or drain excess water without vigorous wringing or twisting. Dry as

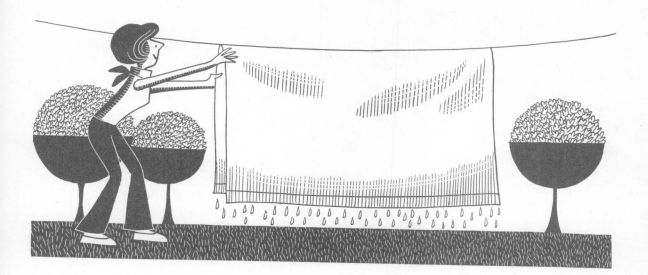

with machine washing. Brushing with a soft brush after blanket is dry enhances its appearance. Blankets of 100 percent Orlon or Dacron may be dry-cleaned, if desired.

(For information about taking care of electric blankets, see October 9.)

**WORN BED SHEETS?** Cut them down the middle and hem the cut edges. Then sew the original sides together to form a center seam—and the thin, worn spots will be switched to the outer edges. Or use good parts to make crib sheets.

"Marriage resembles a pair of shears, so joined that they can not be separated; often moving in opposite directions, yet always punishing anyone who comes between them."
—Sydney Smith

## April 30

**TODAY IN HISTORY:** *Apr. 30, 1889, was once voted a national holiday by an act of Congress. It was the centennial of the inauguration of George Washington as first President of the U.S.*

## April Potpourri for Homemakers

Create your own raincoats. Scotchgard sprayed on any coat will make it water repellent. Follow the directions on the can.

Keep care labels for new purchases where they're readily available until you are sure you will remember washing and cleaning instructions.

Teach all family members to stretch out both the shower curtain and the liner so that they will dry after showering.

Save old socks if you have a small floor which you wax by hand. Just place your hand inside a sock to apply the wax.

Save grocery bags and use them to line wastebaskets and step-garbage cans.

Keep a list of toll calls near your telephone. Check the list against the bills. The phone company isn't always perfect.

**Your Own Reminders:**

## May 1

### Pointers About Storing and Thawing Fish

When you buy fresh fish or someone brings home a catch, wrap the fish and get it into the refrigerator quickly. Always use fresh fish within two days.

If you buy frozen fish and don't plan to use it immediately, put it into the freezer promptly. Leave it wrapped as you bought it. Plan to use it within a month.

When fish has been cooked but you cannot use it immediately, refrigerate it in a covered pan or freeze it in a moistureproof wrapper. Use refrigerated cooked fish within four days, if frozen within a month.

To thaw frozen fish, place it in the refrigerator. Allow 24 hours for each pound package to thaw this way. To thaw it more quickly, put the wrapped package under cold running water. Allow from one to two hours for each pound to thaw this way.

Cook the fish soon after it has thawed. Frozen fillets and steaks may be cooked without thawing; just allow extra time for them to cook. Do not thaw fish sticks or portions before cooking.

Some don'ts: Do not thaw fish at room temperature or in warm water. Do not freeze fish again after it has been thawed.

## May 2

### Where Are You From?

The words you apply to certain household tasks and items may indicate in which part of the U.S. you now live or came from. In the South or Middle West, you may call a paper grocery container a "sack," but in the Northeast you may say "bag." In

the North you may eat corn on the cob or green corn, but in the South the same luscious food is apt to be roasting ears or sweet corn. The North's skunk becomes a polecat in the South.

These regional variations in the choice of words are outlined in a pamphlet "Discovering American Dialects," by Roger W. Shuy, copyright © 1967 by National Council of Teachers of English, 508 South Sixth St., Champaign, Ill. 61820.

If you travel through the U.S. on vacation this summer, you may enjoy listening for such words. Other variations you might hear:

Window covering on rollers: blinds, curtains, roller shades, window blinds, window shades.

Large porch with roof: gallery, piazza, porch, portico, stoop, veranda.

Family word for father: dad, daddy, father, pa,

papa, pappy, paw, pop.

Family word for mother: ma, mama, mammy, maw, mom, mommer, mommy, mother.

Of children: brought up, fetched up, raised, reared.

Melon with yellow or orange insides: muskmelon, melon, mushmelon, lope, cantaloupe, mussmellon.

A carbonated drink: pop, soda, soda pop, tonic, soft drink.

Food eaten between regular meals: a bite, lunch, a piece, piece meal, a snack, a mug-up, munch, nash, nosh.

## *May* 3

### Flue Tiles Make Decorative Planters for Flowers

Planters filled with flowers such as geraniums or petunias are attractive when arranged around a lawn, porch, or patio, but the fancy planters are pretty expensive. An easy and decorative solution is to use ordinary flue tiles, made for building chimneys and available at any building supply house. They come in many sizes and shapes and in a range of clay colors that blend with the landscape. They won't rot out as wooden planters do. For

stability and variety, sink the tiles to different depths.

## *May* 4

> **TODAY IN HISTORY:** *The Woman's Hospital of New York City opened on May 4, 1853, with 40 beds. It was organized by women for the exclusive use of women.*

### "Is There a Doctor in the House?"

Medical emergencies may occur at any time, especially with young children. Prepare ahead of time by knowing exactly what you will do if it becomes necessary to get medical assistance quickly.

You should have a family doctor, but this is often easier said than done. There is a shortage of doctors in many communities. The doctors that do practice are often so overburdened that they are unable to provide the care they would like to give to the patients they already have. What can you do?

Make an attempt to locate a doctor who is able to accept your family as patients. If you're new in the area and there is a Welcome Wagon, the lady who calls on you may be able to offer suggestions. Otherwise, ask one of your new neighbors. Phone the doctor's office. If he is unable to make emergency house calls, he may be able to suggest another doctor who can. If this fails, ask if he would agree to your using his name to secure emergency care at the nearest hospital. This has been the solution for friends of ours who have been caught in a no-doctor bind.

# May 5

## Pointers about Buying Vegetables

Vegetables are low in calories and a number of them rank high in vitamins and minerals. One-half cup of most boiled vegetables contains less than 50 calories. Starchy vegetables like lima beans, peas, corn, and plain boiled potatoes supply from 50 to 100 calories in a half-cup serving.

Most dark-green and deep-yellow vegetables excel as dependable and inexpensive sources of vitamin A. In fact, unless your meals include several servings of carrots, spinach, sweet potatoes, winter squash, broccoli, kale, or other greens each week, your family may not get enough vitamin A. As a bonus, many dark-green vegetables supply valuable amounts of vitamin C, iron, and other vitamins and minerals.

The mature dry legumes—dry peas and members of the bean family including navy, pinto, and soybeans—are outstanding among vegetables for the protein they contain. They also contribute B vitamins, iron, and other nutrients.

And how drab our diets would be without the color and crispness of fresh-tossed salads, the tang and texture of relishes, and the distinctive flavors of our vegetable dishes.

Raw vegetables are becoming increasingly popular as a low-calorie between-meal snack. Weight watchers do well to keep a supply of celery sticks, carrot sticks, radishes, or green pepper slices ready in the refrigerator to eat when hunger strikes.

Besides a variety of fresh vegetables now available the year round, you have the choice of buying other forms—canned, frozen, or dehydrated. (See also February 24 and April 13).

Here are points to consider in making your choice:

Fresh vegetables are generally highest in quality and lowest in price when in season. In selecting, look first for freshness. Vegetables should be comparatively dry; excessive moisture hastens decay.

Canned vegetables are most convenient because they need only brief heating and do not require refrigerated storage until the can is opened.

Frozen vegetables closely resemble fresh vegetables in color, flavor, and texture, but usually cost more than canned vegetables.

Dehydrated vegetables usually take up less storage room than fresh, canned, or frozen vegetables. Some dehydrated vegetables cost slightly more than comparable fresh products, but can be prepared much more quickly.

Dry legumes—including dry beans, peas, and lentils—are inexpensive but take a relatively long time to prepare.

## May 6

### Allowances for Children?

Allowances for children run the gamut from excessive amounts down to a dole given only upon request and when need is justified. An important part of growing up is gaining experience in handling one's own money. A weekly allowance can provide this.

An allowance should not be given, however, without expecting a return—a willingness to share family responsibilities. Initially, these responsibilities can be simple chores the child is able to complete successfully. Very young children can empty wastebaskets, pick up toys and clothes, and help in setting the table. As they become older, they can assume more difficult tasks—dusting, vacuuming, cleaning their own rooms, assisting with garden and yard work, feeding pets, washing cars, and collecting the inevitable garbage for disposal.

Two bits of advice about chores: 1. Remind the child just once that it is time to perform his chore. Two reminders will lead to three and eventually to a shouting match. 2. Make no male-female distinction among chores. Dusting is not just girl's work, nor is collecting the garbage just boy's work. With more and more women entering the job market, such division of labor according to sex is no longer appropriate or right.

How much should the allowance be? Determine this by having the child keep track of what he spends for a few weeks. Discuss these expenses with him and agree on a figure that covers them—with a little left over. As the child becomes older, upward adjustments to take care of added expenses should be agreed upon after discussion.

Adding money to the basic allowance and earmarking it for savings will help the child acquire the virtue of thrift.

## May 7

### Tips on Buying Lamb

A reference to "spring lamb" may make your mouth water—and well it should. For many years, lamb was thought of as a seasonal meat, available only in the spring—an excellent choice for a special Easter dinner. Now, however, lamb is plentiful during all seasons.

Buying lamb presents few problems, but the quality of lamb does vary. Therefore, it is advisable to buy lamb that has been graded by the U.S. Department of Agriculture. Since it is produced from young animals, most cuts of USDA Prime or Choice lamb are tender and can be oven roasted or broiled. Lower grades of lamb (USDA Good, Utility, and Cull) are seldom marked with the grade when sold at retail.

USDA Prime grade lamb ranks very high in

tenderness, juiciness, and flavor. It has moderate marbling—flecks of fat within the lean—which enhances both flavor and juiciness. Prime chops and roasts are excellent for dry-heat cooking—broiling and roasting.

USDA Choice grade lamb has slightly less marbling than Prime, but still is of high quality. Like Prime, Choice chops and roasts are tender, juicy, and flavorful and suited to dry-heat cooking.

Lamb is produced from animals less than a year old. Meat from older sheep is called yearling mutton or mutton, and if it is graded these words —lamb, yearling mutton, or mutton—will be stamped on the meat. Grades for yearling mutton and mutton are the same as for lamb, except that mutton does not qualify for the Prime grade.

The U.S. Department of Agriculture also has yield grades for lamb. Like beef yield grades (see November 5), yield grades for lamb measure the ratio of lean meat to fat and bone. The same rating system of five yield grades is used—with Yield Grade 1 representing the highest yield of lean meat, and Yield Grade 5 the lowest.

Generally, variations in the yield result primarily from differences in fatness on the outside of the carcass and in fat deposited on the inside of the carcass. (See Appendix for chart showing retail cuts of lamb.)

## May 8

### Your County Agents Offer a Lot of Good Help

How much use have you made of the free services offered by your county agent? Today is the anniversary of the Cooperative Extension Service, established May 8, 1914. The service is operated by the U.S. Department of Agriculture, the state land-grant universities, and county governments, but phones are usually listed under the heading of your county. Your county agricultural agent and county home agent offer many free publications about gardening, lawn care, shrubs, trees, flowers, food and cooking, clothing, home furnishing, and household money management. Stop in and see what's available, or write the Department of Agriculture, Washington, D.C. 20250, for a list of their publications. Most county agents also provide useful information to local newspapers, radio, and television. Make use of this valuable source of information—it's reliable and it's free!

## May 9

### Dry Cleaning: Best Control for Clothes Moths

Clothes moths need not cause any problem for homemakers these days. Dry cleaning gets rid of them. Seasonal clothing ought to be cleaned before being stored in any case. So send winter garments to the cleaner during this season. When they are returned, leave them inside the protective plastic coverings and hang them in a closet.

Or perhaps you may want the dry-cleaning establishment to store the garments until autumn. Many dry-cleaning houses now offer to do so at no cost other than the regular charge for dry cleaning.

What about blankets and other items that you may not want to send to the cleaner? Hang them in the sun and brush them well. If you fear the presence of moths, spray lightly with a recommended insecticide.

# May 10

**TODAY IN HISTORY:** *A monument to George Washington's mother was dedicated on May 10, 1894, at her grave in Fredericksburg, Va. The inscription reads: ''Mary, the Mother of Washington.''*

## Store Clothing Properly to Prevent Mildew

Clothing stored in mothproof containers usually is also safe from mildew. Mildew is a thin, often whitish, growth produced by molds that grow on cotton, linen, rayon, silk, wood, leather, and paper. Many man-made fibers are resistant to mildew. As molds grow, they cause damage and often leave a musty odor. They discolor fabrics and sometimes eat into them so severely that the fabrics rot and fall to pieces. They also discolor leather and paper.

Soiled articles are more likely to mildew than clean ones. So in storing clothing or blankets at this time of year, wash or dry-clean them first unless you are certain they have a mildew-resistant finish. And unless you know that your laundry starch contains an inhibitor, do not leave starch in fabrics to be stored. Molds feed on starches.

Certain volatile chemicals, the vapors of which inhibit mold growth, may be used to protect fabrics during storage. One such chemical, paradichlorobenzene, effectively controls mildew on clothing and other apparel when used in packages, trunks, or garment bags kept as nearly airtight as possible. This chemical, which is widely recommended for moth control, is available in groceries and drugstores under various trade names. Check the labels.

Scatter paradichlorobenzene crystals through the folds of garments to be packed in boxes, or hang bags of crystals at the top of garment bags so the heavy vapors settle on the materials being protected. Use about one pound of the crystals for 100 cubic feet of air space, proportionately less for smaller spaces. As the vapors leak out, mildew protection disappears and the chemical must be replenished. Paradichlorobenzene is also available in spray cans. Precaution: The chemical damages some plastics. Therefore, remove plastic buttons and ornaments from garments and use wooden or metal instead of plastic clothes hangers.

Paraformaldehyde is another volatile chemical that has mildew-inhibiting properties. It is sold in powder form at drugstores. Sometimes various-sized bags of the chemical are available. Use paraformaldehyde to protect clothing and bedding (two ounces of the chemical for 100 cubic feet of space). Place bags of the chemical where the vapors can circulate and reach all surfaces of the stored articles.

Precaution: Paraformaldehyde is poisonous. Avoid inhaling the fumes.

Biphenyl is still another volatile chemical that inhibits mildew. It is available in small bags under various trade names. These bags can be hung in closets or put into storage containers to protect fabrics against mildew. Follow manufacturer's directions for use of this chemical.

**MOTHER'S DAY was first celebrated on May 10, 1908, as a city-wide observance in Philadelphia. The observance became nationwide in 1914. Miss Anna Jarvis of Philadelphia had suggested in 1907 that the second Sunday in May each year be so observed.**

days. Bottle, adding to each bottle a handful of seeded raisins. Do not cork for 4 or 5 weeks. (EFW)

## May 12

**TODAY IN HISTORY:** *Today is the birthday anniversary of Florence Nightingale, born on May 12, 1820, in Florence, Italy, of English parents. Her efforts as a nurse to ease the sufferings of soldiers wounded in the Crimean War brought her acclaim throughout the world.*

## May 11

### How to Make Dandelion Wine

Those dandelions blossoming now on your lawn may be blessed as the source of wine instead of cursed as weeds. We have used the following recipe to make a delightful wine.

Pick 2 quarts of the blossoms. Put into a large pan, add 4 quarts of water, and boil until the flowers are soft. Strain out the flowers and add to the remaining liquid 3½ pounds white sugar and 2 lemons, sliced. Boil for 15 minutes. Then cool until lukewarm.

Add to the liquid a piece of toast spread with a cake of yeast. Let stand in a warm place for 2

### Does Your Kitchen Have Two Cutting Boards?

There's a very good reason for having two cutting boards in a kitchen. That reason is one that can't be emphasized too often—the matter of cleanliness.

You need the two work surfaces especially for preparing meat and poultry products. Food experts for the U.S. Department of Agriculture advise that you never should place cooked, ready-to-serve meat or poultry on the same surface or utensil used for the raw product unless you have completely sanitized that surface or utensil. This is to prevent contamination from harmful bacteria present in uncooked meats.

As part of your program for keeping your kitchen clean, use soap and hot water or a suitable cleanser that destroys bacteria to clean all surfaces on which raw meat or poultry has been prepared—especially the wooden cutting boards that absorb juices. Be sure to sanitize these surfaces (and wash your hands) before handling foods that are not cooked or are only partly cooked, salads for instance.

Always wash poultry well before preparing it for cooking.

Thoroughly wash all equipment that has been used in handling meat and poultry and all containers that have been used to store, cook, or serve these products. As part of the cleanup, dismantle all equipment that comes apart for washing. Also wash your hands often when preparing meat and poultry, and before handling other foods.

## May 13

### Your Guide to Spices and Herbs

Spices and herbs include a great variety of vegetable products that are used to enhance the flavor of foods. Spices are defined as parts of plants usually of tropical origin—the dried seeds, fruit, buds or flowers, bark or roots. Herbs are leafy parts of temperate-zone plants.

Strength and quality of flavor and good color are important considerations in buying spices and herbs. They gradually lose flavor and color during storage; therefore, they should not be purchased in quantity.

Spices and herbs should be stored in a cool, dry place in airtight containers. A warm storage area may hasten flavor loss, and a damp environment encourages caking, color change, and infesta-

tion. Containers should be tightly closed after each use so that the volatile oils of the spice or herb are not lost. Under favorable conditions spices will retain maximum aroma and flavor up to six months. Whole spices keep their flavor almost indefinitely. Herbs tend to lose flavor more rapidly than ground pepper, ginger, cinnamon, and cloves. However, if herbs are properly stored they will retain flavor and color for several months.

There is no general rule for the correct amount of a spice or a herb to use, as the pungency of each differs and its effect on different foods varies. Generally, if a recipe is not available, start with ¼ teaspoon of spice per pound of meat or pint of sauce, and increase as desired. When using red pepper or garlic powder begin with ⅛ teaspoon.

The flavor of ground spices is imparted immediately so they may be added about 15 minutes before the end of the cooking period. Whole spices are best in slow cooking dishes, such as stews. Tie whole spices in a cheesecloth bag for easy removal, and add them at the beginning of the cooking period so the long simmering can extract the full flavor and aroma. Whole or leaf herbs should be crumbled finely just before they are used to release the flavor. Flavoring seeds may be toasted before using to enhance the flavor. (See also Appendix and November 11.)

## *May* 14

### Take Cuttings of Favorite Chrysanthemums

Taking cuttings about this time of year is an excellent way to have more of the chrysanthemums that you especially like. Do it when new shoots from

the base of the plant are from three to five inches high. Cut off the top two or three inches of the shoots with a sharp knife.

Dip the lower half inch of the cuttings into a hormone powder that stimulates root growth (these are available at garden shops). Then thrust the cuttings, up to the leaves, into rooting material that you have prepared in shallow pots or wooden trays. Use clean sand or a sterile material such as perlite or vermiculite. Wet this thoroughly and make a cut about an inch and a half deep in it to receive each cutting. Space the cuttings an inch or so apart. Water them at once.

Keep the cuttings at about 65 degrees. Shield them from direct sunlight for several days with newspapers. Water lightly every day or so. After about two weeks, pull up a couple of cuttings to check root development. If they have no roots, reset and wait another week. Then transplant them to a well-prepared bed outdoors.

# May 15

**TODAY IN HISTORY:** *May 15, 1940, was a big day for all women. Stores in all parts of the country placed nylon hose on sale.*

## A Dictionary of Hosiery Terms

If you are one of the many homemakers who also has a part- or full-time job, chances are that the cost of hosiery makes up a good part of your clothing budget. You can do a better job of purchasing if you are familiar with the following hosiery terms:

Afterwelt (or shadow welt). The area directly below the welt at the top of the stocking. Not as heavy as the welt, not as sheer as the stocking. It adds strength to the gartering area and guards against strain.

Boot. That portion of a stocking (or tights, or panty hose) between the welt and the knee.

Color. Should be streak-free, shadow-free, and constant from toe to top. Should never be shiny, but have a matte-like finish.

Course. A row of knitted stitches across a stocking. A high course and gauge count give excellent wear when knit in a low denier yarn.

Defects. Sleazy stitches, uneven welts, vertical lines, and streaks. Can be discovered in a quick hand test.

Demi-sandal. Sometimes called a demi-toe or nude-heel stocking. One with reinforcement only at the very tip of the toe.

Denier. The weight and thickness of a strand of nylon yarn. The lower the denier, the thinner the yarn, the sheerer the stocking.

Dress sheers. Stockings of 15-denier yarn, for daytime wear—sheer yet practical.

Evening sheers. Whisper-weight stockings of 10-, 12-, or 15-denier yarn, usually with nude heel. Recommended for gala occasions.

Filament. A single fiber of indefinite length.

Filament yarn. A yarn made of continuous filaments.

Fishnets. Nylons with an open fishnet design, usually without welts or reinforcements. May be seamed or seamless.

Full-fashioned stockings. Stockings with seams. Vertical seam at back tends to make the leg appear slimmer.

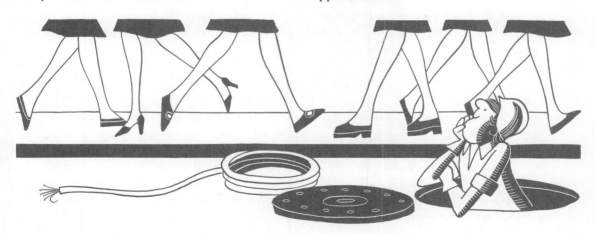

Gauge. The measurement of the closeness or the fineness of stitches, widthwise, across a stocking. (For instance, 60 stitches to every one-and-a-half inches of stocking.)

Leg. That portion of the stocking from the knee down through the ankle.

Mesh knit. A stocking fabric produced by a variety of interlocking loops. It is usually run resistant.

Micromesh. A mesh fabric for seamless stockings, with loops locked in one direction only. Although more run resistant than plain knit, it can run upward.

Monofilament yarn. Yarn made of one single filament of fiber.

Multifilament yarn. Yarn made of several filaments of fiber twisted together.

Panty hose. One-piece sheer or opaque stockings topped with sheer or opaque panties.

Plain knit. The most usual knit for nylon stockings. Similar to hand-knitting and resilient in two directions.

Reinforcements. Found in welt, toe, heel, and sole. Should be in correct proportion to the weight and style of the stocking.

Run-stop stitches. Added safeguards found just under the welt or afterwelt and just above the toe reinforcement which discourage runs that start in those areas from entering the body of the stocking.

Seamless stockings. Made on circular knitting machine, having no seam.

Seams. Should be straight, slim, and trim with no raw edges. Better seams are sewn with nylon thread. Heel reinforcement, welt, and fashion marks should match precisely on each side of seam.

Stretch hosiery. Stockings knit of a processed nylon filament yarn that gives permanent stretch-ability.

Surgical stockings. Doctor's orders stockings. Should be sold as such.

Textured hosiery. Definite patterns, such as diamonds, stripes, jacquards, are knitted into the stockings. May be sheer or opaque. Also called patterned stockings.

Support stockings. Knit of stretch yarns for the purpose of giving support.

Tights. One-piece leg coverings which extend up to the waistline. Usually of opaque stretch yarn.

Walking sheers. Stockings of relatively heavy, 30-denier yarn, worn primarily for sturdy everyday wear. Also called "service weight."

Welt. The hem or foldover at the top of a stocking, knit of heavier yarn, and used for the gartering area.

## May 16

### It's Time to Revive a Poinsettia

Danger of frost is now past in most of the cooler parts of the country. If it is where you live, it's time to get out a poinsettia if you have one in storage.

Cut the plant back to a height of about six inches. Re-pot or plant in the garden. Give full sun and keep watered. You may, if you wish more plants, take cuttings from the new growth when it appears. Put the cuttings into cold water to stop the flow of milky juice and then into rooting mixture.

Bring the poinsettia indoors before the house heating season. It will do best in a sunny window where the temperature is constant—about 65 degrees. Give it lots of water when it reaches the blooming stage.

# May 17

## Hints about Colors When You Redecorate

Use colors thoughtfully when you redecorate any room in the house. Color selection of paints and wall coverings is mostly a matter of personal preference. Your dealer can supply a wide range of colors in paints and wall coverings. For the most part you can choose the colors *you* want. But keep the following points in mind:

Bright walls in a room detract from otherwise decorative furnishings. You'll never go wrong by having white or neutral walls and letting the furnishings provide the colors—all chosen to harmonize.

Light colors make a small room seem larger. Conversely, dark colors make an overly large room appear smaller.

Ceilings appear lower when darker than the walls and higher when lighter than the walls.

Colors often change under artificial lighting. Look at color swatches both in daylight and in artificial lighting.

Paint generally dries to a slightly different color or shade. For a fast preview of the final color, brush a sample swatch of the paint on a piece of clean, white blotting paper. The blotting paper will absorb the wet gloss, and the swatch will be about the color of the paint when it dries on the wall.

## May 18

### Housekeeping without Power: Water Supply?

Homemakers whose plumbing hooks up to the city mains should seldom have any question about an adequate water supply unless a main breaks. But those who depend on their own water supply face real trouble if there's no power to operate a pump.

For all of us, it may be a smart precaution to stock our pantry shelves with a couple of gallons of spring water now available in supermarkets in plastic containers. Or fill clean jars from your tap. Just in case.

People with water pumps might want to consider buying a standby electrical generator, powered by gasoline. One large enough to handle the pump would also be convenient for powering other household conveniences and for lights.

Next possibility to consider, especially in rural and suburban areas where private water supplies are most prevalent, would be a hand-operated pump or a stream or well from which potable water could be obtained. But have the water tested to make sure it's safe for drinking.

Fortunate is the home these days that can be served by gravity-fed spring water. Or is there a constantly flowing stream in your neighborhood? If the stream is at a lower level than your home, you could use the flow-power of the water itself to pump a supply up to your level. This can be done with an amazing device called a hydraulic ram. Information about hydraulic rams can be obtained from Rife Hydraulic Engine Manufacturing Company, Box 367, Millburn, N. J. 07041.

Or—no kidding!—how about a windmill to pump water from your own well? We suspect that you're going to be hearing more about this type of power once again in the years to come.

## May 19

### The Wonderful World of Wall Coverings

Thinking about wallpaper for one or more of your rooms this spring? It's a job you can do yourself. Many women do.

But before you settle on conventional wallpaper, consider some of the other choices in wall coverings that have become available in recent years.

Simulated brick, for instance. Many home decorators think it's great—in a kitchen, perhaps. Some are slices of real brick. Others are made of plastic. Or maybe you'd like to apply waterproof panels in a bathtub area.

Look at the self-stick materials, too. Simply peel off the paper backing and apply to any smooth surface. Some of the designs are really wild. Or how about decorating with burlap?

# May 20

**TODAY IN HISTORY:** *Just five years after Charles A. Lindbergh's solo flight across the Atlantic, Amelia Earhart became the first woman to span the ocean alone. She left Newfoundland on May 20, 1932, and reached Ireland 14 hours and 56 minutes later.*

## Keeping Child Safe While Traveling by Car

You know that the use of seat belts is specified at certain times when you travel by plane, and constantly in a car. But have you heard that ordinary seat belts in a car are often bad for children?

Investigators made this discovery in checking out how and why children died in a number of recent highway accidents. To protect your child, you must have a restraint system especially designed for him—according to his age, weight, and height.

In a booklet prepared by the National Highway Traffic Safety Administration of the U.S. Department of Transportation, it is recommended that you be guided by the accompanying table in choosing the correct type of restraint.

Both infant carriers and car beds should be designed so the vehicle's seat belts can be used to secure them. For maximum protection, carrier and infant should face the vehicle's rear, not the front. Ideally, however, a car bed should go crosswise in the car behind the front seat, with the infant's head at the center of the car. Strong netting or straps should be over the bed to keep the infant from being ejected. Both carrier and bed should have padding to withstand collision forces.

If you decide on wallpaper, give careful consideration to washable vinyl-coated materials. You can even buy washable flocked paper—with raised patterns that have the soft look and feel of velvet. Some of these papers are pre-pasted for easy application. Buy a plastic water tray for use in dipping the paper.

Check out all the possibilities in mail-order catalogs and in your local stores.

Even the best of planners sometimes has wallpaper left over. When you do, don't just put it away. Instead, if you have room in the attic, unroll it and hang it from the highest point. It will then fade gradually, just as the paper on the wall does. Later, if the walls need patching, the attic paper will match the walls.

| TYPE OF RESTRAINT | Infants | Children | | |
|---|---|---|---|---|
| | up to 9 months | 8 or 9 mos. to 4 yrs. | 4 to 5 yrs. old | at least 55 in. tall |
| **Infant Car Bed** | YES | | | |
| **Infant Carrier** | YES | | | |
| **Child Car Seat** | NO | YES | | |
| **Child Harness** | NO | YES | | |
| **Vehicle Lap Belt** | NO | NO | YES | YES |
| **Vehicle Shoulder Belt** (worn only with a lap belt) | NO | NO | YES* | YES |
| *But only if child is at least 55 in. tall | | | | |

Child car seats built since April 1, 1971, must meet Federal safety standards—and must have a label with date of manufacture and maker's name. If you find no date on the seat, better skip it or move with caution. The label also must specify the weight and height of the child and the type of vehicle for which the seat is recommended.

A harness allows greater freedom of movement than child seating restraints, but in choosing give preference to those that either attach directly to the vehicle floor or the vehicle's seat belt, not to the seat back. Choose those with the widest belts. A child using a harness should not be allowed to *stand* on the front seat.

You can obtain additional information from a booklet "What to Buy in Child Restraint Systems," available from the Superintendent of Documents, Washington, D.C. 20402.

## Language Enrichment from the Kitchen

Ever think of how many familiar sayings, quotations, and song titles contain foods and cooking terms used in the kitchen? Or how many kitchen words are used as adjectives to describe people, places, and things?

A person's appearance: fat as a pig, calf eyes, peanut, shrimp, red as a beet (or lobster), peaches and cream complexion, and cheesecake.

A person's age: vintage years or salad years.

Terms of endearment: honey, dumpling, muffin, "You're the Cream in My Coffee," and apple of my eye.

A person's temperament or behavior: crabby, butter up, flounder, have lots of mustard, be hoggish, grouse, throw cold water on, in a pickle, salt of the earth, milk of human kindness, in a stew, meek as a lamb, spicy, silly as a goose, ham it up, has a crust, boiling mad, chicken and chicken-hearted, sweet as sugar, duck the issue.

Expressions of contempt: cheesey, nuts, bologna, sour grapes, hill of beans, chicken, slippery as an eel, raspberries.

The weather: fog thick as pea soup, sizzling hot, hot enough to fry an egg.

Referring to money: beans, bread, bread and butter, bring home the bacon, salt away, cream, don't put all your eggs in one basket, don't count your chickens until they're hatched, kale, roll, cabbage, lettuce, and spinach.

Scores of others, including: that's my cup of tea, "Life is Just a Bowl of Cherries," mushroom, peppery, pea green, in hot water, beef up, close as sardines in a can, that's the berries, bread is the staff of life, an apple a day keeps the doctor away, egghead, cold turkey, make a hash of it, rhubarb, and out of the frying pan into the fire.

# May 22

## Can You Improve Your Home Security?

A house can never be made entirely safe from intruders intent on stealing household goods or doing harm, but a householder can discourage them.

Hardware stores sell a number of items designed just for that. Some of the newest door locks give much greater security than older models. And have you considered a door chain or a two-way viewer? Install these on both front and back doors and you'll be able to let in only those persons you choose.

Do street lights in your neighborhood fail to reach some parts of your property? Your own dusk-to-dawn yard light can contribute a lot to your peace of mind. It will help discourage prowlers, as well as light the way safely for your family and visitors.

Ask your electrical store or electrician about special lights made for the purpose. Good ones have a built-in automatic photoelectric control to turn the lamp on and off. And be sure to specify a shatter-resistant acrylic refractor.

All sorts of electronic devices are now marketed to promote home security. In some communities you can wire your home so that an intruder will sound an alarm in the local police station. Other devices turn on lights and ring bells when tripped by prowlers. Timers turn lights on and off to make an unoccupied house look occupied.

A watchdog is a good idea, too, especially if well trained and kept outdoors.

# May 23

## When to "Look a Gift Horse in the Mouth"

The old saying "Never look a gift horse in the mouth" is unwise advice. If the gift horse (or pony) is to be a mount for your child, someone *should* look in the animal's mouth to determine its age.

A trustworthy pony, chosen with extreme care by an experienced horseman or knowledgeable friend, is a treasure beyond price. Like all treasures, expect to pay a decent price for it.

Looking inside the mouth of a horse or pony can determine its age—accurately, if it is young, within a few years either way if it is old. Few ponies under the age of five are suitable mounts for a child, because they simply do not know enough, have not been broken long enough, and may have been spoiled by inexperienced riding and handling. Older ponies—over 14 or 15 years—may be wise and sensible. But if they have any faults, they are so firmly established as to be probably impossible to cure. Even more important, the pony may have suffered some years of poor care and may not have many serviceable years ahead of him. However, an old, experienced pony may offer advantages to an inexperienced rider which outweigh his possible loss within the next year or two—advantages of wisdom and common sense that can be of great value to a novice.

Unless you are planning to place the animal in the hands of an experienced horseman for three or four years, do not accept, even as a gift, a very young horse or pony. Foals which have just been weaned from their mothers at the age of five or six months are appealing and inexpensive and, almost always, complete disasters in the long run. They must be fed, wormed, innoculated, sheltered, cared for, and expertly handled for several years before they are ready to be ridden. (On top of this expense, colts—male foals—must be gelded or altered, at the age of one or one and a half years.) Very young horses and ponies are exuberant and full of mischief, and this can make them difficult to handle and positively dangerous for a novice or child. (JSD)

# May 24

## Tips on Making Potato Salad

The season for picnics and outdoor dining has arrived in most of the country. These meals won't be complete without potato salad. Whatever your recipe (there are as many variations as people who make it), here are two tips to make it better.

First, use only thin-skinned new potatoes, the kind you can boil in their "jackets," then skin. Other kinds break or become mushy. Slice or dice them into a bowl.

Second, prepare a marinade of two parts olive or cooking oil to one part vinegar, and salt and pepper. The amounts used will depend upon the quantity of potatoes. You may include in the marinade chopped parsley, chopped chives, or minced onions. Pour this over the potatoes. Mix gently (to avoid breaking the potatoes) until each slice or dice is coated with the marinade. Marinate several hours, if possible, before adding your favorite dressing and other ingredients.

## *May* **25**

### Carry Finger-Washing Supplies in the Car

Before you set out on an extended car trip or vacation this summer, stock the car with supplies for washing sticky fingers. The same supplies will also be welcome if you take children to a drive-in snack bar.

You can assemble your own washing supplies by putting a little grease-cutting lemon juice into some tap water and storing the water in a squeeze-type plastic bottle of at least one-pint capacity. Along with the water take one of the reusable cleaning cloths available in supermarkets under such brand names as Wonder Cloths and Handi Wipes. Put both the cloth and squeezable bottle into a polyethylene bag and store in the glove compartment or elsewhere in the car.

In addition to (or instead of) the above, you

might also take along a package of commercially prepared finger-cleaning materials. These are available in drugstores or supermarkets.

If you haven't yet become acquainted with the reusable cloths mentioned in the second paragraph, give them a try. They're handy for all sorts of things. When soiled, they can be hand or machine-washed for use over and over again.

## *May* **26**

### How to Eat a Lobster

If you are a native of the eastern coast of the U.S., the above heading may cause you to remark: "But everyone knows how!" Not so. It's a fact that in the middle and western parts of our country you still can find many persons who do not know the delights of this most delicious of seafoods.

If you, dear reader, are among them, we sug-

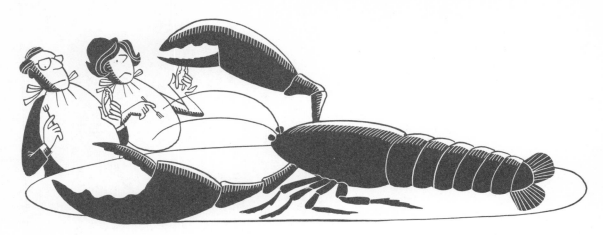

gest that you take a vacation trip this summer to the regions where lobsters are common. Or perhaps you may want to have a lobster shipment sent to you at your home. Several firms on the East Coast specialize in iced express shipments. They're expensive, but you might split the cost with several of your neighbors.

When a whole lobster in the shell is placed before you, what do you do about it? Because eating a lobster, even when experienced, is somewhat messy, most restaurants supply a large coverall bib to protect your clothing. You also need a couple of special tools—a small lobster or cocktail fork and a lobster cracker (a regular nutcracker will serve nicely).

The boiled lobster on your plate will have been placed on its back and split down the middle with a sharp knife. The splitting includes the tail, which has large chunks of delicious meat. Lobster gourmets have their own particular spots for attacking the creature, but this easily gotten tail meat is as good a starting spot as any. Use the small fork to dig out a chunk of the meat. Cut up the chunk with a regular knife and fork. Then fork the bite-sized morsels into the small dish of melted butter served with the lobster. Now eat. And eat.

Use the cracker to break open the shell of the

big claws. Tasty chunks of solid meat are inside. Pull off each of the little claws and suck out the sweet morsels of meat inside.

As you clean out each piece of shell or claw, discard it into a community discard plate that ought to be on the table. Search each piece of shell well before discarding to uncover any tasty tidbits.

Somewhere along the line you also will want to eat the soft greenish liver and the coral roe that you'll find inside the creature. Both are delicious.

Much of the foregoing information came from personal experience. Some came from a government pamphlet you may want to own—"How to Cook Lobster." It's available from the Superintendent of Documents.

## *May* 27

### It's Rachel Carson's Birthday. Use Pesticides Sparingly

At the end of May, with the air full of bird song, it's fitting to remember that today is the birth date of the late Rachel Carson, born May 27, 1907. Her book *Silent Spring*, published in 1962, made the world aware of the dangers of pesticides to our environment, particularly the birds.

Since then a vast movement has coalesced to protect our ecology and improve our environment. One of the major achievements of this movement has been the banning of some dangerous pesticides and the strict control of others. If you must use pesticides, use them carefully. Call your county agent (see May 8) for up-to-date advice on control of specific pests. Read the labels carefully, and use pesticides sparingly.

## *May* 28

### Shop to Avoid Leftover Vegetables

Wouldn't it be great to avoid those containers of leftover food that tend to build up in a refrigerator? You can often get help in that respect by reading the labels on cans and packages of vegetables—and suiting your purchases to the amounts your family normally will consume.

The label may give the number of servings a container yields. If so, you may be able to buy a can or package of the exact size to give what your family will want for a single meal—or two meals if you don't mind leftovers.

One-half cup is the serving size commonly used for adults for most cooked vegetables. Small children and light eaters are often satisfied with smaller portions—¼ or ⅓ cup.

The chart that follows shows the approximate amount of cooked vegetable obtained from average container sizes of frozen and canned vegetables. This chart should help you determine how many, and what size, cans or packages you need.

Frozen vegetables usually do not lose much weight or volume during preparation. Some loss of volume occurs during preparation of canned vegetables for serving if the liquid is drained from the vegetables or if the liquid is concentrated during cooking. From a 16-ounce can of most vegetables you can expect three or four servings (½ cup each) of drained vegetables and two or three servings of canned greens.

Dried vegetables increase considerably in weight and volume during cooking because they absorb water. See the Boiling Guide for Dry Beans, Peas, and Lentils in the Appendix for the approximate yield of cooked food from a cup of dry beans, peas, or lentils.

The inedible parts of fresh vegetables—pods, husks, parings, and trimmings—lower the yield of edible food per pound. Some fresh vegetables shrink because they lose water during cooking, others absorb water and swell as they cook.

Yield from a pound of fresh vegetables may vary from two to six servings (½ cup each) of cooked food. For the approximate amount of each vegetable to buy for six servings, see the Boiling Guide for Fresh Vegetables in the Appendix.

| Approximate amount of cooked vegetables obtained from cans and frozen packages | | | | |
|---|---|---|---|---|
| | Cans | | Frozen packages | |
| | Container size | Cups | Container size | Cups |
| Asparagus, cut | 14 oz. | 1⅓ | 10 oz. | 1¼ |
| Beans, green or wax, cut | 15½ oz. | 1¾ | 9 oz. | 1⅔ |
| Beans, lima | 16 oz. | 1¾ | 10 oz. | 1⅔ |
| Beets, sliced, diced, or whole | 16 oz. | 1¾ | — | — |
| Broccoli, cut | — | — | 10 oz. | 1½ |
| Carrots, diced or sliced | 16 oz. | 1¾ | 10 oz. | 1⅔ |
| Cauliflower | — | — | 10 oz. | 1½ |
| Corn, whole kernel | 16 oz. | 1⅔ | 10 oz. | 1½ |
| Kale | 15 oz. | 1⅓ | 10 oz. | 1⅛ |
| Okra | 15½ oz. | 1¾ | 10 oz. | 1¼ |
| Peas | 16 oz. | 1¾ | 10 oz. | 1⅔ |
| Potatoes, French fried | — | — | 9 oz. | 1⅔ |
| Spinach | 15 oz. | 1⅓ | 10 oz. | 1¼ |
| Summer squash, sliced | — | — | 10 oz. | 1⅓ |
| Tomatoes | 16 oz. | 1⅞ | — | — |

## Shop to Avoid Leftover Fruits

When estimating the number of servings from fresh fruits, allow for waste—the inedible parts, such as parings, trimmings, cores, and pits.

The approximate number of servings you can expect from a purchase unit of fresh fruit follows:

Apples, bananas, figs, peaches, pears, or plums, 3 or 4 per pound; apricots, sweet cherries, dates, or seedless grapes, 4 or 5 per pound; blueberries or raspberries, 4 or 5 per pint; strawberries, 7 or 8 per quart.

There is little or no waste to frozen fruits because they are usually served just as they come from the package. If you drain the liquid from the fruit, however, you get fewer servings.

The approximate number of servings from frozen fruit follows:

Blueberries, raspberries, or strawberries, 2 or 3 per 10-ounce package; grapefruit or pineapple, 3 or 4 per 13½-ounce package; peaches, 2 or 3 per 12-ounce package; red sour cherries, 4 or 5 per 20-ounce package; rhubarb, 4 or 5 per 16-ounce package.

A 16- or 17-ounce can of fruit yields about 4 servings if the liquid is served with the fruit; 2 or 3 servings if the fruit is drained. A 29-ounce can yields about 7 servings if liquid is served with fruit, 4 or 5 servings if the fruit is drained.

Dried fruits increase considerably in weight and volume during cooking because they absorb water. To estimate the servings from a family-size package, see the Guide to Simmering Dried Fruits in the Appendix.

---

**FOR SOME OF THE PUREST** foods, patronize a health-food store in your area. Peanut butter without additives, for instance, is a far different product from what you usually buy in supermarkets. Check the organically grown produce, too.

---

**FOR A DIFFERENT** vegetable casserole, combine 2 packages of frozen mixed vegetables, cooked and drained, with 1 can French-fried onions and 1 can undiluted cream of mushroom soup. Place in a buttered casserole and top with slices of processed cheese. Bake in moderate oven until vegetable mixture is heated through and cheese has melted.

---

**REFRIGERATE PEANUT BUTTER** after opening, and it will always taste a lot better.

## Consider Container Sizes When You Shop

When you shop for canned or frozen vegetables, you may want to know the container size in order to relate the contents to the number of servings of cooked vegetables you will get. See May 28.

Because some recipes refer to the packing industry's common term for a can of a particular size, you also may want to know the net weight of the container's contents.

Here's what the industry commonly calls cans of various sizes and (in parentheses) the usual net weight of the contents:

Eight ounce (8 oz.)
Picnic (10½ to 12 oz.)
No. 303 (16 to 17 oz.)
No. 2 (20 oz.)
No. 2½ (29 oz.)
No. 3 Special (46 oz.)

Common package sizes for frozen vegetables are 8, 9, 10, 12, 16, 24, and 32 ounces. Some frozen vegetables are also packaged in large plastic bags. You may find it more economical to buy the large plastic bag, because you can use part of the contents for one meal and put the rest back in your freezer to serve later.

## May 31

### May Potpourri
### for Homemakers

Get rid of leftovers or other refrigerated foods promptly if you have the slightest suspicion about spoilage. It's better to lose the price of the food than to pay doctor bills.

Keep model numbers and direction booklets for appliances where you can find them in a hurry. The needed information will be at your fingertips when you call the repairman.

To shine a scorched iron, try silver polish.

Rotate linens and towels in closets and clothes in dresser drawers by placing freshly laundered items underneath the piles.

Launder woolen blankets and garments yourself. Set the washing machine for cold water and gentle action and use a cold-water detergent. Set dryer on air or woolen cycle. Press with steam iron set for woolens.

### Your Own Reminders:

## June 1

### Think of Safety When Using an Electric Toaster

Electric toasters have come a long way since they first became common in the 1920s, but they still can be unsafe if improperly used. When a toaster is not in use, unplug it.

Disconnect the power cord before cleaning the crumb tray. If you accidentally depress the bread carriage while the cord is connected and touch the heating elements or wiring, you could be burned or receive a severe shock.

Never try to extract toast with a knife or fork if the power cord is connected. Again you could be either burned or shocked.

No matter what the label says, never put foil-wrapped food into an upright toaster. If the foil touches the heating elements, and you then touch the foil or toaster, you could receive a severe shock.

Never immerse a toaster in water or place it, while it is plugged in, near a sink where it could fall into water, be splashed, or stand in a pool of water. If you touch a wet toaster or water in contact with a toaster, you can receive a severe, even fatal, shock.

Never use an extension cord with a toaster.

## June 2

**TODAY IN HISTORY:** *On June 2, 1886, President Grover Cleveland was married in the White House to Frances Folsom, his ward.*

### Can You Choose a Good Cantaloupe?

Picking any melon for excellent quality and flavor is difficult, challenging the skill of even the most experienced shopper. No absolute formula exists, but the use of several factors in judging a melon will improve the chance of success.

Look for three major signs of full maturity. (1) The stem should be gone, leaving a smooth, symmetrical, shallow basin called a "full slip." If all or part of the stem base remains or if the stem scar is jagged or torn, the melon is probably not fully matured. (2) The netting, or veining, should be thick, coarse, and corky—and should stand out in bold relief over some part of the surface. (3) The skin color (ground color) between the netting should have changed from green to a yellowish buff, yellowish gray, or pale yellow.

But look also for signs of ripeness, for a cantaloupe might be mature, but not ripe. A ripe cantaloupe will have a yellowish cast to the rind, have a pleasant cantaloupe odor when held to the nose, and will yield slightly to light thumb pressure on the blossom end of the melon.

Most cantaloupes are quite firm when freshly displayed in retail stores. While some may be ripe, most have not yet reached their best eating stage. Hold them for two to four days at room temperature to allow them to ripen fully. After conditioning the melons, some people like to place them in the refrigerator for a few hours before serving.

Avoid overripeness. This is shown by a pronounced yellow rind color, a softening over the entire rind, and soft, watery, and insipid flesh. Small bruises normally will not hurt the fruit, but large bruised areas should be avoided, since they generally cause soft, water-soaked areas underneath the rind. Mold growth is a sign of decay.

# June 3

## Serve Fresh Fruits: Excellent Sources of Vitamins

All fruits contain some vitamin C—but in varying amounts. Fruits rich in vitamin C include oranges, grapefruit, cantaloupe, papayas, and strawberries. Fruits containing smaller but worthwhile amounts of vitamin C are fresh apricots, avocados, bananas, blackberries, blueberries, honeydew melon, pineapple, red raspberries, tangerines, and watermelon.

For vitamin A, serve cantaloupe and apricots. Dried apricots are a concentrated source of this vitamin.

Good sources of iron include dried fruits such as raisins, dates, prunes, peaches, and apricots. A half-cup serving of most dried fruits provides at least one-sixth of the iron recommended for a healthy person per day.

Most fresh, raw, unsweetened fruits contain fewer than 100 calories per serving. Sweetened frozen fruits and fruits canned in heavy syrup, however, are considerably higher in calories.

Count as a serving: One medium-sized apple, banana, orange, peach, or pear; two or three apricots, figs, or plums; one-half cup fruit and liquid.

# June 4

## Annual Immunization for Pets

Whether you live in the city, suburbs, or country, your cat or dog should be given annual booster shots against the most common feline and canine diseases. Annual shots are inexpensive life insurance for your pet.

If you are planning to board your pet while you are away for any reason, perhaps on vacation, make sure shots are well up to date: Give booster shots a few weeks before the boarding date if pos-

sible. Though boarding catteries and kennels protect their charges as well as they can, there is no way to be completely sure that a new arrival is not harboring a contagious disease which might well be given to your pet before the new arrival's symptoms become apparent.

No cat or dog should ever be taken to a show without having had recent booster shots. And it would be well to remember that you can carry many of the most common killers of pets home from shows, and even from the street, on your shoes and clothing; you can carry them on your hands if you pat an ailing cat or dog anywhere. So just because your own pet is confined at home does not mean he cannot be exposed to those diseases from which he can be protected so easily. (JSD)

## *June* 5

### What You Can Learn about Vegetables from Labels

Don't take the label for granted on a can or package of vegetables. The information there should enable you to learn exactly what you are getting—and sometimes to compare prices and values. Government regulations require that the following information be given on the label of the can or package as it faces the customer:

The common or usual name of the product and its form or style. The style (for example, whole, sliced, or diced) may be illustrated rather than printed on the label. (See April 13.)

The net contents in total ounces, as well as pounds and ounces, if the can or package contains one pound or more, or less than four pounds.

Labels may also give grade, variety, size, and maturity of the vegetables; seasonings; the number of servings; cooking directions; and recipes or serving ideas. If the number of servings is given, the law requires that the size of the serving must be stated in common measures—ounces or cups—so the buyer will know just how much this serving is.

If the product has been packed under continuous inspection by USDA, the official grade name and the shield indicating that the product has been packed under continuous inspection may also appear on the label.

# June 6

## Care Tips for Garments Made of Qiana

When pressing or ironing garments made of the new fiber Qiana, use a steam iron on a low "wool" setting. This applies both for washable and non-washable garments.

For other care instructions, first refer to February 16. Then read below:

For garments containing nonwashable components, for example silk linings and decorations, dry-clean only.

Spot cleaning above garments: water-based stains (perspiration, dirt, coffee, beverages) —sponge thoroughly with clear water, blot dry; oil-based stains (lipstick, butter, etc.)—use aerosol-spray spot remover according to manufacturer's instructions; stains of unknown origin— try water, then aerosol spray, then dry-clean.

For washable garments (containing low-shrinkage linings, decorations, etc.):

Machine wash in warm water with detergent. Tumble dry at a low to medium temperature. Remove immediately when dryer stops. Or remove from final rinse (without spinning). Drip dry.

Hand wash with detergent. Drip dry. Do not wring.

To spot clean, follow the instructions for spot cleaning nonwashable garments, except launder stains of unknown origin after trying water and aerosol spray.

# June 7

## Broil Fish Outdoors over a Charcoal Fire

It's time once again for cooking some of your meals outdoors over a charcoal fire. Fish is a natural for this form of cookery because it cooks so quickly. Use of a long-handled hinged wire grill is recommended. Rest it on the regular grill of your outdoor cooker.

Pan-dressed fish, fillets, and steaks are all suitable for charcoal broiling. Thaw in advance if frozen (see May 1). Since charcoal broiling is a dry-heat method, thicker cuts of fish are preferable, for they tend to dry out less than thin ones. To ensure serving juicy and flavorful fish, use a sauce

that contains some fat and baste generously before and while cooking.

Fish usually is cooked about four inches above moderately hot coals for ten to 20 minutes, depending on the thickness of the fish.

# June 8

**TODAY IN HISTORY:** *On June 8, 1872, an act of Congress authorized the Post Office Department to issue postal cards. The first one-cent cards appeared the following May 1.*

## "Wish You Were Here"

A new kind of vacation has become popular in recent years. Two families exchange homes for the vacation period—and both benefit. Suppose you live in a Philadelphia suburb and would like to visit San Francisco. Someone in the latter city may want to see the historic sights of Philadelphia. Or maybe a family in England or France is looking for an inexpensive way to see part of the U.S.—and you'd like to go abroad.

You could make your own arrangements by placing newspaper advertising in the city of your choice, while watching the advertising in newspapers covering your area.

There's a better way, however. For a fee, the Vacation Exchange Club, 663 Fifth Ave., New York, N.Y. 10022, will supply a directory listing thousands of persons all over the world who are interested in making a vacation swap. You then make your own arrangements.

"How goes the money?—Sure,
I wish the ways were something fewer;
It goes for wages, taxes, debts;
It goes for presents, goes for bets,
For paint, pomade, and eau de rose,—
And that's the way the Money goes!"
—John Godfrey Saxe

# June 9

## Guard Shoes and Other Leather from Mildew

To remove mildew from shoes and other leather goods, wipe with a cloth wrung out in dilute alcohol (1 cup denatured or rubbing alcohol to 1 cup water). Dry in a current of air. If mildew remains, wash with thick suds of a mild soap or detergent, saddle soap, or a soap containing a germicide or fungicide. Then wipe with a damp cloth and dry in an airy place. Polish leather shoes and luggage with a good wax dressing.

In selecting a wax dressing, read the labels on the packages. Some shoe dressings on the market contain both a fungicide (hexachlorophene or paranitrophenol) to prevent mold growth and wax or a silicone resin to protect against perspiration and wet weather. A thin coat of floor or furniture wax applied to shoes—to both the uppers and the soles—keeps moisture out and thus helps to prevent mildew. Do not use paranitrophenol on white or light-colored leather.

Shoes contaminated with fungus growth on the inside often develop unpleasant odors, and variously colored growths show on the inner sole and linings and up into the toe. You can remove this kind of mildew with formaldehyde solution, obtainable from your druggist. Moisten a cotton-tipped applicator stick with the solution and swab the inside of each shoe thoroughly. Then wrap shoes tightly in a paper or plastic bag and allow the formaldehyde vapors to permeate the shoe materials for at least an hour.

Before wearing the shoes, air them thoroughly out-of-doors. Precaution: Vapors of formaldehyde are very irritating; do not inhale them. Do not get the solution on your skin.

Low-pressure sprays especially intended for freshening shoes are available at shoe and depart-

**TODAY IN HISTORY:** *On June 10, 1952, Haspel Brothers of New Orleans introduced a machine-washable-with-no-pressing seersucker suit made of 60 percent Orlon and 40 percent cotton. It was dubbed "Wash and Wear."*

## What You Should Know about Wash-and-Wear

Wash-and-wear garments tend to retain their original shape and appearance after repeated wear and laundering, with little or no ironing. "Durable-press" (permanent-press) is considered the ultimate in wash-and-wear. Wash-and-wear performance depends on several factors, including the types and amounts of fibers, fabric structure, finish, construction, and washing and drying methods.

Durable-press finishes are also applied to products such as bed and table linens. Fabrics usually are cotton or rayon, blended with polyester, acrylic, acetate, or nylon, and may be lightweight and sheer such as organdy, or heavy such as corduroy.

Buying the correct size is important in durable-press garments because alterations are difficult; original hem and seam lines cannot be removed by home ironing. A "fishy" odor may indicate a finish which has not been fully cured.

To get the best service from wash-and-wear, wash frequently; heavy soil is hard to remove. Pre-treat oily stains before washing by rubbing a small amount of concentrated liquid detergent into the spot. Stains that remain after one washing will generally be removed after repeated launderings.

ment stores. They contain hexachlorophene, dichlorophene, or other fungicides. Use them as directed and repeat as needed.

Another way to stop mold growth in leather goods is to scatter crystals of paradichlorobenzene or to dust paraformaldehyde powder in shoes or luggage, then place in tight containers. The vapors from these chemicals are effective in killing molds that have grown into leather, but they give no lasting protection against future contamination. As the vapors leak out, the chemicals must be replaced. Before using the shoes or luggage, air them thoroughly.

Garments may be laundered in any of the following ways. The manufacturer's labeling instructions should be followed when given.

1. Preferred method: machine wash and tumble dry; remove from dryer immediately after dryer stops and put on hangers to avoid wrinkling.

2. Machine wash and drip dry; remove items from washing machine before spinning cycle; line dry.

3. Hand wash and drip dry; remove from rinse water without wringing or twisting; line dry.

4. Least preferred method: machine wash and line dry after spinning. The spinning cycle adds wrinkles that are difficult to remove.

A fabric softener added to the final rinse water will decrease static build-up and improve wrinkle resistance.

Trademarks of wash-and-wear products: Belfast, Sanforized-Plus, Tebilized, and Wrinkl-Shed; and for durable-press: Coneprest, Dan-Press, Koratron, and Penn Prest.

## Natural Fabrics Are Still with Us

Once upon a time when a woman went shopping, she was sure to come home with clothing and household furnishings made of cotton, linen, silk, or wool. If finances permitted, she may also have added a fur or two for her personal warmth and adornment.

Confronted by a confusing profusion of man-made fibers as you shop today, you might get the impression that the four original natural fibers are no longer being used. Nothing could be further from the truth. Cotton, linen, silk, and wool still are important fabrics.

Cotton, in fact, remains the world's major textile fiber, and is used alone or in blends in an infinite variety of apparel and household and industrial products. New finishes have extended cotton's role in the "easy-care" field and in other fields. Some of the most common are resin finishes used in wash-and-wear, and chemical finishes which make cotton fabrics water repellent or fire retardant.

Cotton quality is dependent on fiber length, fineness, color, and luster. Long cotton fibers can be spun into fine, smooth, lustrous, and comparatively strong yarns from which the better quality cotton fabrics are made. Short fibers produce coarser yarns for use in durable fabrics which are less fine, smooth, and lustrous. (For other facts about cotton, see March 14).

Linen is produced from fibrous materials in the stem of the flax plant. These fibers, in a great variety of thicknesses, tend to cling together, giving linen its characteristic "thick-thin" quality. Compared to cotton, linen is expensive due to its limited production and the hand labor still involved in processing it.

The quality of linen is determined by the length and fineness of the fibers and the degree of bleach, if white, or the fastness of the dyes, if colored. Labels and hang tags should tell you whether these fabrics are made of pure linen, blends of linen with other fibers, or some other fiber which resembles linen.

Silk, the only natural continuous filament fiber, is obtained by unreeling the cocoon of the silkworm. Used alone, "silk" refers to cultivated silk from carefully tended silkworms. By law, "silk," "pure silk," "all silk," or "pure dye silk" must contain no metallic weightings and no more than ten percent by weight of dyes or finishing materials (black silk, 15 percent). Weighted silk contains metallic salts; labels must indicate the percentage of weighting. It may be cheaper and more drapable but less serviceable.

Wool fibers are obtained from the fleece of the sheep or lamb, or from the hair of the Angora or Cashmere goat, the camel, vicuña, alpaca, or llama. Silky Angora hair is called "mohair."

"Wool," "new wool," or "virgin wool" is made of fibers that have never been used or reclaimed. It is usually stronger and more resilient. "Reprocessed wool" fibers have been reclaimed from unused wool products (mill end pieces, for example). "Reused wool" fibers have been reclaimed from used textile products.

"Woolen" fabrics are made from wool yarns containing both long and short fibers. Woolen fabrics are soft, resist wrinkling, but do not hold a sharp crease. "Worsted" yarns, made from the longer fibers, are firm and smooth. Worsted fabrics are more durable. They tailor well, take a sharp crease, but may become shiny with use.

For information about man-made fibers, see tomorrow's article. For information about how to care for products made of natural fibers, see the Appendix.

## June 12

### Man-Made Fibers in Your Wardrobe and Home

Products of man-made fibers are truly interwoven into every phase of your life. There is hardly a moment when you can't reach out and touch something made of man-made fibers.

With their introduction, consumers discovered for the first time a new quality in clothing called "easy care." This highly desirable feature eliminated many tedious washday chores, reduced laundry bills, and provided a lasting neatness not known before. Man-made fibers have brought about a greatly expanded choice of beautiful knitted and woven textiles that can be used in practically every type of apparel at all levels of fashion. The materials are so varied they may appear as sheer nylon hosiery or bulky modacrylic "furs." Blending one fiber with another expands the possibilities even further.

Through the use of man-made fibers, easy care became a reality in products for the home, such as sheets and pillowcases, curtains, drapes, and slipcovers. More than 80 percent of our blankets contain man-made fibers. Ninety-three percent of the carpets produced in America today have surface fibers of nylon, polyester, acrylic, olefin, or rayon. Man-made fibers also are widely used in carpet backings. See table in the Appendix for a listing of major man-made fibers, some of their principal uses, and how you should take care of them.

---

IS YOUR NAME FINK? People by that name gather annually on the third Thursday in June for National Fink Day at Fink, Tex., a tiny hamlet about 80 miles north of Dallas.

---

## June 13

### Housekeeping without Power: Lighting

How can you make your household self-sufficient so far as nighttime illumination is concerned? Candles, flashlights, oil lamps and lanterns, and propane lamps and lanterns will provide emergency lighting. Be sure you have on hand the batteries, wicks, and fuel you need.

Old oil lamps and lanterns are sometimes available in used furniture stores and antique shops. Hardware stores stock new lamps and lanterns, as well as gallon containers of smokeless kerosene and propane tanks to fuel them. If you intend to use oil lamps or lanterns, keep them ready. Wash the chimneys, remove accumulated soot from the wick holders and base, and trim the wicks.

But perhaps best of all, build up your stock of candles—not fancy ones, just good workaday candles that will give you light when you can't get it otherwise. (See September 3.)

## June 14

### Transporting Pets

Even the most stay-at-home pets must travel occasionally, though the trip may be no more than an annual visit to the vet. Whether the trip is short or long, be sure that:

An adequate carrier is available, ready to go at a moment's notice in case of emergency. For a cat, this means a sturdy, safe, well-ventilated carrier made for the purpose. The ownership of a kitten should automatically include the ownership of a proper cat carrier. Picnic baskets, laundry hampers,

trouble or cause accidents when safely confined.

Adequate ventilation is essential; so is control of heat and cold. If the weather is warm, carry a supply of water. Dehydration kills. If the air conditioner in a car breaks down, or if you are caught in a traffic jam—if, at any time during a trip, heat becomes a problem—a Thermos or even a screw-topped jar filled with water can be a lifesaver. Carry a small plastic dish and offer water often; if the animal acts distressed, pour water over its entire body.

Car sickness can be a problem for cats and dogs. If you want your pet to travel with you, let it become familiar with its carrier or crate when it is young and take it on short trips often.

Give water as needed during a trip, but do not feed your pet until the day's traveling is done. If you are spending the night in a strange place, let your pet relieve itself, rest for an hour, and get used to its new surroundings before you offer it food.

If you are planning a long trip with a cat and have room enough in your car, by all means get a wire-mesh crate, big enough to hold a small litter pan and a favorite blanket or bed. Crates made of parallel bars usually will not hold a determined cat. Excellent traveling crates for cats and dogs are made by Kennel-Aire Manufacturing Company, 725 North Snelling Ave., St. Paul, Minn. 55104.

If your pet is traveling in a crate, a blanket or towels can be used to protect it from drafts in the cold weather, or from direct rays of the sun in the summer. Another enormous advantage of crating a traveling pet is that you need not worry about attempts at escape through open windows and doors from the car or a motel room.

Be sure to have all booster shots up to date. Some states require a recent health certificate from a veterinarian; it would be well to travel with a certificate for each pet. (JSD)

or cardboard cartons tied with string are NOT suitable for transporting cats, and it is better to know this in advance instead of finding it out when the frantic cat escapes half-way to its destination!

Small breeds of dogs are safely transported in carriers, too. Carriers and crates are excellent for confining dogs, especially young ones which must travel in a car when the driver has no one to help. A frightened, or rambunctious puppy cannot get into

## *June* 15

### 1853 Advice for Today: Teach Child Daily

Mrs. Abell's advice to parents in 1853 on teaching children at home is still well taken. (See a reference to her book on April 21.) She wrote:

"Few parents realize how much their children may be taught at home, by devoting a few minutes to their instruction every day. Let the parent make the experiment only during the hours which are not spent in school. Let him make a companion of his child, converse with him, propose questions, answer inquiries, communicate facts, explain difficulties, the meaning of things, and the reason of things, and all in so easy and agreeable manner that it will be no task, but serve to awaken curiosity and interest the mind, and he will be astonished at the progress he will make."

---

**TRANSPARENT NYLON THREAD is** a problem solver. Keep a spool in your sewing basket to use when you don't have thread which matches the fabric you want to sew.

---

**SWEET-SOUR DRESSING** for cole slaw or garden leaf lettuce: Moisten ¼ cup sugar, a pinch of salt, and freshly ground pepper with vinegar. Stir in heavy cream until dressing is of the desired consistency.

---

**TURN THE COLLAR** of a man's shirt when it frays a bit on the edges. It's easy to rip loose and sew back on inside out—and the shirt's life often can be doubled.

---

## *June* 16

### Time to Prune Nonblooming Wisteria Vines

Wisterias sometimes develop luxuriant foliage —with nary a blossom. Young vines especially are prone to this deplorable failing. So what to do?

We're told that it's often best to buy a vine that has already blossomed once or twice. If you already have a bloomless vine, however, the time is at hand to attempt a correction. This should take the form of a good pruning. Do it today if you can, but some time soon at least. Midsummer is the time.

Prune away a third or half of all of the viny growths except the main ones. This will induce the growth of new shoots. Cut away a little of the main vine, too.

Make a note to yourself to do some further pruning sometime in August. By that time more new growth should have developed. Prune away part of this, also.

# *June* **17**

## Check Acid Needs of Shrubs near House Foundation

When planning ornamental plantings around your house, remember an old rule that many are unaware of or have forgotten: Don't plant acid-loving shrubs or trees too close to the foundation or, if you must, take care to treat them regularly to a dose of acid soil-conditioner such as aluminum sulfate.

The reason is that masonry walls, whether of stone or cinder-block construction, and no matter how old, continually seep off basic calcium compounds which are poison to such plants as yews, pines, cedars, rhododendron, azaleas, and andromeda.

Ask the county agent or a garden shop for explicit help on this problem. (JOP)

Using the bathroom lavatory for teeth brushing, for instance, becomes possible at a very early age if you have on hand a stool up to a foot high that the child can move in front of the bowl. The stool also may help him return his own face cloth and towel to a rack on the wall. Actually, in a bathroom that's outfitted with children in mind there ought to be a couple of towel racks low enough for tots to reach.

What about the closet in the child's room? Is it possible for him to place his clothes on hangers —beginning at the youngest possible age? Check out a department store or look in a mail-order catalog for a low-hanging clothes rod that you can suspend from an adult-height rod in the closet. The lower rod hooks on the existing rod. The child probably will be able to use the lower one until he

# *June* **18**

## Extending a Child's Reach

When a child wants to begin doing things for himself, he may experience some frustration because certain conveniences of the adult world are just too high for him. So today let's look around the house and see what we can do to bring things down to child-size.

grows enough to reach the upper one.

There's also the matter of door latches and light switches. A stick about a foot long hanging from the toggle of a wall switch will enable the child to turn his light both on and off. Attach the hanging stick with its upper end close to the toggle with a cord. Then liberally douse the cord with household cement.

You can't do much about making door knobs more readily accessible—and perhaps that's just as well, to keep children from wandering. But if an outer screen door has a hook and eye you may want to put it low enough for the child.

## June 19

### Use "Beautiful Junk" for Play Equipment

Many free or very inexpensive materials may be converted into indoor or outdoor play equipment for a preschool child. Painted soft drink "six-packs" become the milkman's bottle carrier, appliance crates become play houses, and empty thread spools become beads with suggestions from you and the imagination of your preschooler.

Think of possible play uses for items such as ice cream cartons, old hats and shoes, and plastic bottles before you put them in the trash barrel. Merchants often have scraps—wood, inner tubes, rug remnants and fabric, among many others —that they will sell for a minimal charge or give for the carting away.

Such play items can be far more educational than the so-called "educational toys," as they require the child to work out and solve his own play needs, thus stimulating his creativity.

For sources of additional scrap and ideas for using it, request a copy of the pamphlet "Beautiful Junk" from the Superintendent of Documents, Washington, D.C. 20402.

---

**A ROLL OF WALLPAPER** usually contains about 36 square feet. When waste and losses from matching are subtracted, the net yield is approximately 30 square feet.

---

**KEEP A LONG-HANDLED BRUSH** near your clothes dryer and use it to remove lint each time you use the dryer. A bath brush for back scrubbing works nicely.

---

# June 20

## Meat Thermometer Best Way to Test a Roast

Using a meat thermometer to measure the internal temperature is the best way to test the doneness of a meat roast or roasted poultry. Use a thermometer that shows temperatures in degrees as well as stages of doneness for various products. Make sure the tip of the thermometer is not touching either bone or fat.

For meat roasts, place the thermometer into the center of the roast in the thickest part.

| | |
|---|---|
| **Fresh Beef** | Rare 140 |
| | Medium 160 |
| | Well Done 170 |
| **Fresh Veal** | 170 |
| **Fresh Lamb** | Medium 170 |
| | Well Done 180 |
| **Fresh Pork** | 170 |
| **Cured Pork** *(Cook before eating)* | Ham 160 |
| | Shoulder 170 |
| | Canadian Bacon 160 |
| **Cured Pork** *(Fully cooked)* | Ham 140 |
| **Poultry** | Turkey 180-185 |
| | Boneless Roasts 170-175 |
| | Stuffing 165 |

When roasting turkey, insert a thermometer into the center of the inner thigh muscle. Treat a boneless poultry roast as you would a meat roast.

Home economics experts of the U.S. Department of Agriculture say roasts are done when your thermometer shows the internal temperature (in degrees Fahrenheit) indicated in the following table:

# June 21

TODAY IN HISTORY: *Columbia Records introduced long-playing (33⅓ R.P.M.) records on June 21, 1948.*

## Good Tips for Buying Canned Fruit

Buy canned fruits according to grade if possible. Grades are: U.S. Grade A or U.S. Fancy, U.S. Grade B or U.S. Choice, and U.S. Grade C or U.S. Standard (thrift quality).

Grades are based on color, texture, flavor, shape, uniformity of size, and freedom from defects. The higher grades are more attractive in appearance, but cost more than the lower grades.

Nutritive values are not necessarily related to grade, so the lower grades at lower prices are often better buys.

Read the labels on canned fruits. Government regulations require that processors state on the label the style of pack, packing medium, and type or variety of fruit. This information helps you choose canned fruits for specific uses.

Fancy pineapple sections or peach halves dress up a salad. But when appearance is less important, as in a gelatin dessert or a cobbler, the broken slices of pineapple or irregular pieces of peach serve just as well and cost less.

Pitted sweet cherries cost more than unpitted ones but are more convenient. Canned clingstone peaches usually cost less than freestone peaches. The clingstones are firm in texture and attractive in appearance, and are desirable in some dishes. Canned freestone peaches do not hold their shape as well as clingstones, but have a more pronounced flavor and are delicious in pies and cobblers.

For desserts, you may prefer fruits canned in heavy syrup. For salads, however, fruits canned in light syrup are just as good. The syrup can be used in gelatin salads or desserts without adding much sweetness.

Water-pack fruits and fruits canned with non-nutritive sweeteners are good for dieters. Canned fruit-pie fillings—which are already thickened,

sweetened, and spiced—save the cook time.

# June 22

## How Long Can You Keep Fresh Fruits?

Before storing fruits, sort them and either use or discard damaged fruits immediately. Most fruits (except berries and cherries) should be washed and dried before storing.

Unripe fruits should be left to ripen in open air at room temperature and out of direct sunlight. They will not ripen in the refrigerator. Some fresh fruits keep best in the refrigerator; others, at a room temperature of 60 to 70 degrees Fahrenheit.

Fresh fruits that may be stored in the refrigerator, and the time they can be held for high quality are listed below.

Apricots, avocados, blueberries, grapes, nectarines, peaches, pears, plums, rhubarb, and watermelons, 3 to 5 days.

Blackberries, cherries, figs, raspberries, and strawberries, 1 or 2 days.

Apples (eating ripe) and cranberries, 1 week.

Storage notes:

Berries and cherries should be refrigerated as soon as possible. Do not wash them before putting them in refrigerator. Leave stems on cherries and caps on strawberries. Sort carefully and place loosely in shallow containers so that air can circulate around them and the weight of the berries and cherries on top does not crush those on the bottom.

Citrus fruits keep for a few days at temperatures of 60 to 70 degrees F., but will keep better in the refrigerator. If they are held too long at cold temperatures, however, the skin may become pitted and the flesh may discolor.

Melons (except watermelons) may be stored at room temperature if they are underripe. Ripe melons should be refrigerated and used within a short time.

Pineapples should be used promptly after purchase. If necessary to hold them for a day or two, keep them in the refrigerator.

## June 23

### Pointers on Judging Freshness of Fish

Certain varieties of fresh fish are most abundant at certain seasons. Ask your local dealer about seasonal offerings and which kinds are most economical. Lesser known kinds of fish often cost less.

Whole or dressed fish should have the following characteristics when fresh:

Flesh: Firm flesh, not separating from the bones, indicates fish are fresh and have been handled carefully.

Odor: Fresh and mild. A fish just taken from the water has practically no "fish" odor. The fishy odor becomes more pronounced with passage of time, but it should not be disagreeably strong when the fish is bought.

Eyes: Bright, clear, and full. The eyes of fresh fish are bright and transparent; as the fish becomes stale, the eyes become cloudy and often turn pink. When fish are fresh, the eyes often protrude, but with increasing staleness, the eyes tend to become sunken.

Gills: Red and free from slime. The color gradually fades with age to a light pink, then gray, and finally brownish or greenish.

Skin: Shiny, with color unfaded. When first taken from the water, most fish have an iridescent appearance. Each species has its characteristic markings and colors which fade and become less pronounced as the fish loses freshness.

Fresh fillets, steaks, and chunks have the following characteristics:

Flesh: Fresh-cut in appearance. It should be firm in texture without traces of browning or drying around the edges.

Odor: Fresh and mild.

Wrapping: If the fillets, steaks, or chunks are wrapped, the wrapping should be of moisture-vapor-proof material. There should be little or no air space between the fish and the wrapping.

## June 24

### Cooking Fresh Vegetables

Remove bruised, wilted, yellowed, or tough portions from fresh vegetables. Trim sparingly to avoid excessive loss of food and nutrients. If root vegetables and potatoes are pared before cooking, make parings thin.

Dark-green outer leaves of cabbage, lettuce, and other leafy green vegetables are high in nutrients, so don't discard them unless they are wilted or tough. Remove woody midribs from kale leaves—there is little loss of nutritive value and the kale will taste better.

Wash vegetables thoroughly before cooking. Use plenty of water for leafy greens; lift them from the water to let sand and grit settle.

Soak fresh Brussels sprouts and broccoli in cold salt water for a short time to remove insects if any are present. Cover potatoes with water to prevent darkening if held after paring. Long soaking of most vegetables is not desirable because some nutrients dissolve in the water.

To insure the best flavor, color, texture, and food value in vegetables, boil them only until they are tender. Vegetables cooked whole in their skins retain most of their nutritive value. To shorten cooking time—cut, slice, dice, or coarsely shred vegetables.

The amount of water used in cooking is

142

important—the less water, the more nutrients retained in the cooked vegetables.

For young, tender vegetables, ½ to 1 cup of water is usually enough for six servings. Water to cover is needed for some older root vegetables that require longer cooking. Spinach and other greens need only the water clinging to their leaves from washing if cooked over low heat in a pan with a tight-fitting lid. Tomatoes can be cooked in their own juice.

To boil fresh vegetables:

Bring salted water to a boil (use ½ to 1 teaspoon salt for six servings of vegetable).

Add vegetable, cover, and quickly bring water back to a boil.

Reduce heat and cook gently until vegetable is just tender. (See Boiling Guide in Appendix.)

Serve immediately; flavor and nutritive value may be lost if vegetables are allowed to stand.

To pressure cook vegetables, see tomorrow's article.

---

**CONTINUE CUTTING asparagus until the first garden peas are ready to be picked—about the middle of June in the Northeast.**

---

**CHECK WITH YOUR DOCTOR before installing a water softener if you will be using the softened water for drinking and a member of your family is on a "salt-free" or "low-sodium" diet.**

---

## *June* 25

### Pressure Cooking Vegetables

In pressure cooking vegetables, follow the directions that came with your cooker, but learn to adjust cooking time to suit the quality of vegetable being cooked. Very young, tender vegetables may require a shorter cooking time than is recommended. Even one or two minutes extra cooking can cause undesirable color, changes in texture, and loss of nutrients.

Directions for pressure cooking:

Bring pressure up quickly.

Time the cooking period exactly.

Reduce pressure as quickly as possible when time is up.

Season pressure-cooked vegetables as you do plain boiled vegetables.

**Variations you may want to try:**

Add a pinch of herbs (see Appendix) or a tablespoon of minced onion, green pepper, or chives before cooking fresh vegetables. These add flavor, without calories.

Season after cooking with a flavorful fat —bacon drippings, butter, or margarine—or with salad oil to which a little lemon juice, horseradish, or garlic has been added.

Sprinkle lemon juice or herb vinegar on vegetables for a pleasantly tart touch.

Mash vegetables, beat in a little hot milk, add butter or margarine, and season with salt and pepper to taste.

Serve with a tasty sauce.

**TODAY IN HISTORY:** *Atlantic City completed its first boardwalk on June 26, 1870. It was eight feet wide.*

## It's Fun to Dig Your Own Clams

Next time you vacation at the seashore, plan to take the youngsters clamming. Check with the local police first, however, for you may need a permit —usually at a nominal fee.

Determine whether you are going after soft-shell or hard-shell clams for the techniques are

**WALDORF SALAD DRESSING:** Mix ¼ cup mayonnaise, 1 tablespoon sugar, ½ teaspoon lemon juice, dash of salt, and ½ cup whipped cream.

**QUICK DESSERT:** Spread slices of angel food or pound cake with butter, top with a little brown sugar, and broil until bubbly.

different. You find soft-shells mostly on the tidal flats at low tide. Spot them as they spurt water from the sand. Uncover them with a special fork and drop into a pail that you carry along. The larger sizes of soft clams are known as "in-shells," the smaller as "steamers."

For the hard-shells, go to the bays and estuaries. In New England, these clams still are commonly known by their Indian name of quahog. Depending on size, hard-shell clams are known as littlenecks (when smallest), cherrystones, or chowders. A larger cousin, the surf clam, is equally good in chowders. It comes from just under the sand in the surf zone.

For the hard-shells, amateurs can use the same technique employed by the Indians who left mountainous mounds of clam and oyster shells all along the Atlantic coast.

Wade out into the bay beyond the sand beach until your feet sink into a layer of soft mud and you are up to your shoulders in water. Pull along a light boat or an inner tube fitted with an inside sack to handle your harvest.

This technique is called "treading" for clams.

You find them with your feet. When you encounter one you'll know it. The trick then is to grasp it with both feet, and quickly raise it high enough to take with your hands.

Some old-time natives in New Jersey bays used to wear oversize woolen drawers and work the clam up inside one pant leg with their toes to waist level. That now is probably a lost art.

For what to do with your seashore harvest, see tomorrow's date. (JOP)

---

CLAM UP! What's the origin of this old phrase? Does its meaning of "shut your mouth" or "keep quiet" come simply from a closed-lip similarity to the tightly closed shell of a live clam? Or could the phrase also have been inspired by the old method of lifting up clams with your feet as described in today's major article? We think it's an interesting supposition. Picture an old-time clammer, each time he raised a quahog, yelling "Clam up!"

---

## June 27

### Buying and Cooking Clams

The clams you buy or harvest from the sea are different on the Atlantic and Pacific coasts of the U.S.—but on both coasts they make great eating. The clams described yesterday are mostly from the East Coast. On the Pacific Coast the most common market species are the butter, littleneck, razor, and pismo clams. The Pacific littleneck is a different species from the Atlantic hard clam.

Although they are served most often in chowders, there are a variety of good ways to serve clams. It is not only the fine distinctive flavor that recommends them as a food; they are also an excellent source of the "protective" nutrients, including proteins, minerals, and vitamins.

Many traditions have grown up around the serving and eating of clams. Annual clam-eating contests are held in various coastal regions of the country. The connotations of the term "clambake" have extended the use of that word far beyond its original meaning. Few controversies (in cookery circles, at least) have more participants than that which centers on the proper way to make clam chowder.

You may have your own method, but we'd like to present the recipe for old-fashioned New Jersey clam chowder that JOP dug up for us. It serves four:

Scrub well 12 to 16 large chowder clams. Put in large pot with ½ cup water and steam for about 2 minutes, or until they open. Put aside the juice from steaming.

Parboil 2 large potatoes and 1 big onion. Dice the potatoes and onion, mince the clam meat, and mix them in a casserole with the clam juice (from steaming). Lard with 6 or 8 pieces of salt pork or fat bacon, and heat in the oven for about an hour at 350 degrees.

When casserole has simmered enough, bring 2 quarts of milk to almost a boil, and pour in contents of the casserole.

## June 28

### All about Hard-Cooked Eggs

When eggs are in good supply and consequently cost less—possibly early summer—hard-cook them and use them in a variety of ways.

Use week-old eggs. The shells of fresh eggs may be difficult to peel. Cover the eggs with cold water. Bring to a boil, lower the heat, and simmer for 25 minutes. Immediately plunge them into cold water. Change the water if necessary to keep it cold. Cooked by this method, the yolks will not darken but will remain yellow.

Quartered hard-cooked eggs creamed with asparagus, either canned, fresh, or frozen, make an excellent luncheon dish. Or serve them this way with ham, hot or cold, for supper or dinner.

Chop hard-cooked eggs for a salad. Add a little salt, freshly ground pepper, and dry mustard, then moisten with mayonnaise. Serve on a bed of lettuce or in a tomato.

Deviled eggs enhance a salad plate or make a good hors d'oeuvre. Halve the eggs, remove the yolks, and place them in a bowl. Work them smooth with a fork. Add salt and dry mustard to taste, and moisten with mayonnaise. Round the mixture into the halves of the whites. Garnish the tops with chopped parsley, chopped chives, freshly ground pepper, cayenne, pimiento strips, or caviar. Deviled eggs on toast, topped with Welsh rarebit, make an appetizing dish.

Pickle whole hard-cooked eggs by placing them in a jar and covering them with the juice of pickled beets.

Whole hard-cooked eggs or deviled halves are a nice addition to the lunch box or picnic hamper. Chopped hard-cooked eggs are good in tuna, chicken, or other salads when a "stretcher" is needed. Chopped whites mixed with yolks that have been pressed through a sieve are a nutritious garnish for vegetables and other dishes.

## June 29

### Dental Checkups—a Must for Young Children

As soon as your child has cut his milk (baby) teeth, about the age of two years, it's time to plan semiannual visits to the dentist. It is important to maintain these teeth in a clean, healthy condition, for they are vital to proper development of gum and bone structure.

You can help the child develop positive attitudes toward his visits to the dentist by having him accompany you to your dental appointments and by reacting in a positive way at these times yourself.

Dentists are acutely aware of the importance of developing these positive attitudes. Some will suggest that you bring the child periodically merely to ride up and down in the dental chair. Later, they will ask the child to open his mouth, then close it, without making an examination. These practices, as well as others, help to dispel any fears the child may have about visiting the dentist.

When the dentist begins actual examinations of your child's teeth, follow any recommendations he makes concerning needed fillings, orthodonture, and fluoride or other treatments.

When the child reaches school age, a good time to schedule one of the semiannual checkups is prior to the opening day of school. Better do this today as there is a waiting period for most dental appointments.

WANT TO GROW a California redwood? Might as well not try. They usually thrive only with special care outside their natural range. They live where they do because conditions are exactly right for them.

THERE ARE DESIGNS all through your house—in wallpaper, upholstery, draperies, and floor coverings. Adapt them to create your very own crewel, needlepoint, or rug-hooking projects.

## *June* **30**

### June Potpourri
### for Homemakers

Save old toothbrushes. Use them to clean appliance knobs, metal edges of kitchen counters, drapery pull knobs, and around faucets.

A bathtub is a good substitute for a washtub for washing items too large to fit into the sink —draperies and oven racks for instance.

Tie the cords on such garments as pajamas, sweat pants, and jackets before washing. If you do lose one, remove the cord completely, pin a safety pin to one end, and feed the cord back through.

Mix minced onion and an egg with leftover mashed potatoes. Shape into cakes, coat with flour, and sauté in butter until brown on both sides.

### Your Own Reminders:

# July 1

## Summer Reading a "Must" for Every Child

Once the child has "unlocked" the reading code—hopefully in first grade—and is able to read independently, it is extremely important for him to read during the summer months to maintain the gains made in reading development during the school year. The child who does not follow a summer reading program may lose as much as a grade level, or perhaps more, between June and September.

What the child reads during the summer months is not as important as the fact that he reads on a regular basis. Any librarian will be able to suggest books which the child can read independently. Teachers have lists of books appropriate to a child's reading level, and they frequently send such lists home with the child during the school year. If you have not received such a list, request one by phoning or visiting your child's school.

Encourage the child to schedule a certain time each day during the summer to read his books. Not only will this help him to maintain or improve his reading ability, but it will have the added advantage of assisting him to develop self-sufficiency.

---

**A GARTER SNAKE on your premises will get rid of garden slugs. The snake is harmless.**

---

**ON JULY 1, 1910, a machine began baking bread. The Ward Baking Company in Chicago opened a fully automatic bread plant. Human hands did not touch the dough or bread except for placing the loaves on the wrapping machine.**

## July 2

### Look Now for Silverfish

Silverfish feed on starchy materials—books, paper, and wallpaper. You may find them at any time of the year in your cookbooks. In the summer, these incredibly thin creatures may congregate in attics where books and papers are stored. So take a look now if you have such storage areas.

Silverfish somewhat resemble another household nuisance—firebrats. Both have two long slender feelers at the head and three tail-like appendages. Silverfish are shiny and silver or pearl gray; firebrats are mottled gray. Adults of both insects are one-third to one-half inch long.

Both pests are active at night and hide by day. Silverfish live and develop in damp, cool places, especially basements. Great numbers may be found in new buildings where the walls still are damp. The firebrat lives and develops in hot, dark places—around fireplaces and furnaces and in insulation around hot water and steam pipes.

In apartment houses, the insects follow pipes from the basement to rooms on upper floors. They may be found in bookcases, behind baseboards, and behind window and door frames. Control them by using sprays recommended for the purpose.

## July 3

### For an Outdoor Barbecue: Glistening Shish Kebab

Looking for a good recipe for an outdoor barbecue on the holiday tomorrow? This recipe provides six servings of glistening shish kebab.

**2 cups red currant jelly**
**⅓ cup lime juice**
**¼ cup butter or margarine**
**1 tsp. salt**
**¼ tsp. pepper**
**¼ tsp. nutmeg**
**1½ lbs. lean lamb cubes,**
 **cut 1½ to 2 inches in size**
**Additional salt and pepper**
**Monosodium glutamate (optional)**
**1 jar (12½ oz.) kumquats, drained**
**12 large fresh mushrooms, wiped clean**

In a saucepan combine currant jelly, lime juice, butter, salt, pepper, and nutmeg. Heat, stirring, until butter is melted and glaze is smooth. Place lamb on skewers; season with salt and pepper, and monosodium glutamate (if desired). Grill over hot coals 15 minutes or until desired degree of doneness is reached, brushing frequently with the glaze and turning often. Skewer the kumquats and mushrooms; grill 5 to 8 minutes or until cooked as desired, brushing frequently with the glaze. Serve kebabs with remaining glaze.

## July 4

### "My Country 'Tis of Thee"

It is especially appropriate to sing the song "America" at any Independence Day assembly, for it was first sung publicly on July 4. This was at a picnic in Boston in 1834. The words for the song had been written only a few days before by the Reverend Samuel Francis Smith, a Baptist minister. The tune came from a collection of German melodies. You may have noticed that persons in the British Commonwealth sing their national anthem, "God Save the Queen" to the same tune. The words of the first stanza of "America" are given below:

> My country 'tis of thee,
> Sweet land of liberty,
> Of thee I sing.
> Land where my fathers died,
> Land of the Pilgrim's pride,
> From ev'ry mountain side
> Let freedom ring.

## July 5

### Sun and Air Stored Articles to Avoid Mildew

From time to time on warm, dry days, sun and air articles stored in closets. It pays to inspect occasionally cotton, rayon, leather, and woolen clothing put away in garment bags. Unless such materials are stored with a mildew inhibitor, they may mildew. A closed bag, dampness, and hot summer weather make ideal growing conditions for molds.

Remove any mildew spots as soon as you discover them. Brush off any surface growth outdoors to prevent scattering the mildew spores in the

house. Sun and air fabrics thoroughly. If any mildew spots remain, treat washable articles as described below. Dry-clean nonwashable articles.

Wash mildew-stained articles at once with soap or detergent and water. Rinse well and dry in the sun. If any stain remains, bleach. Test colored fabrics for colorfastness to the bleach before proceeding.

Bleaches that you can use:

Lemon juice and salt. Moisten stain with a mixture of lemon juice and salt. Spread in the sun. Rinse thoroughly.

Peroxygen bleach. Mix 1 to 2 tablespoons of sodium perborate or a powdered bleach containing sodium perborate or potassium monopersulfate with 1 pint of water. Use hot water if safe for the fabric; otherwise use lukewarm water. Sponge the stain or soak stained area in the solution. Or sprinkle the dry powder directly on the dampened stain. Let solution or powder remain on the stain 30 minutes or longer, then rinse thoroughly. If mildew stains have been on the fabric for some time, it may be necessary to soak in the bleach solution overnight. If safe for the fabric, sodium perborate solution at or near the boiling point may remove stubborn stains.

Chlorine bleach. Mix 2 tablespoons of liquid chlorine bleach with 1 quart warm water. Sponge stain or soak stained area in the solution. Allow bleach to remain on fabric from 5 to 15 minutes, then rinse thoroughly. Never use a chlorine bleach on silk, wool, or spandex fabrics. Some fabrics with wash-and-wear or other special finishes may be damaged by chlorine bleaches. Articles with such finishes should have a warning on the label to that effect.

## July 6

### Cooking Frozen Vegetables

Frozen vegetables may be prepared by boiling in a small amount of water, or you can cook them in a moderate oven while you are baking other foods. Cooked frozen vegetables are seasoned and served like fresh vegetables. If you like, you can cream or scallop them or add them to soufflés, soups, or salads.

Thawing is not necessary for most frozen vegetables. Leafy vegetables, however, cook more evenly if thawed just enough to separate the leaves before you put them into boiling water. It is a good idea to partially thaw corn on the cob before cooking so the cob will be heated through by the time the corn is cooked.

To cook commercially frozen vegetables, follow package directions.

Cook home-frozen vegetables as follows:

Bring lightly salted water to a boil in a covered saucepan. The amount of water varies with kind of vegetable and size of package. For most vegetables, ½ cup of water is enough for a pint package. Use 1 cup of water for a pint of lima beans; water to cover for corn on the cob.

Put vegetables into boiling water, cover pan, and bring quickly back to a boil. To insure uniform cooking, it may be necessary to separate pieces with a fork. When water again boils reduce heat and start to time cooking period (see Boiling Guide in Appendix).

To bake, partly defrost vegetables to separate the pieces. Spread vegetables in a greased casserole, add seasonings as desired, and cover. Bake until just tender.

In a moderate oven (350 degrees) most vegetables require approximately 45 minutes. Cooking time varies with size of the pieces and how much they were thawed before baking.

# July 7

**TODAY IN HISTORY:** *The Territory of Hawaii was annexed by the U.S. on July 7, 1898.*

## Simmering Fresh Fruits

Fresh fruits cooked in a sugar syrup add variety to meals. Use only enough sugar to bring out the flavor of the fruit; too much sugar masks delicate flavors.

To help fruit keep its shape, sugar is generally added before cooking. Firm varieties of fruits, however, should be cooked in water instead of syrup. Add sugar the last few minutes of cooking. Cook the fruit only until tender. This helps retain color, flavor, and nutrients.

For further information on simmering fresh fruits, see guide in Appendix.

# July 8

**TODAY IN HISTORY:** *Nan Jane Aspinwall trotted into New York City on July 8, 1911, becoming the first woman horseback rider to cross the continent alone. She carried a letter to New York's mayor from the mayor of San Francisco, which she had left on Sept. 1, 1910.*

## How to Behave with a Horse in Traffic

Housing developments and indifferent town and city planners are closing off miles of bridle paths throughout the country just when more and more families are discovering the fun of keeping horses and ponies. The family-owned horse population in the U.S. is soaring (more than 13 billion dollars spent on horses each year) and close to half of these horses are owned and ridden by young people.

## July 9

Because of closed bridle paths riders must sometimes venture out into the hazards of main roads for at least part of their rides. There, many car and truck drivers do not realize how dangerously unpredictable a horse can be.

When you are driving: Keep in mind that a horse is easily frightened, no matter how mild and plodding he may look. The sight of a scrap of paper or a rustle in the bushes can send him whirling to one side—very often directly into the path of a car. SLOW DOWN and give the horse plenty of room as you pass—at least as much room as you should allow a child on a bicycle, plus a little more to compensate for the speed and weight of a frightened horse.

Do not blow your horn as you approach a horse and rider. The horse will already have seen you coming; a horse's eyes are set on the sides of his head so that he can see danger approaching from behind, without having to turn his head. The sound of a horn will only scare him and very possibly precipitate the accident you are trying to avoid.

If you own a horse or pony, have your blacksmith put borium on the shoes. Borium, welded in just three or four spots on a horseshoe, prevents slipping on paved or icy surfaces. Helping your horse stay on his feet on the road is a sound safety tip.

When you are riding: Keep to the shoulder of the road, where there is gravel or grass to give your horse better footing. Keep a wary eye out for litter. A broken bottle can sever a horse's tendon. Ride no faster than a walk or slow jog. Then perhaps use this time to try to think of ways to open or protect bridle paths in your area. (JSD)

---

**STOP RUGS FROM CREEPING. Sew rubber rings from canning jars to the underside of the rugs.**

---

---

## Making Fruit Sauces

You can make delicious sauce from apples, cherries, cranberries, peaches, or rhubarb. Serve applesauce or rhubarb sauce as a simple dessert. Cranberry sauce and applesauce are good with meats and poultry. Cherry sauce and peach sauce make colorful toppings for ice cream, puddings, sponge cake, or angel food cake.

When making most fruit sauces, you cook the fruits in water—to soften them—before adding sugar. But for cranberry sauce, add sugar to the water at the beginning of cooking.

In the cooking guide in Appendix, the amounts of water and sugar are for fruits of medium juiciness and tartness. You may need to adjust these amounts because these qualities vary in fruits.

## Know Your Meat Cuts

Perhaps you've·already noticed new meat charts displayed at your favorite stores. Separate charts identify the meat cuts obtained from beef, veal, lamb, and pork carcasses. The National Live Stock and Meat Board, of Chicago, developed the meat charts with the cooperation of an industry-wide committee.

The objective was to eliminate confusion that has long existed in naming meat cuts. In the past identical cuts have often been called different names in different parts of the country. The committee reduced the total number of meat-cut names from more than 1,000 to just over 300.

A few popular names such as porterhouse and filet mignon are retained under the new system, but others that you may have known are not included unless as a supplement to the new nomenclature.

London broil is one of the casualties. This cut henceforth will be known as either "beef flank steak" or "beef chuck shoulder steak, boneless" depending on the area of the steer from which it comes. You also should ask now for a "beef rib eye steak" instead of a Delmonico steak, a filet steak, a Spencer steak, or a beauty steak—all names for the same thing.

For your convenience in studying and learning the new names at home, the four charts are reproduced in the Appendix of this Almanac. Notice that the charts include basic cooking instructions for the various cuts.

## July 11

### Begin Drying Flowers for Winter Bouquets

Many of the flowers now growing in your garden will still be able to bring you pleasure during the cold days of next winter. Dry them, at selected times throughout the summer, and then use them next winter in flower arrangements. After cutting, hang them upside down in a shady place to dry.

Home and Garden Bulletin No. 91 from the U.S. Department of Agriculture, "Growing Flowering Annuals," recommends drying the following flowers at these times:

Baby's-breath, when flowers are well formed; cockscomb, when in color but before seeds begin to shed; gaillardia, when in full color but before petals dry; globe-amaranth, when mature; larkspur, when oldest floret matures (that is, when the plant forms a spike); strawflower, when buds begin to open; zinnia, when in full color but before petals begin to dry.

## July 12

### Storing Frozen Fruits and Vegetables

Store both frozen fruits and vegetables at zero degrees Fahrenheit or lower if you plan to keep them more than a few days. A home freezer, a freezer locker, or the freezer section of a combination refrigerator/freezer can all maintain a safe zero temperature. Remember, however, that freezing compartments of most home refrigerators cannot. Frozen food placed there should be used within a few days.

How long will commercially frozen fruits retain high quality stored at zero? Perhaps as long as 12 months. This depends on their quality at time of purchase. (See Appendix.)

Most home-frozen fruits keep high quality for eight to 12 months at zero or below. Home-frozen citrus fruits and juices, however, maintain high quality for only four to six months.

Frozen concentrated juices should be used within two or three days after they have been opened and reconstituted.

Exactly how long commercially frozen vegetables will retain high quality when stored at zero also depends on the kind of vegetable and condition at time of purchase. Maximum storage suggested for commercially frozen asparagus, beans, cauliflower, corn, peas, and spinach is eight months. Home-frozen vegetables should maintain high quality eight to 12 months.

## July 13

### Use Flowerpots as Outdoor Candleholders

Candlelight at an outdoor party on a warm summer evening will add a festive air. You probably will not want to use your good silver candlesticks outdoors, but there is an attractive and simple alternative. Take a few clay flowerpots of varying sizes, paint them and decorate them, turn them upside down, and insert candles in the holes. Place them around the patio or lawn and you'll have lovely light—and a lot of compliments! (JOP)

## July 14

### Two Garden Uses for Aluminum Foil

Rather than discard or recycle all of the aluminum foil used in household packaging and cooking, perhaps you can find secondary uses for it in your garden. Lots of people cut it into strips and hang them over ripening fruit to scare away destructive birds. It's doubtful whether this works for long, because birds soon learn that aluminum strips aren't all that scary. But there is another use for aluminum foil in the garden. Use the flattened sheets as a ground cover under melon and squash vines. So used, it is said to repel hungry aphids and increase crop yield. The theory of agricultural research men is that the foil reflects ultraviolet rays which confuse the aphids and send them elsewhere.

## July 15

### Clean Filters Often on Air Conditioners

Some of us have felt for a long time that living in an air-conditioned atmosphere may not always be conducive to good health. Now a researcher has found that if air-conditioning filters are not changed often they may be the source of an illness with symptoms similar to flu. The moist air inside the air conditioner promotes the growth of a mold, or fungus, on the filter—and its spores are carried out into the air you breathe.

To reduce the chances of this sort of contamination, clean or change the filter frequently during the hot periods of the year. In any case, air conditioners are designed to operate most efficiently with relatively clean filters. If a filter is allowed to become clogged with dust, the overworked cooling coil may become covered with a build-up of frost and ice that will further impede air flow.

## July 16

### Will You Do Some Canning This Summer?

With food prices what they are, home canning makes a lot of sense. Even if you don't raise your own fruits and vegetables, buying and canning foods while they are fresh and plentiful should enable your family to eat better at a lower cost. You can also can meat and poultry.

Your own cookbooks may give you canning procedures, especially if you plan to use a boiling-water-bath canner. Once again you may want to seek information from your county home agent or write to the Superintendent of Documents in Washington. Two excellent government bulletins are available: "Home Canning of Fruits and Vegetables" and "Home Canning of Meat and Poultry."

If you're really serious about home canning, we suggest that you consider doing it with a pressure cooker-canner. You will find a pressure cooker a practical piece of equipment for other uses as well. See August 23.

Excellent pressure-cooker canning and recipe booklets are distributed by the two principal manufacturers of pressure cookers—National Presto Industries, Inc., Eau Claire, Wis. 54701; and Mirro Aluminum Company, 1512 Washington St., Manitowoc, Wis. 54220.

# July 17

**TODAY IN HISTORY:** *Spain ceded Florida to the U.S. on July 17, 1819.*

## Storing Fresh Vegetables

Even under ideal storage conditions—the right temperature and humidity—most fresh vegetables retain top quality only for a few days. Green, leafy vegetables quickly wilt and change flavor as water evaporates from tissues. Other vegetables—corn, beans, and peas—lose sweetness within a short time as sugar converts to starch.

Most fresh green vegetables keep well and stay crisp if put in covered containers or plastic bags and stored in the refrigerator. If you wash lettuce, celery, and other leafy vegetables before storing, drain thoroughly because too much moisture can hasten decay. Tops should be removed from beets, carrots, and radishes.

Always sort vegetables before storing. Discard or use at once any bruised or soft vegetables; do not store them with sound, firm vegetables.

To maintain high quality in the following fresh vegetables, store them in the refrigerator in the crisper or in plastic bags, and use within the time specified below:

Asparagus, broccoli, Brussels sprouts, spinach, kale, collards, chard, beet greens, turnip greens, mustard greens, lettuce and other salad greens, green onions: 1 or 2 days.

Snap beans (green or wax), cauliflower, celery, cucumbers, okra, peppers, and summer squash: 3 to 5 days.

Beets, cabbage, carrots, and radishes: 1 or 2 weeks.

Specific directions for storing other vegetables and the length of time they can usually be held:

Beans, lima. Store uncovered in pods in refrigerator—1 or 2 days.

Corn. Store with husks on and uncovered in refrigerator—1 or 2 days.

Eggplant. Store at cool room temperature (approximately 60 degrees F.). If air is dry, keep eggplant in plastic bag to retain moisture—1 or 2 days.

Onions, mature. Store at room temperature or slightly cooler (60 degrees is best). Put in loosely woven or open-mesh containers with good circulation of air. Onions sprout or decay if temperature or humidity is high, but will keep several months in a cool, dry place.

Peas, green. Store uncovered in pods in refrigerator—1 or 2 days.

Potatoes. Store in a dark, dry place at 45 to 50 degrees, with good ventilation. May be held several months under these conditions.

Squash. Store hard-rind winter varieties in cool, dry place (about 60 degrees). Keep several months.

Sweet potatoes, rutabagas. Store at cool room temperature (about 60 degrees). Temperatures below 50 degrees may cause chilling injury. Stored this way, these vegetables keep several months.

Tomatoes. Store ripe tomatoes uncovered in the refrigerator. Keep unripe tomatoes at room temperature away from direct sunlight until ripe, then refrigerate. Too much sunlight prevents development of even color.

NOTE: Mature onions, potatoes, winter squash, sweet potatoes, and rutabagas can be kept at room temperature for a short time if it is not possible to store them at the temperatures recommended. Buy only enough for a week.

---

**PARFAITS ARE ELEGANT and easy do-ahead desserts.** Alternate layers of ice cream, crème de menthe or crème de cacao, and whipped cream to fill parfait (or other) glasses. Fruits with their juice may be used instead of a liqueur.

---

"I have heard with admiring submission the experience of the lady who declared that the sense of being well-dressed gives a feeling of inward tranquillity which religion is powerless to bestow."
—**Ralph Waldo Emerson**

## 1853 Potpourri for Homemakers

We have included in our potpourri for each month useful hints for homemakers. You may find interesting some hints as they were given to housewives by Mrs. Abell (see April 21) more than 120 years ago:

"Save all your suds for gardens and plants, or to harden cellars and yards when sandy.

"Count your clothes pins, spoons, knives and forks, towels, handkerchiefs, &c., every week.

"A hot shovel on a warming pan of coals, held over varnished furniture, will take out white spots. The place should be rubbed while warm, with flannel.

"In laying up furs for summer, lay a tallow candle in or near them, and all danger of worms will be obviated.

"Scotch snuff put on the holes where crickets come out, will destroy them.

"Starch all kinds of calico, but black; use potatoe water for black, as that will not show. If there are many in a family that wear black, save the water when potatoes are boiled, for this purpose.

"Oat straw is best for the filling of beds, and it is well to change it as often as once in a year.

"Wood ashes and common salt, wet with water, will stop the cracks of a stove, and prevent the smoke from penetrating.

"It is said that the half of a cranberry bound on a corn will eradicate it in the course of a few nights."

**TODAY IN HISTORY:** *Bloomers were introduced on July 19, 1848, at a national women's rights convention in Seneca Falls, N.Y. They were named for their sponsor, Mrs. Amelia Bloomer.*

## Buying Stockings and Panty Hose That Fit

Yes, you've come a long way—from bloomers to hose to panty hose. When you buy, do you have problems with fit? By following Du Pont's instructions for saleswomen who handle hosiery, you can do a better job of purchasing hosiery and get greater mileage from the hosiery you buy. The instructions, adapted for your use, follow:

The fact that you "always wear that size" doesn't necessarily mean it's the right size. If you have the slightest doubt, check with a tape measure: Measure your leg from the bottom of your heel straight up to your garter. Gartering heights have much to do with proper stocking lengths. You may need two separate stocking lengths for two different foundation garments.

Is the shape of your leg slender, average, or full? Hosiery is made in proportioned lengths; a very generous leg that measures 30 inches in length will need a slightly longer stocking than a slim or average leg of 30 inches. Also, your stocking size may be affected by a gain or loss in your weight.

If your stocking fits the way it should, it is smooth and snug at arch, ankle, and knee. There are no wrinkles, no stress, no strain, no taut streaks. It can be gartered without folding or stretching the welt. There is no discomfort when you bend, stoop, or sit. Proper fit is important to your comfort and your budget.

Sizes vary from brand to brand. To help you purchase hosiery that fits well, we have included a size chart in the Appendix.

## July 20

**TODAY IN HISTORY:** *Here's the tale of a big cheese. Early in 1801, dairy farmers in the vicinity of Cheshire, Mass., organized a cooperative to make quality cheeses. Apparently as a publicity stunt, a big cheese was pressed on July 20, 1801, at the Elisha Brown farm. Later it was found to weigh 1,235 pounds, a big wheel indeed—a fitting gift for President Thomas Jefferson, to whom it was presented on Jan. 1, 1802.*

## Facts You May Want to Know about Cheese

Cheese has a high food value and comes in a wide variety of flavors to suit every taste. Natural cheese is cheese made directly from milk. There are virtually hundreds of varieties of natural cheese.

Processed cheese is a blend of natural cheeses that have been shredded, mixed, and heated. This type of cheese may contain pimientos, fruits, vegetables, or meats.

If the label says "processed cheese food," other ingredients such as nonfat dry milk have been mixed in. "Processed cheese spread" has higher moisture content and lower milkfat content than processed cheese and cheese food. It's more

spreadable. Processed cheese products are usually packaged in slices, loaves, and jars.

Cottage cheese is a soft, unripened natural cheese that can be bought in cup-shaped containers or tumblers. It may be bought plain or creamed and in different curd sizes. Creamed cottage cheese contains a minimum of four percent fat.

Cheddar cheese packages may carry USDA grade labels when packed under inspection of the U.S. Department of Agriculture. Grade AA is the best, Grade A is almost as good.

---

**ARE EGGS FRESH?** Check by putting them in a pan of water. A fresh egg will sink. Get rid of those that float.

---

## Defrosting a Food Freezer

Unless your freezer defrosts automatically, you should defrost it periodically. A logical time to do this is when the supply of stored food is low —perhaps just before you begin to put in this season's stock of new vegetables and fruits. The reason for removing frost: A heavy build-up causes the freezer temperature to rise.

If thin layers of frost are scraped off as they form, complete defrosting need be done less frequently. Just move the packages to another shelf or side of the freezer and scrape the frosted surfaces.

Defrost completely before frost reaches a depth of one-half inch over a large area of the refrigerated surfaces. Defrost also whenever frost begins to accumulate on packages that have been stored in the freezer only a few hours.

To get the food as cold as possible before defrosting, set the temperature control of the freezer at its lowest setting for a few hours or overnight. If freezer space can accommodate large cartons, put the food in large cartons during this period. (Food can be left in these cartons after you take it out of the freezer.)

Disconnect the freezer and remove the food. Setting the cold cartons in larger cartons will help keep the food cold. Place several layers of newspapers on the cartons if they have no tops.

Work quickly. Scrape as much of the light frost from freezer walls or shelves as you can. Placing pans of hot water in the freezer speeds defrosting.

Work at the edges of the ice so you can remove it in chunks as it comes free. Use a thick, flexible spatula or similar tool. Do not use sharp or rigid instruments which might damage the walls.

When all ice and water have been removed, wipe the surfaces dry. Close the freezer. Set the control at its coldest setting. Run the freezer at least 10 minutes before replacing the food; if defrosting

has taken more than an hour, run the freezer 15 to 20 minutes.

Wipe or scrape each food package quickly to remove any frost or moisture and replace it in the freezer. Run the freezer with the control at its coldest position long enough to be sure the food is thoroughly frozen. Then turn the control to the position that will maintain zero degrees Fahrenheit in the warmest part of the freezer.

## July 22

### Good Rules for Cooking Meat and Poultry

Keep all meats and poultry refrigerated until you are ready to prepare them. Serve them immediately after cooking, or refrigerate them promptly. Keep foods that are to be eaten cold in the refrigerator until mealtime.

It is usually best to cook any meat or poultry product in the frozen state. This is especially important for frozen combination meat dishes and commercially frozen poultry. Do not thaw these before cooking. If it is not practical to cook other meats and poultry while frozen, defrost them in the refrigerator when possible. Do not let frozen products, particularly chicken or pork, thaw on surfaces where other foods are kept. Harmful organisms from those foods (which will be killed in cooking) may contaminate the surfaces. Cook foods promptly after thawing.

Be sure processed meat or poultry products that are heated, or leftovers that are reheated, are hot throughout before serving. Bring broth or gravy to a full rolling boil and allow to boil for several minutes.

Pork and pork products must be cooked long, slowly, and fully. When baking pork, be sure the oven is at least at 350 degrees.

Cook poultry completely. Never cook it partially and finish cooking it later. It is safest to cook poultry dressing outside the bird. If you want to stuff the bird, do so immediately before roasting. Never stuff raw poultry and then refrigerate or freeze it.

**MOLES IN YOUR LAWN? Ask a garden center where to get the commercial preparation of milky-spore disease that kills the Japanese beetle grubs on which moles often feed. Treat the lawn with this, and you ought to reduce the numbers of both Japanese beetles and moles.**

## Eliminating Odor from a Garbage Disposal Unit

You may notice an objectionable odor coming from a garbage disposal unit, especially in hot summer weather. Put several orange or lemon rinds and a tray of ice cubes through it, and the disposer usually will be an acceptable member of society again.

In operating a disposal unit, start cold water running before adding the garbage. If your dishwasher drains through the unit, run the latter briefly each time after the washer is used.

---

**"There's no sauce in the world like hunger."**

**—Miguel de Cervantes**

---

## Turn Off Home Motors During "Brownouts"

During periods of exceptionally hot weather be alert for signs or announcements of voltage reductions in electrical power—a situation known as a "brownout." Signs of a brownout include dimming of lights and a reduction in the size of a TV picture.

Turn off as many of the motor-driven appliances in your home as you can when you know or suspect that voltage has been reduced. This will help conserve the power available in your neighborhood. But there's a selfish reason, too, for turning off the appliances. If left on, the motors may overheat and eventually burn out, requiring expensive replacement.

Appliances that have heating elements instead of motors (clothes dryers and water heaters, for instance) will continue to operate during a brownout, but you ought to minimize their use. Keep refrigerators and freezers closed after turning them off. Food should keep safely for up to 24 hours.

## Care Tips for Bedding of Man-Made Fibers

Many pillows filled with polyester fiberfill carry hang tags giving tested care instructions. Some of these are washable, some are not, DuPont notes. When no instructions are given, and the pillow is designed to be washed, the following suggestions may be followed after you refer to general instructions (see February 16).

Immerse the pillow in lukewarm water with detergent added. The use of a non-sudsing detergent facilitates rinsing. Create a flow of wash water through the pillow by compressing repeatedly by hand. Severe twisting of the pillow should be avoided. Do not wash in a machine.

Rinse thoroughly in clear water and press or squeeze the pillow to remove excess water. Remove remaining water by spinning in an automatic washing machine and drying in a tumble-type dryer on a low temperature setting.

For "Sontique" pillows:

Refluff after each use by holding diagonal corners and shaking a few times. If outer ticking of polyester and cotton becomes soiled, unzip and remove for machine washing and drying just as you would a pillowcase. Durable press ticking needs no ironing.

Several times a year, depending on usage, refresh and refluff the pillow batt. Remove the zippered ticking. Place batt still encased in its marquisette cover of polyester in the dryer set to maximum temperature for 20 minutes. If pillow batt becomes soiled, wash by hand and machine dry.

"Adoration" pillows are machine washable if desired. Immerse the pillow in water before putting into machine. Pillows should be thoroughly wet before starting wash cycle. Use the wash-wear cycle and machine dry at the maximum temperature setting.

For comforters and mattress cushions filled with fiberfill, when no instructions are given on the label, and the article is designed to be washed, the following suggestions may be followed:

Machine wash in warm suds (100 degrees Fahrenheit) using detergent. Set machine for a three- to five-minute wash cycle. Use "Special Fabric" cycle if available.

Remove the comforter from machine after the spin-dry cycle. It may then be tumble dried at low temperature setting for 15 to 20 minutes. In order to assure the original fresh, fluffy appearance, remove from the dryer as drying is complete.

Comforters filled with Dacron may be commercially laundered using the wool wash system.

"Sontique" mattress pads: This mattress pad can be washed as often as needed to keep it clean and fresh. Machine wash on regular cycle just as you would a sheet. Machine dry on "Medium" for 20 to 30 minutes or until dry.

## July 26

### Care Tips for Upholstery of Man-Made Fibers

Man-made fibers can be cleaned as well or better than other upholstery fibers; even so, the cleaning of upholstery requires special techniques because only one side of the fabric can be cleaned, and it is impossible to flush dirt from the fabric. Also, in upholstered furniture the stuffing material frequently contains dust and dirt, which further complicates the cleaning procedure. Because of the wide variety of fabric types and fiber combinations, the following care suggestions for upholstery containing man-made fibers are general in nature.

It is recommended that spots be removed promptly and soil not be allowed to build up as it will be more difficult to remove. Vacuum furniture thoroughly to remove dust from stuffing.

Oil-based stains can usually be removed with standard household cleaning solvents, some of which may be flammable and should be used with caution. Test solvent on inconspicuous area before using on stain. Work from the edges toward the center of the spot to avoid enlarging it.

For general cleaning, use a low sudsing detergent, or use one of a number of good upholstery cleaning agents. Apply with a soft brush or sponge. Remove foam promptly using clean cloths, toweling, or a dry sponge. Repeat process where necessary. Allow to dry.

## July 27

### What to Do about Ants

Ants are a summertime thing—big ones, little ones, red ones, or black ones. If they show up inside your house or apartment, what do you do?

First try to locate where they are coming from, the location of the nest. In some cases, you can follow them back to a nest in the ground outside the house. But all too often, they may be coming from a nest inside the walls of the house or perhaps under it.

Dust or granules containing five percent of chlordane are effective when sprinkled over ground nests and washed into them. They also make a killing barrier against ant invasions when applied over the ground under porches and houses. The dust is often effective for treating hard-to-reach places indoors. With a hand duster you can puff it into cracks where a spray will not reach.

To prevent ants from entering the house, apply a two-percent oil-base chlordane spray to the

outside walls, from the ground up to the windows. Apply it also to the lower part of window frames and around doors. If you have a porch that is open underneath, or if there are other open areas under the house (as may be the case if there is no basement), apply the insecticide to the underside of the structure. As you do this, treat thoroughly all supports, posts, pillars, and pipes that the ants might use as runways into the house. One or two applications should provide control for a season.

You may decide that the ants have nests inside the house. Use the same two-percent oil-base chlordane spray mentioned above. Apply it as near as possible to where you believe the nests are located. Put it into any cracks or openings that ants can use to enter a room, and on nearby surfaces.

By using a small paintbrush you can get the insecticide exactly where you want it, and there is no drifting spray mist. This method is desirable in the kitchen.

If ants continue to appear after one treatment, it is likely that they are entering over surfaces that have not been treated. Re-treat surfaces, taking care to cover any that may have been missed before.

When ants infest apartment houses or row houses, control efforts made by different individuals at different times are likely to be unsuccessful. Simultaneous cooperative efforts are needed to rid an entire structure of the pests.

## *July* 28

## How to Reduce Noise "Pollution" in Your Home

While you read this, can you hear the loud whine of a rotary power mower somewhere in your neighborhood? In a 1972 report submitted to Congress, the U.S. Environmental Protection Agency found yard-care tools the worst offenders among modern appliances and tools in creating noise levels high enough to cause human annoyance and stress or perhaps actually injure the ear. (See the article on April 14.)

Local governments, the construction industry, and tool and appliance manufacturers must all

a power mower, operate it at reasonable hours.

Use a headset when you are the only one interested in listening to the hi-fi. Also, keep the volume down when you're not wearing a headset.

Place window air conditioners where their hum can help mask objectionable noises. However, try to avoid locating them facing your neighbor's bedrooms.

Be aware that children's toys need not make intensive or explosive sounds. (Some can cause permanent ear injury, as well as getting on your nerves.)

Compare the noise levels of different makes of an appliance before making your selection.

share in the job of reducing noise in modern society, but the EPA suggests that each of us can create a quieter home by remembering the following points:

Use noise-absorbing materials on floors, especially in areas where there is a lot of traffic.

Hang heavy drapes over the windows closest to outside noise sources.

Put rubber or plastic treads on uncarpeted stairs. (They are safer, too.)

Use upholstered rather than hard-surface furniture to deaden noise.

Install sound-absorbing ceiling tile in the kitchen. Wooden cabinets will vibrate less than metal ones.

Use a foam pad under blenders and mixers.

Use insulation and vibration mounts when installing dishwashers.

Install washing machines in the same room with heating and cooling equipment, preferably in an enclosed space.

Remember that a hand-powered lawnmower does the job and gives you exercise, too. If you use

## July 29

### Screen Your Compost

Almost every home owner has a compost heap these days, which should include not only leaves and grass clippings, but such good nutrients as ashes from the fireplace and dog droppings from the kennel (they melt away to clean dust in the composting process).

One problem comes when you want to use the finished product: sticks and stones and bones, which you don't want on the lawn or garden. An easy solution is a screen, made of ½" mesh on a frame of 1" x 2" scantlings, of a size to fit over your wheelbarrow. Sieve enough compost to fill about three-fourths of the barrow, and then mix in about three shovels of 5-10-5 fertilizer, or whatever variation you wish, and you have a fine all-purpose grass and plant food. You can add special foods, such as bone meal, to those areas which require them. (JOP)

## July 30

## Sauces to Use with Vegetable Dishes

It's simple to make sauces that add variety and distinction to vegetable dishes. The right sauce can add contrast in color, flavor, and texture. From a basic white sauce you can concoct many pleasing sauces to serve over cooked vegetables or in scalloped vegetables.

Thin white sauce is usually preferred with starchy vegetables like peas or lima beans; medium white sauce with other vegetables.

**How to make white sauce.** For a smooth white sauce, blend the flour with fat or cold liquid; then combine with remaining liquid, stirring constantly over low heat until thickened. For amounts of ingredients, see the accompanying table.

Fat may be omitted if white sauce is to be used in cream soups, casseroles, or other recipes where fat is not needed for flavor or texture.

**White sauce variations.** Certain vegetables are enhanced by special sauces. The following sauces taste particularly good with the vegetables listed with them.

Cheese sauce (asparagus, broccoli, cabbage, cauliflower, potatoes, and summer squash). Cook 1 cup of thin or medium white sauce. Remove sauce from heat; stir in 1 cup shredded Cheddar cheese. Blend well.

Mock hollandaise sauce (asparagus and broccoli). Make 1 cup of medium white sauce. Beat 2 egg yolks, stir in a little hot white sauce, then stir this mixture into rest of sauce. Stir in 2 tablespoons butter or margarine. Cook over hot water about 1 minute. Remove from heat and stir in 1 tablespoon lemon juice. Serve at once.

(NOTE: In above recipe use only clean eggs with no cracks in the shells.)

Mushroom sauce (asparagus, green beans, and peas). Use proportions of fat and flour for 1 cup of medium white sauce. Cook 1 cup small whole or sliced fresh or canned mushrooms in fat. Add flour. Use liquid from canned mushrooms to replace part of milk.

Onion or celery sauce (carrots, green beans, and peas). Use proportions of fat and flour for 1 cup of thin white sauce. Cook ½ cup finely chopped onion or celery in the fat until tender, stir in flour and salt, and slowly blend in liquid. Cook over low heat, stirring constantly until thickened. Add 1 teaspoon Worcestershire sauce before serving.

| Ingredients for 1 Cup of White Sauce | | |
|---|---|---|
| | Thin Sauce | |
| | Standard | Low-fat |
| Butter or other fat | 1 tablespoon | 2 teaspoons |
| All-purpose flour | 1 tablespoon | 1 tablespoon |
| Salt | ¼ teaspoon | ¼ teaspoon |
| Milk[1] | 1 cup | 1 cup[2] |
| Calories in 1 cup white sauce | 290 | 180 |
| | Medium Sauce | |
| | Standard | Low-fat |
| Butter or other fat | 2 tablespoons | 1 tablespoon |
| All-purpose flour | 2 tablespoons | 2 tablespoons |
| Salt | ¼ teaspoon | ¼ teaspoon |
| Milk[1] | 1 cup | 1 cup[2] |
| Calories in 1 cup white sauce | 420 | 245 |

[1]Vegetable liquid may be used in place of part of milk.
[2]Use skim milk or reconstituted nonfat dry milk for low-fat white sauce.

**TODAY IN HISTORY:** *On July 31, 1918, a set of china ordered by President Woodrow Wilson was delivered to the White House by Lenox, Inc., of Trenton, N.J. The set consisted of 1,700 pieces, each bearing the seal of the President of the United States.*

## July Potpourri
## for Homemakers

Have a long coiling cord installed on the telephone in your kitchen. You can then reach the sink and range without asking your caller to hold on.

Press let-out hems and shiny trousers with a cloth which has been dipped in a vinegar-water solution, then wrung out. The old hemline won't show and the trouser shine will disappear.

Rotate canned and packaged foods and cleaning supplies on shelves. When you unpack the groceries, place your purchases behind similar items you already have.

Invert liquid detergent or hand-lotion bottles with caps on when nearly empty and let stand in the sink drain basket. You'll get the last drops.

## Your Own Reminders:

# August 1

**TODAY IN HISTORY:** *A patent was granted on Aug. 1, 1893, to William H. Ford, of Watertown, N.Y., for a machine to make shredded wheat biscuits. The Cereal Machine Company was formed the same year in Denver, Colo., to produce this popular breakfast food.*

## Bedmaking—Miter Those Corners!

Arrival of August reminds us of a housekeeping procedure that is constantly used in the Stevenson household—making beds with mitered (square) corners. The procedure was learned years ago during an August Girl Scout encampment. Besides being neat, square corners hold sheets and blankets securely in place.

Watching someone else is the ideal way to learn how. Perhaps you have a friend or relative who can teach you. Do you know a nurse? Nurses in training learn to make beds this way. Consequently, square corners also are called "hospital" corners.

Center the bottom sheet lengthwise on the bed, leaving about 18 inches of sheet to tuck under the upper end of the mattress.

Stand at one side of the head of the bed, grasp the edge of the sheet at a point about 18 inches toward the foot, and lift it until it forms a right angle with the top surface of the mattress. Hold the sheet in this position while you tuck the hanging part under the mattress. Release your hold, letting the sheet fall, then tuck the overhang under the mattress. *Voilà!* You have made a square corner. Now tuck the rest of the sheet under the mattress on that side. Proceed in the same way on the other side of the bed.

Center the top sheet lengthwise on the bed leaving enough to fold over the blanket at the head. Next, center the blanket on the bed with the top edge slightly above shoulder height of the sleeper. Fold the top of the sheet over the blanket.

Tuck the sheet and blanket that overhang the foot of the bed under the mattress. Make square corners at each side of the foot, this time working with the blanket together with the top sheet.

The portion of the top sheet and blanket that still overhangs the sides of the bed may be left that way or tucked under the mattress.

---

**WOMEN PILOTED PLANES** very early in aviation history. On Aug. 1, 1911, Harriet Quimby of New York passed a license test given by the Aero Club of America.

---

**SHOPPING TIP:** You will find broccoli in the markets during July and August, but it may not be a good buy. Broccoli grows best in cool weather.

---

**NIGHT PASSENGER FLIGHTS** across the U.S. began on Aug. 1, 1934. A twin-engine monoplane took off from Newark airport at 5:24 P.M. At Kansas City, Mo., passengers transferred to another plane and reached Glendale airport in California at 7:13 A.M.

---

## *August* **2**

### Circular Mat Keeps Down Grass around Shrubs

Nobody likes to get down on hands and knees to trim around shrubs and trees each time the lawn is mowed. To avoid this, consider a fairly new product—a circular rubber mat designed to encircle bushes and small trees. It looks like red bricks, and besides keeping down grass and weeds, it conserves moisture. Or you could put down real bricks and accomplish the same thing.

## August 3

### Do Wild Berries Grow in Your Region?

A passage that Shakespeare wrote in *As You Like It* is particularly appropriate at this season: "O, how full of briers is this working-day world!"

In the early days of August, you will find abandoned or untilled fields full of clinging, grasping, scratching briers, in many parts of the country. For those who have the temerity—and permission from the landowner—to force a way through these brambles, there's a rich reward waiting to be brought home: literally gallons of luscious blackberries. In the early days, homemakers found the effort of picking them definitely worthwhile. Back home, they converted their luscious loot into mouth-watering pies, jams, jellies, and muffins. What's wrong with us moderns? Rising food prices make it worthwhile once again to go aberrying. If you do, wear a heavy jacket with sleeves. But no gloves. You can't pick berries while wearing gloves.

## August 4

### Save Energy—and the Window Air Conditioner

In these days of energy conservation one piece of household equipment to watch is the window air conditioner. Don't leave it on in all kinds of weather just because it's there; if you do, you'll be wasting energy, money, and the life expectancy of the machine itself. Operation during mild weather results in heavy frosting of the cooling coils, causing the conditioner to work harder than it should. When the ice on the coils finally melts, dripping

water will damage window, walls, or furnishings below the window. Wait till the temperature gets up to between 75 and 80 degrees before you turn on your friend in the window.

## August 5

### Water Hanging Plants with Ice Cubes

Place a few ice cubes among the plants of a hanging planter as a no-mess method of providing water for the plants. The ice will melt at room temperature and the water will seep slowly into the growing medium. Experience will teach you the number of cubes to use for a typical watering.

## August 6

### Ratatouille Is in Season

All of the ingredients for making ratatouille are plentiful now. Take advantage of their availability by making several casseroles of this delicious "vegetable stew," which consists mostly of zucchini, eggplant, and yellow squash. Serve it as a vegetable main dish, hot or cold, or as a casserole when guests stop in to accompany cold meat. The extras may be frozen for later use.

The name of this stew is derived from the French word meaning "to stir." How do you pronounce it? The "experts" on radio and television frequently manage to mutilate it. Give it three syllables only, not four. Pronounce it "rah tah tooeh," with the accent on the last syllable. Pronounce the "rah" as in a high school cheer, and elide the two apparent parts of the final syllable into one. Don't say "too ee."

In making ratatouille, suit yourself as to proportions of the vegetables and spices used. Our version is baked in a casserole, ideal for serving or freezing.

Sauté separately in oil unpeeled cubed eggplant, zucchini, and yellow squash. Add sliced onions, green pepper strips, and quartered tomatoes. Pepper and salt to taste, and add any or all of the following: garlic, bay leaf, basil, thyme, and parsley. Mix and pour into a greased casserole. Top, if desired, with bread crumbs, Parmesan cheese, or both. Bake 20 minutes at 350 degrees.

---

**FOR NEW DRY WALL, apply a first coat of latex primer or paint. Solvent-thinned paints tend to create a rough surface. Later coats can be of either type—water- or oil-based.**

---

## August 7

### What You Should Remember about Rabies

Most dog owners are aware of the ever-present danger of rabies. Most are aware, too, that if their pet nips, or even scratches someone, the cry of "rabies" will be heard throughout the land, usually accompanied by calls from the police and hostile lawyers and former friends.

Protect yourself from these unnecessary worries by having your dog inoculated against rabies at whatever intervals your veterinarian recommends and according to your state laws. Ask for, and keep, a dated certificate of inoculation and put the rabies inoculation tag on your dog's collar.

Don't forget to inoculate your cats. Cats get and carry rabies, too. If yours is allowed outside, it is far more likely to be exposed to rabies than a dog, for all cats capture small wild animals.

Do not handle—and teach your children not to handle—any usually wild animal which appears to be strangely tame or unafraid. Rabies can cause such animals as foxes or skunks to wander about in daylight without their usual fear. Bats are common carriers of rabies and should never be picked up or handled in any way.

If you should see a wild animal acting strangely, call your pets and children into the house and immediately notify the police, the humane society, or the health department. Rabies may be more common in some states than others, but its dangers are real and should not be ignored, no matter where you live. (JSD)

## *August* **8**

## Pointers about Taking Care of a Refrigerator

You can't expect your refrigerator or refrigerator-freezer to continue to do its job of preserving and conserving your foods without attention from you. You have to take care of it.

Make a regular check of the defrost drainage system of frost-free models. You can expect the water to evaporate from the collecting pan under normal conditions. In periods of high humidity, it probably will not. Empty the pan at such times and clean out any collected dust.

Check your instruction manual about how often you ought to vacuum dust from the condenser coils. Use the crevice tool of the vacuum and/or a long-handled brush. Unless you keep dust off the coils, temperatures inside the appliance will rise and running time will increase.

Make up a solution of baking soda and water and wipe out the interior regularly. Store an open box of soda in the refrigerator to keep it sweet and odor-free.

Never let frost build up excessively in the freezer compartment.

## Why Not Have a Yard Sale?

Give any home a few years and it seems certain to collect a lot of useful—but unused—items in attic, garage, basement, or utility room. August is a great time to get all of these still-useful items together and have a yard (or porch) sale.

Teen-age youngsters may like to plan and conduct the sale, especially if you promise them part or all of the profits. It will give them something interesting to do during this sometimes-dull period before school reopens. Perhaps several neighbors may want to join you or the kids in having the sale. The bigger the sale the better.

Most home-type sales seem to be held on weekends—Friday, Saturday, and sometimes Sunday. Make your plans early enough so you can insert a classified advertisement in a newspaper that circulates in your area. The advertisement doesn't need to be extensive, but do be sure to list certain items that you feel will attract buyers.

In setting your prices don't be greedy. Remember that sales-goers are looking for bargains. Give them bargains—and you'll be surprised at how quickly your sales totals mount up. Have a good supply of change on hand the morning the sale is scheduled to open.

Home sales are not restricted in any way in most communities. But check with your local government headquarters if you have any doubt. The police might like to know—just in case the response is so great it creates a traffic problem.

## August 10

### Improving Your Time:
### 1853 Fashion

We think that Mrs. Abell's recommendations for making best use of your time are as good today as when first given in 1853. See April 21 for more about her book. Her recommendations:

"Do small things, as writing a letter, making a sketch, reading a review, etc., in your leisure moments; leaving the body of the day to more important affairs. Instead of SAYING much about your employments or wasting time in procrastination and dread of them, set yourself quietly, promptly, resolutely about your work, and you may save hours for the acquisition of some important Art or Science. Always have convenient work at hand, that your time may be usefully employed during a social call or in moments of leisure. Much time and labor will be saved by always keeping things in order. Devise methods of expediting labor, and give to each branch its due importance. There is time enough for every work and duty; if any thing is neglected from a supposed want of time the fault is ours."

## August 11

### Do I Still Love You Truly?

The song "I Love You Truly" written by Carrie Jacobs Bond, born on this date in 1862 in Janesville, Wisconsin, has been played at countless weddings. For how many years after the couples leave the churches do the words still apply?

One way to assure that they continue to hold true is to create an atmosphere of romance each night when you dine. Light candles and have on the table an arrangement of flowers.

Good candles cost comparatively little, even if several are burned at one time.

Flowers needn't be expensive. Make it a point to grow some that last well when cut. Take advantage of the goldenrod that blooms in wide areas of the U.S. this month and next (it does not cause hay fever), day lilies in July, meadow rue in June, and other blooms that may be found on roadsides in spring, summer, and fall months. A dried arrangement or a green house plant can be your winter centerpiece. Consider, too, using artificial flowers in the winter. Some of today's are lovely.

This attention to your romantic life each day

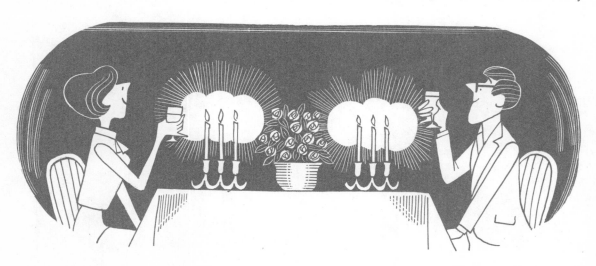

may then remind you of another song favorite of your grandmother's lifetime—"A Perfect Day," also written by Carrie Jacobs Bond. Your festive dining "at the end of a perfect day" will become, as the song says, part of "the joy that the day has brought."

# August 12

**TODAY IN HISTORY:** *A sewing machine with a rocking treadle was patented on Aug. 12, 1851, by Isaac Singer, of New York City.*

## Housekeeping without Power: Sewing

Fortunate is the woman these days who has her grandmother's foot-operated sewing machine, still in working condition. Those machines did good work half a century ago, and they'll do so again today.

Perhaps you can locate one in someone's attic or in an antique shop or secondhand store. If your quest is successful, oiling and a new drive belt may be all that's needed to make the machine workable. You might also check a local department store for an inexpensive battery-operated machine that sews a chain stitch.

Otherwise (and even if you find a machine) you may want to brush up on the techniques of hand sewing.

Basic hand repair stitches may be used to accomplish any sewing ordinarily done with a machine. The back stitch is probably the most helpful—it gives the appearance of machine stitching and provides the strength needed in underarm and other seams subject to a lot of stress. The underneath stitch of the back stitch is twice the length of the top stitch. Top stitches look like machine stitching because each top stitch meets the next stitch.

Hand stitches are described and illustrated in "Clothing Repairs," Home and Garden Bulletin No. 107. The bulletin also contains instructions and illustrations on darning, patching, and mending. To obtain a copy, ask your extension home economist or send a post card to the Superintendent of Documents, Washington, D.C. 20402.

**HERALDED AS THE FIRST WOMAN** to sail alone across the Atlantic, Ann Davidson reached Miami, Fla., on Aug. 12, 1953, in a 23-foot sailboat. She left Plymouth, England, on May 18, 1953. She made several stops en route.

## August 13

### What to Do When Salt Won't Pour

During months of high humidity, especially those that often come in late summer, salt in shakers cakes up and refuses to pour. Sugar gives the same problem.

Mixing rice with the salt lessens the problem, although you may not consider this entirely satisfactory. During humid periods, some of our friends serve salt at the table in open containers. A "pinch" then provides seasoning.

Some time ago we encountered what seems to be the perfect solution—moistureproof salt and pepper shakers and sugar dispensers. A spring-loaded cap closes the shaker automatically when it's not in use. An absorbent pad within the cap takes up any moisture before it can reach the salt. Load the shaker with dry salt, and it should remain dry. Just don't try to use the shaker over a cooking pot while the steam is rising. The salt and pepper shakers sell for about $2 a pair. For information write to Daniell's Shaker Company, Box 84, Thomasville, Ga. 31792.

## August 14

### Zucchini and Cheese Custard

This is a fine way to use the zucchini which is in plentiful supply now. It may be served as a vegetable main dish or company casserole.

Place a lump of butter or a tablespoon of cooking oil in a saucepan. Slice into the pan 2 pounds of unpared, tender young zucchini and half an onion. Cover and cook over low heat until tender. Do not add water unless needed. Mash but leave lumpy. Add 1½ cups grated sharp cheese, 4 beaten eggs, a pinch of basil, a pinch of oregano, and salt and pepper to taste. Pour into a greased casserole and bake at 350 degrees until custard is set and lightly browned on top (about 40 minutes). (RP)

## August 15

**TODAY IN HISTORY:** *A storm of hurricane intensity on Aug. 15, 1635, caused damage near the Plymouth colony in Massachusetts.*

### Spray to Lubricate Wood Surfaces

About this time of year we usually get a spell of humid weather which can cause all kinds of troubles in the house. The dampness causes wood to swell, making doors, windows, and drawers stick and jam, and reluctant to open or close.

There's a simple solution—a spray can of lubricant containing a fluorocarbon resin, which can also be used to lubricate metal, rubber, plastic, or glass surfaces. Read the label carefully when buy-

Both afternoon and evening sessions are included in offerings which vary from "A to Y" (antique appreciation to yoga). Treat yourself to an afternoon away from the house and children—get a baby-sitter and learn a skill or hobby that you are especially interested in.

Help keep your husband in shape by getting him to enroll in an evening course in golf or gymnastics. Or, go with him to learn first aid, wild-game cooking, or a foreign language.

"Education is a lifelong process" according to those in the know. Adult education courses offer an opportunity to continue learning, a welcome change of pace, and fun!

ing to make sure the contents include the fluorocarbon compound. Then be careful to keep the spray off your skin, your food, and your smokes. Wash thoroughly after using.

Another way to lubricate sticking drawers is to rub a cake of soap over the sliding surfaces.

## *August* 16

### A More Interesting You through Adult Education

Become a more interesting person by expanding your interests through adult education programs. Announcements of course offerings are in the mail about now giving information about times, places, and tuition (which is modest).

## August 17

### Take Your Choice of Melons during This Season

Various melons are in season at this time, some of them not very widely known. An example is the Cranshaw, a large California melon. Peak shipments of these are made during August and September. A deep golden yellow rind, a surface that yields to moderate pressure of the thumb, and a pleasant and distinctive aroma are signs that the melon is ripe.

You should also find Persian melons in the markets at this period. They resemble cantaloupes but are more nearly round and have a finer netting. Persians are about the size of honeydews.

Honeydews are abundant from July through October. Casabas also are in season now, as are perfectly round honey-ball melons.

## August 18

**TODAY IN HISTORY:** *Home grounds were assured of more floral color on Aug. 18, 1931, when Henry F. Bosenberg, of New Brunswick, N.J., was granted plant patent No. 1. It was for the climbing rose "New Dawn" that blooms steadily through the summer season. It was derived from "Dr. Van Fleet," a rose that blooms only in June.*

### Make Jelly with a Kit?

The season is at hand when our grandmothers converted various fruits into jellies. If the idea interests you, but you don't want to start from scratch, consider buying a jelly-making kit. Check your local stores to see if they have kits available. If not, you might want to write to Specialty Products Division, Welch Foods, Inc., 2 South Portage, Westfield, N.Y. 14787, and ask where you can get a kit. The Welch company has been offering kits to make grape, strawberry, apple, and cherry jellies, and orange marmalade. The kits come with or without a set of glasses and caps.

**NEATNESS HELPS control slugs and snails in a lawn. Boards, stones, trash, and compost piles all serve as shelters, and their removal will reduce the number of snails in an area. Hand picking is also a practical means of reducing populations. The snails may be placed in a paper bag and disposed of in the trash or by burning or burial.**

# August 19

## Easy Desserts That Use Condensed Milk

Two easily prepared desserts which use condensed milk follow. In addition to these, you might like to try some of the other recipes which come with some brands of the milk.

Lemon Icebox Cake: Line a 10″ x 6″ x 2″ dish with graham crackers. Pour over a mixture of 1 can condensed milk, 1 beaten egg (use an uncracked egg), the grated rind of 1 lemon, and the juice of 2 lemons. Top with graham crackers and refrigerate for several hours or overnight. Cut in squares and serve topped with whipped cream.

Caramel Pudding: Remove the label from 1 can of condensed milk. Place the can in a pan and cover completely with water. Bring to a boil and simmer 3 hours. Cool to room temperature, then refrigerate. Remove both ends of the can and use one end to push the can's contents onto a plate. Slice and serve as is, or top with milk or cream or whipped cream. The long, slow cooking carmelizes the milk to a deep brown. This dessert is very sweet and rich—a little goes a long way.

"Heaven has no rage like love
to hatred turned,
Nor hell a fury like a woman scorned."
—William Congreve

USE SHEARS to cut off the leaves of iris plants about two inches above the ground during August.

## August 20

### No-Egg Recipe for Corn Pudding

There are two schools of thought about corn pudding. One school uses eggs as an ingredient. The other claims that eggs do nothing good at all for this delectable baked dish.

We bring up the subject now for a good reason. Corn pudding is a great way to use fresh corn that's just a bit too mature for good eating on the cob. Some cooks contend, in fact, that you should use only mature corn in pudding. This should be in good supply now.

If you want a recipe that includes eggs, check your own cookbooks. Otherwise, try ours.

Scrape (don't cut) the kernels from 9 large or 12 small ears. Add up to 1 quart of milk, the amount depending upon the age of the corn and the amount of liquid it still contains. Aim for the consistency of a thick cake batter. The older (and drier) the corn, the more milk you will need. Add a moderate amount of salt and pepper, and put the mixture in a shallow baking pan, the shallower the better. Dot the top with pieces of butter. Bake in a slow oven for an hour or so until the pudding has a crust on the top. (LSS)

## August 21

> **TODAY IN HISTORY:** *A patent was granted on Aug. 21, 1841, to John Hampson, of New Orleans, for a "manner of retaining in any desired position the slats of Venetian blinds."*

### Storage of Purchased Frozen Foods

Food freezers are a great thing. No one would want to keep house these days without one. But some of us may tend to think a freezer is actually a better appliance than it is, that frozen food can be stored

indefinitely. This is not true if you want to eat food of the same quality that you bought.

Storage at zero degrees Fahrenheit or lower is needed to maintain quality. At those temperatures, bacteria in food multiply at a slow rate. As the temperature rises, bacterial action speeds up and quality is lost. So today, during a season when many of us may be thinking about restocking our freezers, let's consider facts concerning storage.

Determine if your freezer provides the recommended temperature—or, if not, how close it comes to it. You'll need to know this temperature to determine how long to store foods. To check, use an accurate thermometer and take the temperature in several locations. Regulate the temperature control to lower the warmest spot to zero, if possible.

How long commercially frozen food retains good quality in a home freezer at zero or lower depends on (1) the kind of food and (2) how long and at what temperature it was stored before you bought it.

A table in the Appendix gives suggested maximum home-storage periods for frozen foods that are of good quality when purchased. Recommended periods are approximate. They are for foods that have been subject to good commercial freezing, handling, and storage before you purchased them. If there is any question about the quality of the frozen food, reduce storage time. If your equipment does not maintain a temperature of zero or lower, plan to hold frozen foods only a few days before you use them.

When shopping, select frozen food last—to shorten the time the food is without refrigeration. Protect frozen food with an insulated bag or a double paper bag during the trip home. Put food in your freezer promptly after you arrive home.

During the transfer from store to home, temperature of the food may rise somewhat. To lower it, place the packages in contact with a refrigerated surface in the freezer or freezing compartment. Leave space around packages for air to circulate. After temperature of the food has been lowered to the proper storage temperature, pack containers close together to save space.

Mark the date stored on packages. Store like

foods together, placing the most recently purchased products underneath or behind foods already in the freezer. Keep a record of frozen foods in storage. Record date of purchase and date by which it should be used. Refer to this record when you plan purchases and meals.

## August 22

TODAY IN HISTORY: *A patent was granted on Aug. 22, 1865, to William Sheppard, of New York City, for liquid soap.*

## Housekeeping without Power: Dishwashing

The order in which dishes should be washed by hand may have been forgotten by some and never

known by others, for automatic dishwashers have made this an unnecessary bit of knowledge. Supplies needed for hand washing include:

Detergent or soap powder recommended for hand washing, drain basket to use in one side of a double sink or on the counter with a mat under it to funnel rinse water back into the sink, a silverware basket, which hooks over one end of the drain basket, sponge or dishcloth, dish towels.

Wash the glasses and cups first and rinse under the tap, or stand them in the drain basket and rinse with the faucet spray or by pouring water from a kettle over them. Invert to drain. Next, wash the silverware and stand the pieces with handles up in the silverware basket. Rinse. Then wash and rinse the plates, cooking utensils, and pots in that order.

Dry the cooking pots and utensils with a towel but leave the rest of the dishes in the drain basket to air dry. This not only saves time but also is more sanitary.

Wash greasy iron skillets last and dry them with a paper towel.

## August 23

### Pressure Cooking Saves You Time—and Money

Strangely enough, many cooks are not aware of the virtues of pressure cookers. This method of cooking deserves wider use, for it saves both time and energy. (Because less gas or electricity is needed, it saves money, also.) If you don't have a pressure cooker, take advantage of housewares sales that occur this month or next.

A "must" for the homemaker who also holds down a part- or full-time job, a pressure cooker makes it possible to prepare quickly main dishes which require a long period of cooking by other methods. The recipe book which comes with your cooker will suggest some of these.

Pressure cooking is the ideal way to cook less tender cuts of meat. Lamb shanks, for instance, require 90 minutes to two hours cooking time. Using a pressure cooker, they are tender and succulent in just over half an hour.

Pressure saucepans are made of heavy gauge aluminum with steam-tight covers. Two types of closures are used: a flexible cover which is slipped under the rim of the pan and pressed or flexed into position, and a domed cover that slides into grooves of the pan and locks into place. A gasket provides a tight seal. Temperature-controlled burners on gas and electric ranges relieve the cook of constant watching. Manufacturers' direction books state specific temperatures to use. Electric pressure pans feature automatically controlled heat and require even less attention from the user. Look for a UL (Underwriters' Laboratories) seal as a safeguard against unsafe construction.

## August 24

### Pressure-Cooked Spaghetti Sauce

In the pressure cooker, sauté 2 large onions, minced, and 1 finely chopped clove garlic in ¼ cup olive oil until the onion is transparent. Remove to a plate and brown 1 pound ground beef in the same pan. Return the onions and garlic to the cooker and add the following:

> 1 large can tomato purée
> 1 can tomato paste
> 1 can mushrooms (use the liquid to rinse out the purée and paste cans, and add)
> 1 Tbs. salt
> ¼ tsp. ground pepper
> 1 tsp. sugar
> 1 tsp. chili powder
> 1 tsp. oregano
> 1 tsp. basil

Stir just until mixed. Pressure cook at cooking pressure ½ hour, remove from heat, and let cool until indicator returns to off position.

If the sauce is not prepared in a pressure cooker, it should simmer for 3 hours.

Any leftover sauce may be frozen for use at a later time. (ADS)

---

**AMELIA EARHART PUTNAM was the first woman to pilot a plane non-stop across the U.S. She left Los Angeles at 4:26 P.M. on Aug. 24, 1932, and arrived at Newark, N.J., 19 hours and five minutes later.**

---

## *August* 25

### The Delights of Blueberries

Besides supplying a crop of delicious berries, the blueberry bush is ornamental. Its shiny green leaves, attractive in the summer, turn a brilliant red in the fall. The berries will attract many birds to your grounds. If you are a bird fancier, this in itself is a reason to include blueberry bushes in your yard.

At this time of year the berries are ripening. In some years there will be enough for you *and* the birds. In lean years, you will have to protect the bushes from feathered predators if you want berries for your own use.

The berries ripen gradually. Each day pick those that have turned to their characteristic blue. Keep them refrigerated until you have enough for immediate use or to fill a freezer container. Pick over and discard stems or imperfect berries. Wash and drain well. To freeze, mix the berries with sugar (¼ cup to a quart of berries) before filling the freezer container. When you use the frozen berries in a recipe later, subtract this amount of sugar from the quantity called for in the directions.

## August 26

## Dry Out the House to Avoid Mildew

Muggy weather during the late summer may bring dampness into your home. Conditions become ideal for growth of the molds that cause mildew. That's your cue for doing something about drying out the atmosphere within.

This is the time of year in many areas where a dehumidifier can earn its keep. You may want to consider buying one with a humidstat. Air-conditioning systems also remove moisture from the air by taking in warm air, cooling it, and circulating the cool air back into the room.

Even though it is hot, it would be wise to start up your heating plant if the humidity is very high to get rid of excess household dampness. Then open the doors and windows to let the moisture-laden air out. Use an exhaust fan if you have one. An extra benefit from this heating-plant operation: The heating plant itself will be dried out, preventing metal parts from rusting.

Burning an electric light continuously in a closed closet and other small areas will reduce dampness and prevent mildew. On the other hand, you may want to leave the closet doors open to improve ventilation. Hang clothing loosely so air can circulate.

You can also use chemicals to reduce atmospheric moisture. See tomorrow's article about this.

*August* **27**

## Chemicals Dry Air, Combat Mildew

Silica gel, activated alumina, or calcium chloride may be used to absorb moisture from the air. They are sold in department stores and drugstores and by building-supply dealers, sometimes under various trade names.

Silica gel and activated alumina are not harmful to fabrics. The porous granules still feel dry even when saturated—they hold half their weight of water. To use, hang cloth bags of the chemical in clothing closets. Or place an open container of it in the closet—on a shelf preferably, or on the floor. Keep closet doors closed so that moist air from outside will not get in. You may scatter the dry granules through layers of clothing and other articles that are to be stored in tightly closed chests or trunks.

Both silica gel and alumina can be used over and over, if dried between times. To dry, simply place moist granules in a vented oven at 300 degrees Fahrenheit for several hours. Then put the granules in an airtight box and cool before reusing. Silica gel specially treated with a color indicator is pink when filled with moisture, blue when dry.

Calcium chloride also absorbs moisture from the air. It is available both in small white granules, and in specially prepared products that employ calcium chloride soaked on a claylike material.

Calcium-chloride-on-clay products do not drip when saturated; they can be regenerated by driving off the absorbed moisture in an oven. To use one of these products, hang cloth bags that contain it in closets, basements, pantries, or any enclosed space.

Granular calcium chloride holds twice its weight of water. But as it absorbs moisture it liquefies. Do not let this chemical come in contact with clothing or textiles; it can eat holes in them.

To use, put it on a nonrusting screen supported in an enameled container. Then place the open container in the closet and keep the door shut. When it becomes liquid, replace with fresh chemical.

*August* **28**

## Use Washable Slipcovers

Protecting your upholstered furniture from the grubby hands of small (and older) children is best done, we think, by slipcovering with fabric that you can machine wash and dry yourself.

Use the washing machine cycle, water temperature, and soap or detergent recommended for the particular slipcover fabric. Wash as frequently as necessary—don't wait until accumulated grime makes pre-treatment or soaking essential.

Remove the slipcovers from the dryer when they are still slightly damp. As you put them back on the furniture, "iron" out wrinkles with your hands.

## August 29

## Protect Ripening Grapes

Check ripening grapes frequently to see if bees, wasps, or birds are damaging the fruit. If so, tie a paper or plastic bag over each bunch, cutting a few holes in the bottom of the bag to release any moisture that develops.

REVIEW PEDESTRIAN traffic rules with your youngsters before they set off for school again. Make an opportunity to take them into a congested area of your community—and see that everyone heeds traffic lights and looks both ways before stepping off the curb.

## Banana Pickles—Made from Cucumbers

Yellow in color like a ripe banana, these pickles are sure to please the palate of those who like their pickles sweet. They are made from a recipe that came out of the hills of southwestern Pennsylvania's Greene County through Dr. Mildred Van Zandt, beloved guidance counselor and teacher for many years in the Point Marion (Pennsylvania) High School and the Albert Gallatin Senior High School a few miles away. The turmeric gives the pickles the banana color.

The recipe:
**1 peck (or less) cucumbers**
**2 cups cider vinegar**
**1 cup water**
**3 cups granulated sugar**
**1 Tbs. salt**
**1 tsp. turmeric**
**1 tsp. celery seed**
**1 tsp. mustard seed**
Peel the cucumbers and cut into long narrow strips. Remove the seeds. Pack vertically in sterile jars. Combine all other ingredients in a saucepan, bring to a boil, and pour over the packed cucumbers. Process 10 minutes in a hot-water bath in a canner. (PSL)

# August 31

## August Potpourri for Homemakers

At the end of summer, mark canned goods on your pantry shelves with a marking pencil or magic marker. A quick slash down the front of each can will indicate these cans should be used first, and make sure there's no chance of them sitting on the shelves too long. (HD)

Cucumbers, plentiful now, may be used in many ways. Peel and slice very thinly, cover with salt water, and let stand at least 1 hour. Squeeze out the water, and mix with sour cream, chopped fresh dill or dried dill weed, and salt, pepper, and vinegar to taste.

Another cucumber dish: Grate peeled cucumbers using the coarse side of your grater. Squeeze out liquid, and mix with mayonnaise and salt, pepper, and dry mustard to taste.

Fry some of the green tomatoes available now. Coat slices with flour, and saute in butter until browned on both sides. Season to taste with salt and pepper.

Cook summer squash without water. Slice them onto a lump of butter in a saucepan. Cook slowly over low heat, watching carefully to see that they do not burn.

## Your Own Reminders:

## September 1

### How Are Your Children's Telephone Manners?

"Hi" or "Who's this?" are not appropriate ways to answer the telephone. Such salutations, we suspect, would have been deplored by Emma M. Nutt, who began work in Boston on September 1, 1878, for the Telephone Despatch Company as a telephone operator. Operators before that had all been men.

Children are often judged on their telephone manners. So teach your junior miss to answer "Hello, this is Emma Nutt," rather than just "Hello." This saves time and makes a much better impression.

## September 2

### Tips about Keeping Plants Healthy Indoors

It's time now in many parts of the country to bring indoors any frost-sensitive plants that you have had outdoors for the summer. Many plants thrive indoors when you give them the care they need. Some tips:

Keep plants out of drafts. Many plants, especially African violets, need protection from extreme changes of temperature. Move them away from windows during cold weather.

Water plants when they need it, usually twice a week in winter when humidity is low indoors —once a week at other times. It is best to check the soil twice a week. Take a pinch of it; if it crumbles and does not stick to your fingers, watering is indicated.

While you're away, keep plants watered by inserting one end of a few feet of old cotton clothesline or wicking in a jar of water—the other end into the soil.

Turn a plant at regular intervals so light reaches all sides to enable the plant to grow evenly. A floor-size plant in a corner, of course, should be allowed to grow unevenly to fit into the location.

Use artificial light (such as a spotlight) to supplement natural light in dark locations. In a dark basement, for example, two 40-watt fluorescent tubes, lighted for 18 hours a day, will supply enough light for growing plants. Place the fixture one foot to 18 inches above the plants.

Keep the plants clean. For large plants in floor containers (like philodendron) wipe off dust with cotton moistened with water. Use a soft brush to dust hairy leaves. Most small plants (like ivy) can be showered weekly with a gentle sink spray. Do not clean leaves while plants are flowering—you could injure the petals. And never use oil—it

## Candlemaking: It's a Great Hobby

Some folks spend their spare moments during the fall making candles for Christmas gifts and home holiday decorations. We think this is a great idea. If you agree, get started soon.

Around our home we never seem to have enough candles. If that's the case with you, you have reason enough to make some candles of your own. Everyone who has tried it tells us making candles gives one a lot of fun and satisfaction.

Check locally for candlemaking kits. If you can't find them, write to Candle Mill Village, 1027 Main Street, East Arlington, Vt. 05252, and ask the proprietors for their catalog. Enclose a quarter to cover cost of mailing. You'll find all sorts of candlemaking supplies and instruction books offered in the catalog, as well as other interesting items.

might clog the leaf pores.

Examine house plants periodically when watering or cleaning. At the first sign of insects, spray with a bug killer.

The foregoing tips are from a colorful booklet, "How Does Your Garden Grow?" It contains much more information about growing plants and protecting them from insects. Get a copy free by writing to Johnson Wax, 1525 Howe Street, Racine, Wis. 53403. Another good publication for your homemaker-gardening library is "Insects and Related Pests of House Plants," available from your county home agent or the Superintendent of Documents, Washington, D.C. 20402.

## September 4

### Would You Like to Make Your Own Wine?

Lots of people are making their own wine these days—and you can, too. Now's a good time to consider it, for the grapes and other fruits you might want to use are generally available.

If you wonder about the legality of wine making, Federal regulations permit you to make up to 200 gallons of taxfree wine per year for your own use—not for sale. (You are prohibited from making beer.)

You may already have instructions on how to make wine. If not, most public libraries have books that will help you. The easiest way to get into wine making as a hobby, however, is to write to Welch's, P.O. Box 7455, Rochester, N.Y. 14615, for information about instructions and all supplies needed. Local stores also may have wine-making kits.

## September 5

### For Meals in a Hurry, Try Seafood

Time today is more valuable than at any period in history. This is especially true for homemakers who hold down paying jobs outside the home. The Bureau of Commercial Fisheries of the U.S. Department of the Interior had the hurried homemaker in mind when it produced a booklet of new seafood recipes. Each recipe can be prepared in just a few minutes. Fish and shellfish are among the best timesavers. They cook quickly and easily.

The recipe booklet is called "Time for Seafood." It is available through the Superintendent of Documents in Washington.

## September 6

### Some Thoughts about Household Adhesives

Every homemaker should have on hand a selection of adhesives to use with different types of materials. A squeeze bottle of white glue will fill the need for a wide range of jobs. You may also want a bottle of mucilage for paper and cardboard.

Want to mend a prized china or pottery item? A number of suitable products are available. Two that have given us good results are Weldit Cement and Scotch Super Strength Adhesive. The makers also recommend these for glass.

Plastics require special adhesives. Vinyl products such as inflatable toys and wading pools can be repaired with a vinyl adhesive and film patches sold in kits at toy and swimming-pool stores.

Polystyrene items such as toy cars, planes, and

ship models can be bonded with adhesives available at hobby shops for use in the assembly of such models.

Polyethylene, one of the most commonly used plastics, can sometimes be bonded together with heat—or taped—but otherwise you might as well discard the item that needs repair.

## September 7

## Cooperate with Your Child's Teachers

Home-school cooperation is vital if your child is to make optimal academic progress. To help you do your part, we offer the following suggestions:

Get to know your child's teacher by attending the "get-acquainted" tea or similar function at the start of the school year, back-to-school night, parent-teacher organization meetings, and other school functions.

Make it a point to attend parent-teacher conferences. Most schools schedule these at least once a year. They offer an opportunity for you to find out how your child is progressing—both demonstrated performance in the classroom, including relationships with his peers and with those in authority, as observed by the teacher; and his performance in relation to others in the same class, both locally and nationally, as determined by standardized achievement test scores. The conference is the time, too, when you can get specific suggestions from the teacher as to the ways you can help your child at home.

If you have questions concerning your child's schoolwork at any time, a phone call to the school is in order. Teachers stand ready to schedule conferences with parents, in person or over the phone, to discuss a child's performance.

Most schools welcome volunteer help from parents, and you can cooperate in this respect by assisting in the school library, for instance.

## September 8

---

**TODAY IN HISTORY:** *Sextuplets were born on Sept. 8, 1866, in Chicago to Mr. and Mrs. James Bushnell. There were three boys and three girls. One girl died at age two months and one boy at eight months. Of the four survivors one lived to be 68, the others more than 70.*

---

## Does Your Child Have a Place to Do Homework?

Sitting in front of the TV set is definitely not the place and position. A child should study away from the center of family activities, preferably at a desk in his own room. Make sure there is good lighting. Help your child develop the good habit of doing his schoolwork at the same time each day and without musical accompaniment of radio, TV, or record player. Help him develop pride in neatness of his work—compliments from you will help.

If your child requests assistance to complete homework, comply by explaining or working out a sample problem. Doing the work for him will only give him a crutch which he very quickly will not be able to do without.

## September 9

## Seal Home from Insects Seeking Warmth

Many kinds of insects survive from generation to generation by wintering in cracks and crevices in woodlands. Some also crawl into any available cracks in a home at this time of year. During the winter, they may continue on through the wall and show up, sometimes in numbers, inside the house.

Keeping out these insects is another good reason for using caulking compound to seal all outside cracks in a house. Caulking usually is done, of course, to keep warmth in. Apply the caulking compound to all cracks you can locate around windows, doors, and pipes and wires that go through walls. Weather stripping on doors and windows will serve the same double purpose.

If insects do manage to get in, the safest way to fight them is by spraying with a chemical recommended for indoor use.

# *September* **10**

## Tips on Buying a Sewing Machine

An electric sewing machine, cabinet or portable, is a long-time investment. It should last for years with only minor replacements of parts. There are many choices in a wide range of prices, so it pays to do a careful job of selecting the machine which will best fill your present and future sewing needs.

There are four main categories of sewing machines: straight stitch, basic zigzag, more versatile zigzag, and most versatile zigzag. Which you choose depends upon the kind of sewing you will be doing.

Most home sewing needs can be filled by the straight-stitch machine which does only straight stitching, forward and reverse, and is the simplest and least expensive machine. Attachments are provided or can be bought to make a zigzag stitch, buttonholes, ruffles, overcasting, or to do blind hemming. However, if you have to buy too many extra attachments, the total cost may be more than a machine with a few more built-in stitches.

If your sewing needs include a variety of stitches or decorative stitching, one of the more complicated (and more expensive) machines may better suit your purposes. However, be sure that you will use the special stitches often enough to make the added cost worthwhile.

When shopping for a machine, test at least three makes in order to have a basis for comparison. Can you sit at it comfortably? How noisy is it? Will you be able to care for it and keep it in good running condition easily? Part of the test should include actual stitching of fabrics. At this time check the operation, lighting, threading, stitching, and speed control.

Other considerations: Will the dealer provide good reliable service? Is there a guarantee? What is the total cost?

## September 11

### If Your Family Dog Is a Female

If your dog is a female, you may plan to raise a litter of puppies. But first consider the complications.

Puppy raising is expensive. Before she is bred, your female must have a health checkup, booster shots, and worming if necessary. All this must be done before the beginning of her heat period. She must then be confined after she is bred until she is safely out of heat (puppies born in a single litter can have different sires if their mother is bred by more than one male).

The stud fee may be paid in cash, or by giving the owner of the stud one of the expected puppies. Make sure there is a written agreement about what constitutes a litter. In drawing up the agreement, consider the following possibilities: Your female does not conceive, or has just one live puppy, or the entire litter dies before the stud-fee puppy is old enough to be taken away from its mother.

Even if all goes well during the birth of the litter, after the puppies are born they should be checked, and the mother examined by your veterinarian and given any post-partum medication he thinks necessary. Puppies should be tested, and wormed if necessary (but only by your veterinarian) three or four weeks after birth. Temporary protective shots against common puppy diseases should be started at about five weeks. Even at a discount "litter rate," these shots are expensive.

A well-balanced diet, and a good vitamin-mineral supplement are essential for the expectant mother. A weaning formula, vitamins and minerals, and feedings every four hours for several weeks are essential for the puppies when they start to eat on their own (at about four weeks).

Once the puppies are up on their feet, they must have a sturdy, roomy, clean, bright, and draft-free pen suitable for confining them until they are sold or given away—and this may be for a

longer period of time than you'd planned.

Of course, you will not breed anything but a registered purebred female to a registered purebred male. There are too many mongrel puppies today dying on the roads or being put to death in humane society shelters without deliberately adding to this list. A mongrel litter costs just as much as a purebred one. With purebreds you have a chance of selling a few to help cover expenses.

If you do not want to spend the time and money necessary to raise a litter of planned and purebred puppies, for the sake of your pet have her spayed. This operation, though not inexpensive, removes the female reproductive organs and frees you from the endless worry of confining her during heat periods and from the dangers of attentive strange male dogs coming onto your property. Under these conditions, even normally friendly male dogs may fight or bite and are a hazard to children. (JSD)

BOTTLE BRUSHES made of nylon bristle were introduced on Sept. 11, 1939.

# September 12

## Use Apples for Norwegian Pie

Use some of the apples that are in season now to make this dessert that is more of a chewy cake than a pie. The recipe is a favorite among Point Marion, Pennsylvania, women for a quick dessert at luncheon meetings.

1½ cups sugar
1 cup flour
2 tsp. baking powder
½ tsp. salt
2 unbeaten eggs
1 tsp. vanilla extract
2 cups apples, diced fine
1 cup walnuts or pecans, chopped fine

Mix all ingredients through the vanilla together well by hand (the batter is too stiff to mix with an electric beater). Add the apples and the walnuts or pecans. Spread in two 9-inch pie pans which have been well buttered and floured. Bake 30 minutes at 350 degrees.

The pie freezes well for a long time, but do not place it in a plastic bag or it will become soggy when thawed. (MLR)

## September 13

### What Education Should Be: 1853 Advice for Today

Whether the responsibility for the moral education of children lies in the home, in the school, or both, is frequently the subject of debate among parents and educators. Here's what Mrs. Abell had to say about it over a hundred years ago. (See reference to her book on April 21.)

"The foundation of education should be laid in the knowledge and love of God. Education, without MORAL TRAINING, is like a sword in the hands of a madman. 'Knowledge is power' for good or for evil. See to it then, that your children are trained in the principles of religion, honesty, integrity and virtue, in obedience, self-government, benevolence and kindness. They need line upon line, precept upon precept, and constant watchfulness over faults and habits. No schools however well conducted, no colleges however high in literary advantages, without this care and effort to establish correct principles, and form the character to virtue, can be safe for your children. They should be taught moreover, that they must be, under the blessing of God, the manufacturers of their own fortunes. Many parents toil and labour, and deny themselves the comforts of life to hoard up wealth for their children. But fit them to take care of themselves, and it will be of more value than the wealth of the Indies. The earlier you teach them to depend upon their own resources the better. See that their morals are pure, the mind cultivated, and the whole nature subservient to the laws of God, and it will be of greater value than the riches of the world. Train them up to habits of industry, economy and virtue, and it will be the best estate they can have."

# September 14

## Scrub and Wax Linoleum Now

Now that the muggy days of late summer are over and the children back in school, it may be a good time to tackle the scrubbing and waxing of a linoleum floor. Do it today if you anticipate a minimum of traffic and if the moisture content of the air is low enough to speed the drying process.

If this is a job you do thoroughly only once or twice a year, the linoleum no doubt is pretty scruffy looking. You may want to call in a professional or rent a power scrubber and waxer to do large rooms that are linoleum-covered. But, if you have a small area that you do by hand, we have found the following procedure will change the scruffiest floor to a "see-your-face-in-it" brilliance.

Scrub the surface with steel-wool soap pads and scouring powder to remove embedded dirt and any old wax. Rinse thoroughly and let dry completely. Use a liquid wax recommended for linoleum floors. When dry (see label for drying times), apply a second coat. A third coat will provide the protection needed for floors that are cleaned thoroughly only annually or semiannually. Regular vacuuming and occasional wiping up with cool water will maintain the floor until the next thorough cleaning.

# September 15

## Do You Have Firewood on Hand?

If there's a wood-burning fireplace in your home, you ought to think now about getting in a good supply of wood. Burning wood is an economical and pleasant way of taking the chill off the house quickly in early fall before you start up the household heating plant.

In buying your wood, or cutting your own if you have the trees available, remember that oak produces a steady glowing fire. Softwoods like pine, spruce, and fir are easy to ignite, but they burn rapidly and need frequent replenishment. The U.S. Forest Service recommends combining softwoods with a hardwood (ash, beech, birch, maple, or oak) to create the best fire.

Slabwood available from sawmills is usually less expensive than regular firewood, especially if you pick it up yourself.

## September 16

### Use Ornamental Gourds for an Autumn Centerpiece

Ornamental gourds may show up in markets about this time. Don't overlook their uses for filling an autumn centerpiece or otherwise decorating the house.

Or perhaps you grow your own. If so, try to pick them just before frost strikes in your area. The more mature they are, the better they will keep. Sponge them off with a mild antiseptic solution, leave for a few days to dry, and finally give them a coat of clear varnish or paste furniture wax.

Gourd growers have their own club, organized "to promote . . . research; to publish books, pamphlets, bulletins; to encourage the use of gourds in decorative art; to hold exhibits." For information, write to The Gourd Society of America, Inc., Elmwood, Mass. 02337.

## September 17

**TODAY IN HISTORY:** *This is Constitution Day. The new U.S. Constitution was signed in Philadelphia on Sept. 17, 1787.*

### Some Facts about Potatoes

Most of our year-round supply of fresh potatoes is harvested in September or October. These fall-crop potatoes are stored for one to nine months before shipment to retail outlets. Some potatoes, however, are freshly harvested and marketed from January through September. These are called "new" potatoes. This term is also used to describe freshly dug fall-crop potatoes which are not fully matured. New potatoes are best when boiled.

Use of U.S. grade standards is voluntary except where required by state law or other local regulations. U.S. Extra No. 1 potatoes are the premium grade; potatoes in this grade can only be slightly affected by internal defects or sprouts. The minimum size is 2¼ inches in diameter or 5 ounces in weight. Variation in size of potatoes within a package is limited. Generally, they must vary by no more than 1¼ inches or 6 ounces.

You may find U.S. No. 1 potatoes labeled Size A. Such potatoes must be at least 1⅞ inches in diameter, and 40 percent of the potatoes must be 2½ inches in diameter or 6 ounces in weight or larger. If the size is not designated, the minimum for U.S. No. 1 potatoes is 1⅞ inches in diameter; there is no maximum.

When shopping for potatoes, look for those that are firm, well shaped, and smooth, with few eyes. Potatoes should be free from large cuts, growth cracks, bruises, skinned areas, and decay. Some amount of skinning is normal in new pota-

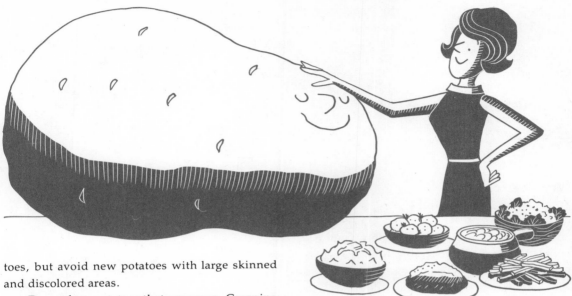

toes, but avoid new potatoes with large skinned and discolored areas.

Do not buy potatoes that are green. Greening is caused by exposure to natural or artificial light. Sometimes only the skin is affected, but greening may penetrate the flesh. The green portions contain an alkaloid which causes a bitter flavor and is said to be poisonous to some people.

You may find potatoes with second growth. These irregular, knob-shaped growths are considered defects because they are likely to cause waste.

A "smell test" can also help you select potatoes. If the potatoes smell musty or moldy, the flavor may be affected.

It is impossible to detect internal defects without cutting the potato, but if you find that some of the potatoes you have bought are hollow in the center or have severe internal discoloration, take them back to your grocer for replacement.

If stored properly, general purpose and baking potatoes will keep for several months; new potatoes will keep for several weeks. Look potatoes over before you store them. Set aside any that are bruised or cracked and use them first. Don't wash

potatoes before you store them. Dampness increases the likelihood of decay.

Store potatoes in a cool (45 to 50 degrees Fahrenheit, if possible), dark place, with good ventilation. Potatoes stored at 70 to 80 degrees should be used within a week.

---

**YOUR LOCAL SCHOOLS** may be seeking volunteer workers for various activities. That's a great way to become involved in your community. Telephone the principal.

---

"This be the verse you grave for me:
Here he lies where he longed to be;
Home is the sailor, home from sea,
And the hunter home from the hill."
—Robert Louis Stevenson

---

# September 18

## Dry Berries for Autumn Bouquets

Some of the colorful autumn berries and fruits now found in woods and fields can be dried and kept for weeks as autumn bouquets. Among those that last well are the red fruits of the multiflora rose, the yellow-and-orange bittersweet, the steel-blue berries of Virginia creeper, and the grayish-white bayberries. Red barberry lasts well, too, but prickly stems make them hard to handle.

Cut branches with any of these fruits attached, tie them into bunches, and hang them for a few days in a dry attic or closet.

ANN HUTCHINSON and her husband arrived in New England on Sept. 18, 1634. An advocate of personal religion without regard to church or minister, she soon became a center of controversy. In 1637, she and her followers were banished from Massachusetts. Indians killed her and all members of her family except one child at Pelham, N.Y., in 1643.

# September 19

## You Can Use Carpet Sweeper and Vacuum Cleaner

The advice of home-care experts makes a lot of sense: Own a carpet sweeper as well as a vacuum cleaner for the best and most efficient care of the carpets and rugs in your home.

The vacuum removes soil that has worked down into the pile and helps keep the pile upright. The carpet sweeper removes lint, surface soil, and such things as pieces of thread. It is also handy for quick pickup cleaning.

In areas that have constant use, daily cleaning is advisable with either vacuum or sweeper. Three sweeps over each section are usually enough —forward, back, forward. The care program should also include a thorough weekly cleaning —seven strokes of the cleaner over each area. This cleaning should remove both surface soil and embedded dirt.

Periodic cleaning by yourself or a professional cleaner will restore the rug to its original beauty and assure longer life. You can do the job yourself by either the wet or dry method, carefully following the directions that come with the cleaning material. If you prefer professional cleaning, send the rug out if it can be easily taken up. It may be more convenient and economical for wall-to-wall carpeting to be cleaned right on the floor. Be sure to have this done before the carpet is badly soiled.

To extend the life of your floor covering, put down throw rugs in areas of heavy traffic. Extra pieces of carpet are ideal for this. Have the edges of the carpet bound.

# September 20

## Housekeeping without Power: Heating

One-room living is the best rule if you must get along without twentieth-century heating conveniences. A room with a fireplace is the obvious choice. Make sure you have wood or coal on hand. Newspapers tightly rolled will extend your supply of firewood. The kitchen is a second choice if there is a gas range and a dependable supply of gas—or if you have and can install an old wood-burning range. (CAUTION: A gas flame can quickly use up all oxygen in an enclosed space. If you use this form of emergency heat, be sure to ventilate.) If there aren't doors, consider hanging blankets over inside-the-house door openings to keep as much heat in the room as possible. Draperies or window shades will also provide some insulation—close the draperies and pull down the shades. This is the time when insulation in all walls and ceilings of a house pays off. Make sure, especially, that there's good insulation in your emergency-heat room.

If you must rely on either a gas oven—remember the need for ventilation—or a fireplace for temporary house heating, think about making double use of the fuel by preparing some meals with the unit at the same time. See October 25 for emergency cooking ideas.

If temperatures in other rooms go below freezing, house plants and bouquets may freeze. Move them to the room in which you have heat.

Remember your water pipes, too. Open all taps and let them drip to keep water flowing to prevent freeze-ups. Flush toilets periodically. If temperatures are likely to drop to near zero, drain

210

all household systems that use water. Does some-one in the household know the location of the drain valve that will accomplish this?

If you have space, you may want to install a standby heating system—a wood-burning Franklin stove, for instance.

---

**A PLASTIC LID** from a one-pound coffee can is just right for sealing a quart can of oil.

---

## September 21

### Green-Tomato Relish for the Season's End

When an impending frost at the end of summer leaves you with a large supply of green tomatoes from a garden, one excellent way to make use of them—right away—is to make green-tomato relish, using the following recipe. Of course, you don't have to wait until the end of the season. You can make this delicious relish any time during the year that you can pick or buy green tomatoes.

1 peck green tomatoes
1 head cabbage
5 green peppers
5 red peppers
2 pounds onions
½ gallon vinegar
8 cups sugar
2 Tbs. mustard seed
2 Tbs. celery seed
1 tsp. whole cloves
1 Tbs. cinnamon
1 tsp. allspice

Grind the tomatoes and cabbage. Let stand overnight. Drain. Grind the peppers and onions, and add to the tomato mixture. Bring the vinegar, sugar, and spices to a boil. Add the ground vegetables and cook very slowly 2 to 3 hours. Place in sterile jars and seal while hot. (PSL)

---

**MILKWEED PODS** make attractive additions to winter bouquets. Spray them or not, as you like.

---

"Train up a child in the way he should go: and when he is old he will not depart from it."

—Proverbs XXII, 6

## September 22

### Run Car Air Conditioner Five Minutes Weekly

Now that winter is approaching, we tend to forget about the air conditioners in our automobiles. We shouldn't. Car manufacturers advise that an air conditioner ought to be run for about five minutes every week during the winter. This, they say, will help keep it in good condition. Better decide now which family member will be responsible for remembering to do this during the coming winter.

The manufacturers also suggest that a specialist service the air conditioner once a year, or every 10,000 miles.

## September 23

### Are You a Proficient Family Chauffeur?

Homemakers with children growing up in a sprawling suburb must often transport them to and from distant parties and school events. As one mother says, she almost lives in the family's second car.

Besides driving the car, you must accept the responsibility for keeping it in safe operating condition, for the man of the house may have neither the time nor the opportunity.

Keep your eye on the gas gauge. Running out of gas in the middle lane of the three-lane interstate can put your family in peril. Take a look at the tires every time you go out. If you hear an unusual noise, or the car begins to behave in an unusual way, get to a service station as soon as possible.

Mothers often overlook the fact that these trips provide basic training for children in how to handle a car in traffic. Set a good example. Drive safely and legally.

"For better or worse, today's mothers are the primary teachers of tomorrow's driving habits," says our good friend Edward D. Fales, Jr., in his book *Belts On, Buttons Down,* subtitled *What Every Mother Should Know About Car Safety.* A Seymour Lawrence Book from Delacorte Press, New York, N.Y., Ed's book is one of several publications for parents backed by the Children's Hospital Medical Center of Boston, Massachusetts.

---

**"That man is richest whose pleasures are the cheapest."**
**—Henry David Thoreau**

# September 24

## Plan for Winter Blossoms

For indoor winter blossoms, plant bulbs of China lily and paper-white narcissus now in bowls and pots. Choose large bulbs, place them on a layer of crushed rock, fill in with enough rock to hold them upright, and cover the bases of the bulbs with water. Keep in a cool place until tops form. Replenish the water as necessary.

# September 25

## Make Your Own Spoon Rings

One of the crafts which has caught on in recent years, especially among young people, is making rings from silver spoons. You might like to try this now and make Christmas gifts for family and friends.

Any teaspoon may be used. Silver is easier to work than stainless steel. For your first endeavor, practice on a silver-plated spoon which needs to be resilvered.

Equipment needed includes a vise, a pair of needlenose pliers (preferably with a half-rounded

nose), a rawhide or wooden mallet, a hacksaw or file, a piece of soft cloth, and a ring mandrel or ring sizer.

The mandrel is required to size the ring and assure its roundness. This is a tapered steel bar available for less than $10. Two sources are William Dixon Company, Carlstadt, N. J. 07072; and Paul H. Gesswein & Company, Inc., 235 Park Ave. South, New York, N.Y. 10003.

Follow these steps to make the ring:

1. Roughly measure off a section of the spoon handle from its end to a point that's equal to the circumference of the mandrel at the desired ring size. Leave a little extra, say one-eighth inch, for overlap.

2. Cut the handle with a hacksaw or file. Once the cut has been started, you can complete it by bending the handle.

3. File the cut smooth. Discard the bowl of the spoon or use it for another purpose.

4. Place the mandrel horizontally between the upper edge of the vise jaws. Put the sawed end of the spoon handle between mandrel and vise (with handle placed vertically). Assemble mandrel and handle of the spoon with a soft cloth between them to protect the handle.

5. Gently tap the spoon with your mallet, forming the spoon around the mandrel, until the metal touches the vise.

6. Remove and again place the spoon handle vertically between the mandrel and vise.

7. Repeat steps 5 and 6 until the ring is relatively round.

8. Tap down the original end of the spoon handle over the cut end.

9. Loosen the ring from the mandrel, but don't remove it.

10. Gently tap all around the ring until it is uniformly round.

11. Try the ring on your finger for size. To

enlarge it, place it on the mandrel and tap downward. To make it smaller, gently squeeze with a pair of needlenose pliers. In both cases, protect the ring with a soft cloth.

12. Check size and roundness on the mandrel.

Your ring is ready to wear. A more professional appearance results if the ends are soldered together—but this is not really essential. (JKS)

## September 26

### Recipe for Mead

Wouldn't it be fun to make a little mead—the fermented drink enjoyed by Robin Hood and other early Britons? Autumn is the traditional time for putting down a crock or two, for that's when you are able to get fresh honey. Our recipe comes from England.

To make your sample of mead, buy 4 pounds of strained fresh honey. Dissolve this in 1 gallon of water and boil the mixture for 45 to 60 minutes. Remove the scum from the surface and pour the liquid into a wooden or earthenware receptacle.

When your cooking thermometer shows that the temperature has dropped to about 70 degrees Fahrenheit, dissolve an ounce of yeast in a little of the liquid and add it to the container.

When fermentation begins (that is, when the mixture starts to bubble), strain the liquid into a clean earthenware jar, filling it to the brim. Cover lightly with a piece of foil and set the container in a warm room. After fermentation has stopped, in a matter of several weeks, stir in a half ounce of isinglass (available at drugstores) to clear the mixture. Strain the mead into clean bottles. Cork and seal them. Wait at least six months before using.

---

**THE LOWER THE SETTING of your thermostat, the less water your house plants will need.**

## September 27

### Wash Silk Lampshades Now

If you have soiled silk lampshades that you feel are not worth a professional dry cleaning, try washing them yourself before buying replacements. There is risk involved, but they may turn out so well that you'll decide replacements aren't necessary. The sunny, breezy, low-humidity days that are common at this time of year are ideal to take on this task, as the shades must dry quickly to avoid the possibility of rust stains.

Before starting, check to see that the shades are sewn, not glued; glued shades may come apart.

Wash the shades one by one in the sink or washtub using a mild detergent, warm water, and a soft brush. Rinse under running water. Tie a piece of string through the hole of the fixture that fits over the finial screw, then tie the string to your clothesline.

## September 28

**TODAY IN HISTORY:** *Kate Douglas Wiggin was born on Sept. 28, 1856, in Philadelphia. Her novel,* Rebecca of Sunnybrook Farm, *was popular reading for children of many past generations—and would be for today's youngsters if they were introduced to it. While writing, she also taught school, and in 1878 in San Francisco organized the first free kindergarten west of the Rocky Mountains.*

### Importance of Pectin

To make a jellied fruit product, you need the proper amounts of four ingredients: fruit, pectin, acid, and sugar. Some fruits, such as crab apples, have enough natural pectin to make a jelly. You must add commercial pectins to others.

Underripe fruit has more pectin than fruit fully ripened. Acid content also is higher in underripe fruit. These facts often make underripe fruit the better choice for jelly making.

# September **29**

## You Can Preserve Fall Colors

Trees will soon be resplendent with their autumn colors, especially in northern states. A treatment with glycerin can preserve some of this color indefinitely.

Cut small branches at the first sign of color, before the leaves have begun to dry. Oak, beech, and mountain ash leaves respond well to the glycerin treatment. Maple leaves do not because they are too thin. Choose a pitcher or small vase with a narrow top for your spray of leaves.

Buy a small bottle of glycerin at the drugstore. Make a solution of two parts of water to one of glycerin. The stems should be immersed in three or four inches of the solution. Before placing the branches in the vase, clip off any small twigs at the bottoms so that a considerable length of the main stem is bare. Slit the bottom of each stem up about three inches. Place the stems flat on a board and bruise the ends thoroughly with a hammer, meat tenderizer, or similar object to allow the stems to absorb liquid.

Arrange the leaves in the vase, making sure each stem is at the bottom of the solution. Place the bouquet in a cool room for a week or so. The solution will be drawn up into the leaves, which will continue to change color as if they were still on the tree. Solution remaining at the bottom of the vase can be discarded.

Leaves preserved this way will retain their color for years.

**TOO FEW PIECES of furniture to fill your rooms? Let house plants fill some of the empty space. They're soothing to the nerves also.**

## September Potpourri for Homemakers

Parsley, chives, and basil freeze well. At the end of summer, wash the herbs well in several changes of water and blot dry with paper towels or a terry towel. Using a kitchen shears, snip the herbs into small freezer containers. In the winter, use as much as desired and return containers to freezer.

Pick figs for preserving several days before they are fully ripe. This reduces damage from souring and splitting.

Simmer stick cinnamon and whole cloves in water on top of the range when you are entertaining in the fall or winter. The spicy odor will perfume the house.

Create your own flower color schemes. Stand Queen Anne's lace (wild carrot), which blossoms in summer and early fall in many areas, in food coloring to which you have added just a little water. Remove when desired color has been achieved.

Bait mousetraps soon. These rodents tend to seek warmth indoors at this time.

Do you recognize high bush cranberries when you see them? They are bright red at this time of year and grow in the wilds on shrubs about six feet tall in the northern states and southern Canada. They can be used in place of the regular bog-grown fruit for sauces and jellies. Birds like them, too, during the winter months. A few of the shrubs are worth adding to your grounds.

## Your Own Reminders:

# October 1

## Facts about Floor Polish

Buy floor polish to suit the surface on which you'll use it. Two types of polish are available—water-based and solvent-based. Water-based polish is usually best for resilient flooring. Solvent-based polish is designed to preserve wood and cork floors. Either might be used on stone, brick, or other hard surfaces.

Beware of using a solvent-based polish on resilient flooring. The solvent can cause a severe softening on some asphalt or rubber tile, although it may be safe to use on other resilient surfaces. Be sure before you use it.

Finishes generally can be divided into two other basic kinds—hard and glossy, or soft and satiny.

A hard, glossy look can be achieved on resilient and hard-surface flooring by using water-based, self-polishing liquids—particularly those containing polymers such as acrylics. A hard, glossy finish will minimize scuff marks and protect against spills, spots, and black heel marks.

Although all water-based polishes protect, some brands protect better than others. Experiment to see which polish works best on your floors.

On resilient or hard-surface flooring, water-based buffable paste or liquid polish gives a soft, satiny look. This polish will protect your floor, but must be buffed regularly in heavy traffic areas for an unscuffed appearance.

On wood and cork floors, a relatively hard, glossy finish is produced with a solvent-based, self-polishing liquid. It may give a harder finish than a buffable paste polish because of its polymer content.

A soft, satiny look can be achieved on wood floors by using an electric buffer and buffable solvent-based polish in paste or liquid form.

# October 2

**TODAY IN HISTORY:** *A patent was granted on Oct. 2, 1866, to J. Osterhoudt of New York City for "an improved method of opening tin cans." This was a key opener on cans.*

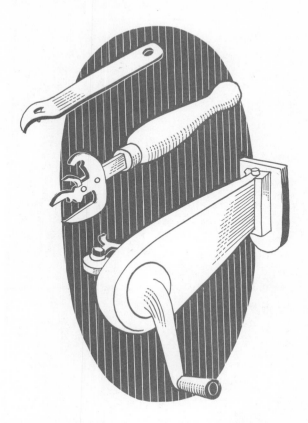

## You Should Own Several Can Openers

Every kitchen should be equipped with at least three can openers. First on the list is a "church key" beverage can opener, the hooked piece of metal you use to puncture holes in cans that contain liquids. Use it also to pry up jar lids and open bottles.

The second type of opener likewise is a hand tool. You use it to remove a can lid by working the opener around the container rim with an up and down motion. This tool can usually be used to open bottles and puncture beverage cans also, and sometimes has a corkscrew.

For the third opener choose between an electric opener or a wall-mounted swing-out manual opener. A refinement worth owning, if you can find one in a local or mail-order market, is a slide-out bracket for mounting a wall-type manual opener under an above-counter cabinet. While not in use, the opener slides out of the way under the cabinet.

Electric openers are a boon to recyclers, who must open both ends of a can before flattening. They open cans quickly and cleanly. They are easy to clean and do not require oiling. Some electric openers also are equipped with a knife sharpener and bottle opener. Electric openers are useless, of course, during electric failures or brownouts. For that reason, it's wise to have the hand-operated types also.

221

# October 3

**TODAY IN HISTORY:** *A patent was granted to John S. Thurman of St. Louis on Oct. 3, 1899, for a "pneumatic carpet renovator." It was motor driven.*

## Housekeeping without Power: Cleaning

Because of the pressure of many duties, your grandmother may have moved so fast to complete her weekly cleaning that she literally stirred up a whirlwind of dust. When the dust settled, you could properly have questioned—but not within her hearing, of course—whether cleaning was worthwhile.

That's why we suggest you include among your nonpower cleaning supplies a supermarket product which you spray on a dry mop to keep dust down. Look for it among the other cleaning supplies in the store. You will also need a good broom, dust brush and pan, a carpet sweeper—and a rug beater (especially for periodic cleaning of throw rugs).

Look for the rug beater in an antique shop. Even though it is not old enough to be a true antique now, it will be eventually. So keep it. You might fashion your own rug beater by wiring a loop of heavy wire about a yard long to a piece of wooden broom handle about a foot long.

Our grandmothers hung rugs over clotheslines for cleaning. Then the beating activity not only got rid of the dirt but also any pent-up emotions, perhaps even anger at those in the house whose carelessness made the cleaning necessary.

# October 4

## Cricket on the Hearth Not So Good

Cool nights at this time of year may bring crickets indoors. During the night their chirps may keep you awake. But that's not all. These insects can cause damage. They love to eat holes in woolen blankets and clothes and any starched articles.

Your best precaution against such damage is to try to keep them out of the house. Check basement windows and doors for cracks where insects might enter. Seal such cracks with caulking compound.

If you hear a cricket inside, seek it out and destroy it or carry it outside the house.

## Tips about Buying Canned or Frozen Vegetables

When you buy canned vegetables, be sure the cans are not leaking or bulged at either end. Bulging or swelling indicates spoilage. Small dents in cans do not harm the contents. Badly dented cans, however, should be avoided.

Vegetables sold in glass jars with screw-on or vacuum-sealed lids are sealed tightly to preserve the contents. If there is any indication the lid has been tampered with, return the jar to the store and report the matter to the store manager.

For good-quality frozen vegetables or fruits:

Select clean, firm packages. If packages are soft, you can be sure the food has already lost quality. Frozen food is safe to eat as long as the package remains frozen, but a storage temperature of zero degrees Fahrenheit or lower is necessary to maintain high quality.

Buy only frozen foods that are displayed in a properly refrigerated cabinet made for that purpose. Do not buy frozen vegetables stacked outside the frozen-food cabinet even if they are packed in dry ice.

Select packages only from clean cabinets in which foods are stacked no higher than the proper fill line. This line is marked on the inner side of many cabinets. Look for a thermometer in the cabinet; if there is one, it should register zero.

---

**SHOPPING REMINDER: Brussels sprouts should be coming into peak supply at this time—and they'll remain so through December. Avoid those that have yellow or greenish leaves, loose or wilted leaves, and leaves with small worm holes.**

---

## October 6

### Christmas Shop by Mail? Do It Soon

Mail-order shopping is a great way to save both time and effort in your Christmas shopping. But you ought to do it soon, not later than November 1, according to the Direct Mail Advertising Association. The association offers other suggestions:

Beware of exaggerated claims for products or price.

Read catalogs carefully. Determine if merchandise is offered on a satisfaction-guaranteed or money-back basis.

Pay by check or money-order; do not send cash with the order. Avoid delays by including shipping and handling fees and taxes noted in catalog or advertisements.

Clearly indicate names and addresses where gifts are to be sent and whether a gift card is to be enclosed; keep a complete record of your order.

Check order carefully upon receipt. Register any complaint or refund or exchange request immediately. If you exercise exchange or refund option because of valid dissatisfaction, insure the return package, including a letter of explanation, order number, shipping label, and all pertinent information.

If you question a company's reputation, check through the Better Business Bureau, Chamber of Commerce, or state and local consumer offices before placing an order.

If you experience difficulties, write the company stating details of your problem. Register the letter and keep the receipt. If you hear nothing within three to four weeks, send a second registered letter reiterating the details with copies to the U.S. Postal Service, Consumer Affairs Office, Washington, D.C. 20260; and the Direct Mail Advertising Association, 240 Park Ave., New York, N.Y. 10017.

---

**A FAMILY BIBLE** once was part of almost every household. Our ancestors often kept a record of births, weddings, deaths, and other events in the big volumes—a custom you might like to revive.

---

## October 7

### The Children's Poet

James Whitcomb Riley once referred to himself as "an elderly child." This approach to life certainly helped him win a place in American literature as the poet of childhood days and happenings. Today is his birthday anniversary. He was born on October 7, 1853, in Greenfield, Indiana.

Even before his death in 1916, schoolchildren in Indiana were celebrating the anniversary. In 1912, he wrote the following to be read in Indiana public schools on the anniversary:

"It may be well for you to remember that the day you are about to celebrate is the birthday of many good men, but if I may be counted the least of these I will be utterly content and happy. I can only thank you and your teachers with a full heart and the fervent hope that the day will prove an equal glory to us all. To the very little children I would say, be simply your own selves, and though even parents, as I sometimes think, do not seem to understand us perfectly, we will be patient with them and love them no less loyally and tenderly."

After Riley's death a hospital for children was built in Indianapolis as a permanent memorial to the poet.

powder are available today, so why not try it?

"Curry-powder. Six ounces of pale-colored turmeric, five ounces of black pepper, 13 ounces of coriander seed, three ounces of cummin seed, two ounces of fenugreek seed, one ounce of Cayenne pepper. All these ingredients are to be ground fine, separately, and well mixed.

"To make curry. Take a fowl, or any white meat, cut it up in joints or small pieces, fry them a light brown in a little butter, and put them on a plate; have ready three middling-sized onions cut fine, and fry them also; then add a tablespoonful and a half of the curry-powder, and two of flour. Mix it smooth, and moisten with a pint of weak broth or water; peel and core a good-sized apple, and cut it in small pieces, and add to the sauce; put the meat in and let it stew gently for an hour. Before serving, skim very carefully and strain the sauce. Plain boiled rice should be served with it."

## October 8

### Mrs. Abell's 1853 Receipt for Curry

From the *Skillful Housewife's Book*, published in 1853 (see April 21), Mrs. Abell first tells the reader how to make curry powder, then gives instructions on making curry. All of the spices called for in the

---

CANNING IDEA: Quinces should be turning golden yellow now, after the first frosts in the North. That's an invitation to a thrifty housewife to make tasty quince jelly or honey.

---

# October 9

## How to Take Care of Electric Blankets

Electric blankets require gentle treatment, both in use and in laundering, to prevent damage to the heating wires and thermostats inside. Be aware that manufacturers always specify laundering, not dry cleaning. Dry cleaning solvents could dissolve plastic insulating coatings on the fine electrical wires that heat the blanket. Avoid bleaches, too.

Never stick pins into the blanket. These also could damage the wires. While the heating controls are turned on, avoid bunching or folding the blanket, tucking in wired areas, or placing anything (a book or pet, for instance) on top of the blanket. Don't sit on the blanket. All of these practices can cause undesirable and potentially damaging hot spots. In an extremely cold room, an ordinary blanket (but only a lightweight one) may be used over an electric blanket if desired. Otherwise, the blanket itself should provide all the warmth you need.

Operate the blanket according to the instructions that come with it. Use the blanket only on the size bed for which the blanket is intended. Place the control where it will sense an average room temperature—not near a window or radiator, in a cold draft or warm-air flow, or under a pillow. Turn off the control in the morning. Do not use an electric blanket on a baby or a person insensitive to heat.

You can wash an electric blanket, either by machine or by hand. But washing restrictions are imposed both by the blanket's electrical components and the type of fibers from which the blanket was manufactured. You ought to know—and follow—the maker's laundering instructions. You should have found these, in brief, on a care label attached to the blanket when you bought it. See April 29 for washing instructions for two fabrics of which some electric blankets are made.

If improperly washed, a blanket may shrink. Shrinkage will bunch up the heating wires. In general, you should use only lukewarm water (100 degrees Fahrenheit). Dissolve a minimum amount of all-purpose detergent in the water and soak the blanket for 15 minutes or so, whether you wash by hand or by machine. If washing by hand, rinse twice in lukewarm water and remove excess water

by squeezing gently. Do not twist the blanket or put it through a wringer.

If you wash in a machine, be sure to keep agitating and tumbling to a minimum. Some makers tell you to limit agitation to one minute at slow speed. Rinse on the regular cycle at slow speed. Spin dry or squeeze gently.

Air drying is the preferred method. Use two parallel lines, placed several feet apart, in the shade outdoors. Drape the blanket across both lines. Use no clothespins. As the blanket dries, return it to its original size by stretching it gently, both across and lengthwise, at the same time smoothing it all you can.

Although drying in a dryer is usually not recommended, it's possible to do so if you use extra care. Follow the maker's instructions for drying a nonelectric blanket. Keep the heat low and use a slow tumbling speed. Avoid excessive tumbling since tumbling tends to shake the wires and electrical parts out of place. If you preheat the dryer for ten minutes before putting the blanket in, you will get more drying action with less tumbling.

You should not iron an electric blanket, but you can use a cool iron to smooth the binding if you wish.

---

DRIP! DRIP! DRIP! Repair dripping faucets at once. A recent study showed that a very small leak can waste as much as 200 gallons of water in a single month.

---

# October 10

**TODAY IN HISTORY:** *Proctor & Gamble began marketing a detergent on Oct. 10, 1933.*

## Dry Fabrics Well to Avoid Mildew

Dampness promotes mildew. Because of this, never let clothing or other articles of fabric lie around damp. Dry soiled clothes before putting them into the hamper. Wash out dishcloths and hang them to dry. Spread out washcloths and damp towels in the bathroom. Stretch out a wet shower curtain. It is the wet curtain left bunched together or sticking to the wall or tub that is most likely to mildew.

Wash soiled garments and household fabrics in plenty of hot sudsy water; rinse well and dry thoroughly and quickly. Fabrics dried slowly may get musty smelling—a sign of mold growth.

When washing musty white cotton materials, add diluted chlorine bleach. (Never use chlorine bleach on silk or wool. Some colored fabrics and some fabrics treated with special finishes may also be affected by chlorine.)

When you iron, sprinkle only as many articles as you can complete that day. Shake out and dry those articles that you will iron another day.

To help keep moisture out of clothing and household fabrics and thus make them less susceptible to mold growth, treat them with water-repellent sprays. Use the sprays on draperies, slipcovers, mattresses, golf bags, overshoes, jackets, and outer garments.

Fungicide products that can be sprayed on fabrics to give them mildew protection are available in aerosol containers. Some germicidal, mothproofing, and water-repellent sprays may also protect against mildew. Read the labels.

# October 11

## Remedies for Special Carpet Problems

Special carpet problems occasionally arise, either through normal wear or from accidents. Here are some you may encounter:

**Fluffing or shedding.** Balls of fluff that appear on the surface of certain new carpets are bits of fiber left in the pile during manufacturing. They do not indicate poor quality and are gradually removed by vacuum cleaning.

**Rippling.** A rise in humidity may cause temporary rippling in wall-to-wall carpet. If the ripples do not disappear with drier weather, a carpet installer probably can correct the problem.

**Static electricity.** If static is a problem in your carpet, it can be reduced by using a humidifier or an anti-static spray. If static becomes serious, call a professional rug cleaner and ask his advice. (See also December 14.)

**Sprouts and pills.** Sometimes a tuft will rise, or "sprout," above the surface of a carpet. Don't pull it out. Snip it off with scissors. Use the same technique if little balls, or pills, appear.

**Burns.** A small burn can be improved by clipping off blackened fiber ends with scissors, dampening with a detergent solution, and then blotting. A deep or wide burn can be corrected only by retufting or patching.

**Indentations.** Use rustproof cups under heavy pieces of furniture to help prevent permanent indentations in carpet. When furniture is moved, an indentation can often be remedied by gently rubbing it with the edge of a plastic ruler. If the pile is still matted, hold a steam iron an inch above it just long enough for the fibers to absorb the hot moisture. Then fluff the pile with your hand.

## *October* **12**

### Do You Understand All Meat-Cooking Terms?

What's the difference between "pan-frying" and "pan-broiling" a piece of meat? When we encountered these terms in the revised meat charts that are reprinted in the Appendix, we checked several good cooks and found considerable confusion. So it seems advisable to offer definitions for all terms applied to cooking meat:

**Roasting.** The meat is placed fat side up on a rack in a shallow roasting pan in the oven. No water is added and the meat is not covered. Roasting is a dry-heat cooking method. If the pan is covered or water added, the meat becomes a pot roast.

**Broiling.** The oven regulator is set for broiling. The meat is placed on a rack in the broiler pan, two to five inches from the source of heat—the distance depending on the type of meat. After the top side has been browned, this side is seasoned (if desired) and the meat is then turned and browned on the other side.

**Pan-broiling.** Meat cuts one inch or less thick are pan-broiled in a heavy frying pan or on a griddle. No fat or water is added and the meat is not covered. The meat should be cooked slowly and turned several times. Fat is poured off as it accumulates.

**Pan-frying.** A small amount of fat usually is added to the pan or allowed to accumulate. The thin slices of meat are browned on both sides. The pan is not covered.

**Deep-fat frying.** Here, as with other foods that are deep-fried, the meat is immersed in hot fat.

**Braising.** The meat is browned slowly on all sides and the drippings are poured off. Fat is usually added during browning to keep the meat from sticking. After browning, a small amount of liquid is added if necessary—and the pan is covered tightly. The meat is then simmered on top of the range or in a slow oven.

**Cooking in liquid.** The meat can be browned on all sides if desired, then covered with water or stock. Simmer (do not boil) in a covered utensil until tender.

## Panning—a Good Way to Cook Some Vegetables

Panning—cooking shredded or sliced vegetables in a small amount of fat and water on top of the range—is a good way to prepare snap beans, cabbage, carrots, corn, spinach, and summer squash. See the Boiling Guide in the Appendix for length of time to cook and amounts of vegetable and other ingredients needed for six servings (½ cup each).

Directions for panning:

Shred or slice vegetable.

Heat fat (butter, margarine, or drippings) in a heavy frying pan over moderate heat.

Add vegetable and sprinkle with salt.

Add water and cover pan to hold in steam.

Cook over low heat until vegetable is tender; stir occasionally to prevent sticking.

For a variation, add finely chopped onion or onion juice before cooking. Or add bits of crumbled crisp bacon or diced ham to cooked vegetable.

# October 14

## Do You Know the Many Kinds of Lamb Chops?

Like lamb chops? Most people do. But do you recognize—and know how to cook—all of the various kinds of chops? Here's a rundown:

From the loin: loin chop and boneless double loin chop. Both cuts can be broiled, pan-fried, or pan-broiled.

From the rack (the body section just behind the shoulder): rib chops and Frenched rib chops. Cooking choices are the same as for loin chops.

From the shoulder: blade bone chop, arm chop, and Saratoga chop. Braise, broil, or pan-fry these chops.

For identification of these and other lamb cuts, see the chart in the Appendix.

Your choice of chops may be the result of personal preference, the cooking method to be used, or your budget. For an unusual way to cook lamb chops, see tomorrow's recipe.

# October 15

## Broiled Parmesan Lamb Chops

The Parmesan topping of this recipe gives a flavor which beautifully complements the broiled lamb.

**4 shoulder or loin chops about 1-inch thick**
**¼ cup grated Parmesan cheese**
**2 Tbs. butter or margarine, softened**
**½ tsp. salt**
**⅛ tsp. pepper**

Broil chops 3 to 4 inches from the source of heat for 8 minutes or until lightly browned. Turn; broil 5 more minutes or to desired degree of doneness. Meanwhile, combine remaining ingredients and blend well. After broiling second side, spread cheese mixture on chops; broil 2 to 3 minutes longer or until cheese is lightly browned. This will serve 4.

# October 16

## Make Pomander Balls for Christmas Gifts

Pomander balls are easy-to-make gifts that children can help make and that will be well received by anyone on your Christmas list. Their spicy odor will perfume closets and dresser drawers and last for a long time. They are said to repel moths.

To make them, you will need oranges, lemons, or limes, whole cloves, ground cinnamon, oris root (obtainable in drugstores), net, ribbon, paper bags, a skewer or other sharp-pointed instrument, and newspaper or foil.

Wash the fruit and wipe dry. Insert the cloves in the skin so that the entire surface is covered. Use the skewer to start the holes if the skins are hard to penetrate. Do not insert the cloves in straight lines or the skins may split.

Put each clove-covered piece of fruit into a paper bag together with a heaping teaspoon of cinnamon and oris root, which have been mixed in equal parts. Shake the bag so that the fruit is well coated with the mixture. Remove the fruit, wrap it loosely with newspaper or foil, and store in a dry place until hardened (three to four weeks). Wrap each ball in net and tie with ribbon. Leave a loop of ribbon so that the ball may be suspended from a clothes hanger.

# October 17

## Does Your Kitchen Have All Essential Cookware?

Every homemaker has her own preferences about what cooking equipment she wants in her kitchen. Some items, however, must be considered essential for everyone. We have seen an interesting list, made up for the Committee of Stainless Steel Producers of the American Iron and Steel Institute. The list was aimed at helping brides-to-be select an essential kitchen trousseau. Perhaps you'd like to check off any items that you don't now have—and consider buying them.

Saucepan (1 quart), saucepan (2 quart), saucepan (3 quart), double-boiler inset (2 or 3 quart), skillet (8 inch), skillet (12 inch), Dutch oven (5 to 8 quarts), pressure cooker, and a roasting pan and rack.

Kitchen tool set (usual set includes spoon, pierced spoon, fork, narrow spatula, pancake turner, soup and gravy ladle), and a set of kitchen knives—a paring knife, with a short tapered blade 2½ to 3½ inches long; a utility knife, with a slender blade from 5 to 7 inches long, useful when the

## Make Warm Shearling Clothing Now

If you like to sew, plan now to make clothing that is so warm it will fend off the coldest temperatures winter is likely to bring.

Wool shearlings (sheepskins with the wool left on) may be fashioned into mittens, vests, hats, and coats. A coat, if purchased ready-made, could cost more than $200. Home sewing of shearlings saves a considerable amount of money. Perspiration-absorbency combined with warmth makes shearlings perfect for ski jackets and winter boots. A special tanning process only recently developed makes shearlings washable—they remain soft and flexible even after repeated launderings.

Since leather is more difficult to sew than fabrics, it's best to select a pattern simple in design —either homemade or selected from a pattern book. Place the pattern on the leather side of the shearling (wool side down), hold it in place, and trace around it with chalk. After tracing the pattern, cut the shearling by slicing the leather side with a safety razor. Use caution in cutting so that you do not damage the wool on the opposite side. Because the size of shearlings is limited, you may have to piece them together to fit a particular pattern. When the garment is completed this piecing

paring knife is too small; narrow slicer, with a narrow, flexible blade 7 to 12 inches long; a chef's knife (also called a French knife), with a sturdy angled blade 8 to 10 inches long; and a carving knife, with a blade 9 inches or longer—colander, grater, meat thermometer.

Measuring spoons (¼ teaspoon, ½ teaspoon, teaspoon, tablespoon), measuring cups (¼ cup, ⅓ cup, ½ cup, 1 cup—or a marked glass measuring cup), mixing bowls.

Covered casserole, tea kettle, coffeemaker (4-cup electric or top-of-stove), coffeemaker (12-cup electric for company), toaster, can opener, canister set (for coffee, tea, flour, and sugar), and a baking or cookie sheet.

**SHOPPING REMINDER:** Winter squash should start to be plentiful now. A hard, tough rind indicates full maturity. A squash that seems heavy for its size will have a thick wall and therefore more edible flesh.

is not noticeable.

The shearling pieces may be sewn together in two ways: By carefully stitching by hand, using heavy-duty needle and thread, or by punching holes at regular intervals along the edge of the pieces and lacing them together with leather. Leather laces are oil tanned and can be washed with the garment.

Shearlings can be washed in an automatic washer using warm water. Hot water will shrink the leather and make it hard and brittle. Use a small amount of mild soap or detergent. A detergent that contains sodium perborate will cause the shearling

to deteriorate (check the detergent label). Air dry in a warm room or tumble dry on the lowest heat setting in a dryer. Never expose shearlings to direct heat, such as a radiator. When the shearling is dry, lightly comb the wool with a comb that has widely spaced teeth, such as that found in pet supply stores. If you use a fabric softener in the rinse water, the wool will not mat as much and less combing will be needed to fluff the wool.

Other uses for shearlings are suggested in a pamphlet "Washable Shearlings" for sale by the Superintendent of Documents, Washington, D.C.

Washable shearlings are available from the following distributors: Alconox, Inc., 215 Park Ave. South, New York, N.Y. 10003; Bucks County Fur Products Company, 220 North Ambler St. Rear, Quakertown, Pa. 18951; Deltan Company, c/o Alfred C. McIlvaine, Box 560, Bristol, Pa. 19007; Pierini Tanning and Dyeing Corporation, 28 Paris St., Newark, N.J. 07105; Evenpressure Company, 2501 7th St., Box 25, Tuscaloosa, Ala. 35404; and Thera-Fleece Company, 2650 Ocean Parkway, Brooklyn, N.Y. 11235.

## *October* 19

### What Homemakers Should Know about Butter

Butter is made by churning pasteurized cream. It must have at least 80 percent milkfat by Federal law. Salt and coloring may be added. Whipped butter is regular butter that has been whipped for easier spreading. Whipping increases the volume.

Unsalted butter may be labeled sweet or unsalted. Some prefer the flavor of unsalted butter.

When using whipped butter in recipes in

place of regular butter, use one-third to one-half more than the recipe calls for if the measurement is by volume (in cups). If the measurement is by weight, use the amount called for in the recipe.

Butter readily picks up odors, therefore store it in its original wrappings or container or in a tightly closed dish. It should always be refrigerated.

Butter is usually sold in pound, ½-pound, and ¼-pound packages. It may be less expensive in larger packages. Butter not to be used immediately may be frozen. It can be kept frozen up to a month.

To be assured of high quality butter, look for the USDA grade shield on the package. The grade shield (AA, A, or B) means that the butter has been tested and graded by government graders. Butter graders also test the keeping quality.

U.S. Grade AA butter is made from high-quality fresh sweet cream, has a smooth and creamy texture with good spreadability, and has salt completely dissolved and blended in the right amount. It has a delicate, sweet flavor with a pleasing aroma. U.S. Grade A butter is made from fresh cream, is fairly smooth in texture, and has a pleasing flavor. U.S. Grade B butter, usually made from selected sour cream, may have a slightly acid flavor.

## *October* **20**

### Do You Take Proper Care of Your Dishwasher?

Automatic dishwashers in our opinion rank near the top of homemaker aids that have been developed during this century. But yours will give you good service only if you take proper care of it.

Clean the inside of the door and the outside of the dishwasher occasionally with a damp cloth and mild detergent. The interior and the tub are essentially self-cleaning.

Check the bottom of the tub and the filter now and then and remove any insoluble food particles that may have accumulated. Be careful not to burn yourself on the heating rod or coil if the dishwasher has just stopped.

If you live in a hard-water area, lime deposits may form on the bottom of the tub and on the door. To remove them, start the dishwasher on the rinse action. While the tub is filling, open the door and add one-half cup of white vinegar. Do not use detergent. Then let the dishwasher finish its cycle.

If your dishwasher doesn't operate, make sure the door is tightly closed and the latch is in the lock position. Check to see if a household fuse may have blown or a circuit breaker may have tripped. If this has happened, unplug other appliances from the circuit before trying the dishwasher again. Make sure the plug is firmly in the electric outlet if your dishwasher is a portable model.

If your dishwasher fails to clean properly, test

the water temperature with a metal cooking or baking thermometer after the second fill. If it is below 140 degrees Fahrenheit, adjust your water heater, making an allowance for loss of heat in the pipes between the heater and the dishwasher. Also, check to see that filters and screens inside the dishwasher are clean and that hoses are free of kinks.

## *October* **21**

### Prepare for Fabric Stain Removal

Removing stains from fabrics is a problem that has no easy solution. The problem increases somewhat in complexity with introduction of each new

fabric—and there have been many new fabrics developed in recent years. Different stains require different removal methods; what removes one stain may set another. Different fabrics also require different stain treatments. These two variables—the kind of stain and kind of fabric—have resulted in the need for a long list of removal methods. Some stains can be removed at home. Some need professional treatment.

Prompt treatment is essential in any case. Many stains that can be removed easily when fresh are difficult or impossible to remove later, especially if they are set by heat.

This means being prepared for stain emergencies. You should have the necessary supplies on hand, and you should have a source of instructions to suit the removal method to the kind of stain and fabric.

Four kinds of remover materials are needed—absorbent materials (powders, cloths, blotters, etc.), detergents, solvents, and chemical removers such as bleaches. You must know how to use each of the four materials—under a great variety of conditions and for a long list of stains and fabrics.

Where do you get this know-how? We investigated the problem, hoping to bring you necessary information. But we soon found that the subject of stain removal is too extensive for the scope of this Almanac.

Instead we urge you to include in your homemaker's library an excellent government bulletin, "Removing Stains from Fabrics," Home and Garden Bulletin No. 62. This 32-page pamphlet is being constantly updated by the Consumer and Food Economics Research Division of the Agricultural Research Services. We have a succession of editions, dating back to World War II, our latest costing 20 cents. Each has been very helpful.

# October **22**

## What to Do about Spills on Carpets and Rugs

Act promptly. Have on hand a special purpose carpet-cleaning detergent available in supermarkets or hardware stores. Also keep a nonflammable dry-cleaning fluid. When an accident occurs, take these steps:

1. Remove the excess immediately. Take up semisolids with a spoon. Soak up liquids with a clean white cloth, facial tissue, or paper towel.

2. Apply a small quantity of dry-cleaning fluid. Do not use carbon tetrachloride, gasoline, or lighter fluid. The fumes could be toxic if the room is not well ventilated. Pat gently with tissue, working from edge to center of stain. Do not rub.

3. Dampen the spot with a solution of one teaspoon of a mild powdered detergent in one cup of water.

4. Apply a pad of tissue one-half-inch thick and hold it in place with a weight. Check occasionally to see if the tissue has absorbed all the liquid. If some liquid remains, apply a new pad. The carpet should be dry within six hours.

If some stain remains, repeat steps 2, 3, and 4.

When dry, brush gently to restore fluffiness.

Spills such as blood, furniture dyes, lipstick, indelible ink, paint, and rust need special solvents and professional care.

You can get further information from a useful booklet, "Carpet and Rug Care Guide," published by the Carpet and Rug Institute, Inc., Dalton, Ga. 30720, and possibly available from a carpet store in your vicinity. Also see October 21.

# October 23

## Our Indian Succotash, a One-Dish Meal

In pioneer days when warm southwest winds brought mild weather at this time of year, early Americans called it Indian summer. This was the time when pioneer cooks were likely to prepare a seasonal feast of succotash, using the autumn's harvest of beans and corn as the Indians had taught them to do.

Our recipe came from a friend whose family traced it back to the Indians of early Rhode Island. According to the story told through generations of our friend's family, the Indians combined the beans and corn with bear meat. Our friend substituted pork sausage—and that's what our recipe calls for.

Cover 2 10-ounce or 1 18-ounce package of frozen speckled butter beans with water, bring to a boil and simmer until almost tender, about 20 minutes. Add 2 10-ounce boxes frozen cut corn, and continue cooking just until corn is thawed. Add 1 pound link sausage which has been cooked, drained, and cut into bite-sized pieces. Season with 1 teaspoon sugar and salt to taste. Mix well and serve immediately. This, with crusty bread, will make a one-pot meal for 6.

If speckled butter beans are not available, you may substitute lima beans.

**BLANCHE STUART SCOTT made a solo airplane flight on Oct. 23, 1910, at Fort Wayne, Ind. She had received instructions from Glenn Curtiss.**

## Tips for Cleaning Kitchen, Laundry, and Bathroom

So many different finishes are found these days on kitchen, laundry, and bathroom equipment that you can't always be sure what products are safe for cleaning exterior or interior surfaces. Some cleaning products may cause staining, discoloring, or even scratches on the finish that you hope to keep spick-and-span.

To avoid this, your first good tip is to consult any literature that may have come with the equipment and any cleaning directions given. A second good tip is to try to identify the finishes the manufacturer applied to your major appliances and then suit your cleaning to what you find. Half a dozen different finishes may have been used on a single appliance.

You may hope that your appliances are coated with porcelain enamel, a durable and easily cleaned glasslike coating that is fused to the base metal (steel, iron, or aluminum) at furnace temperatures up to 1,600 degrees Fahrenheit. Some finishes may resemble porcelain but actually be any one of several plastics or other less durable coatings. We are told that acrylic enamel has been applied to practically all refrigerator exteriors and to the tops of about half of all clothes dryers manufactured since 1965. Such finishes require special treatment.

The question is, how can you distinguish porcelain enamel from ordinary baked enamel or plastic coating? That's a toughie.

If you're buying a new appliance, ask to see the maker's "spec" sheet. Or ask the salesman to take a dime and rub it firmly across a *hidden* area of the finish. If the dime leaves a permanent scratch, the finish is not porcelain enamel. On the other hand, rough usage can chip porcelain enamel, but

modern coatings have been so improved that this damage is less likely to occur. Chipped porcelain can be repaired by professionals (refer to the Yellow Pages).

How do you suit your cleaning methods to other surfaces? If you have any doubts, use nothing more than a mild detergent—and never anything abrasive. Wipe up spills promptly. Check the directions before using commercial cleaners.

A helpful booklet, "Cleaning Tips for Kitchen, Laundry, and Bathroom," is available from the Porcelain Enamel Institute, Inc., 1900 L St. N.W., Washington, D.C. 20036. If you are considering buying a new appliance, the institute has another helpful booklet, "Knowing Your Home Appliances."

# October 25

**TODAY IN HISTORY:** *The Tappan Company demonstrated an electronic range at a press conference in New York City on Oct. 25, 1955.*

## Housekeeping without Power: Cooking

Feeding your family in the absence of both electricity and gas is a tough proposition. But it has been done—through much of world history. And it can be done again.

A return to a wood-burning stove or range may make sense if you can locate one, have the space for it, and can get fuel. This type of cooking also provides heat for the home. See September 20.

Can you place a wood-burning range in the garage? Perhaps there's clearance to one side of the space needed for the car. Run a smoke pipe through the wall or roof. For safety, do not use the range until you have moved the family car outside. You may also have an outbuilding you can use, or you may want to build a small addition to the house.

Camping or backyard cooking equipment, of course, is a less strenuous choice for feeding your hungry horde. This equipment, however, may be fueled with charcoal, briquettes, Sterno, or propane, which may be in short supply or not available. Perhaps you can burn wood instead, in a brick or stone backyard fireplace. (Be sure that there is good ventilation if you use any camping fuels indoors or in a sheltered spot.)

Adjustable grills are available to fit any fireplace. They move up or down and swing in or out. Look, too, for a hinged wire grill that you can hold over the fire to cook meats and toast bread.

Be sure to include among your supplies a hand can opener and a hand eggbeater.

Stock your pantry shelves with some main dish canned foods that can be easily heated —hearty soups, stews, hash, and chili, for instance. Dried foods, including milk, cocoa, instant tea and coffee, would also be helpful to have on hand. A stroll up and down the supermarket aisles with powerless cooking in mind will suggest many other canned and dried foods for emergency use.

**TRANSFERRING AUTUMN LEAF patterns to white paper, in color, is an appealing activity for children during the fall days. Use wax crayons to apply one or more colors to one entire surface of the leaf. Place the leaf waxed side down on paper, cover with another sheet of paper, and press gently with a hot iron.**

# October 26

## Caring for Stainless Steel Pots and Pans

Before using a new stainless steel utensil, check the manufacturer's instructions on care and use. Wash the utensil thoroughly in hot detergent suds to remove any packing dust.

When cooking, make sure pots and pans sit evenly on the heating unit.

Washing by hand in hot sudsy water or in a dishwasher with conventional detergents usually is the only requirement for keeping stainless utensils bright and shiny. Prompt drying prevents water spots.

A cloth, a sponge, or a fiber pad can be used for cleaning stainless steel. Stainless steel pads or sponges, available at houseware and hardware outlets, are also ideal cleansing utensils. Always rub in the direction of the polishing lines of the metal to retain the finish.

For really stubborn deposits and burned-on food, either add baking soda to the water or use a paste made with ammonia, water, and a fine scouring powder.

Dark areas may have formed because you have inadvertently overheated your cookware. They won't harm the metal, but you may want to clean them for the sake of appearance. To do so, scour vigorously with stainless steel wool and a mildly abrasive household cleanser. There are also several very good commercial cleaners designed just for this task. But prevention is better than a cure. Use even heat when cooking, and don't leave empty equipment on the lighted burners.

## You Can Harvest Jerusalem Artichokes Now

Jerusalem artichokes are native to North America, yet these vegetables are not as well known as they should be. A member of the sunflower family, the plants grow from seven to 12 feet tall and bear small flowers in late September.

You can make your first harvest of the white-fleshed, knobby tubers about now—after the first frosts have killed the stalks. Loosen the soil with a spade and pull up the mass of tubers at the base of the stalks. Turn over the soil carefully so as not to miss tubers which sometimes develop as much as a foot away from the stalk. Since the tubers keep best in the ground, you may want to dig only a hill at a time, or what you need for one or two meals. Old-timers thought Jerusalem artichokes were best when dug in the spring after the ground thawed.

Standard cookbooks will give you recipes for preparing them. Creaming is our favorite. For a lucious pickle recipe, see the entry for October 28.

---

**TWO PEOPLE** are much better than one when it comes to making a dress. Ask a friend to check whether the pattern fits and to mark the hems.

---

**LUBRICATE A ZIPPER** when it becomes hard to work by rubbing the "lead" (actually graphite) of a soft pencil over the metal.

---

**SAVE WATER** and heating fuel by taking showers instead of bathing. A quick shower uses far less water than a bath.

---

## October 28

### A Recipe for Jerusalem Artichoke Pickles

½ large cabbage
3 lbs. red onions
1½ red bell peppers
Salt
6 lbs. Jerusalem artichokes
1 cup dark brown sugar
¾ Tbs. turmeric
1 Tbs. mustard seed
¼ tsp. red pepper
¼ tsp. black pepper
1 Tbs. dry mustard
2 Tbs. celery seed
2 qts. cider vinegar
½ cup flour

*Note: Round all the spice measurements.*

Cut the cabbage, onions, and peppers into small pieces and place in a kettle. Cover with salt water (use about ½ cup salt) and let stand overnight. Scrub and scrape the artichokes, cutting out any discoloration. Cut them into small pieces, place in a second kettle, cover with salt water, and let stand overnight.

In the morning, drain all of the vegetables. Add ½ cup of the brown sugar and the spices to the vinegar, and bring to a boil. Add the cabbage, onions, and peppers, and boil for 20 minutes. Add the artichokes and boil for an additional 5 minutes.

Make a paste with the flour, the remaining sugar, and some vinegar from the kettle. Add this to the mixture and stir until it begins to thicken. Depending upon the sharpness of the vinegar, it may be necessary to add more sugar in order to sweeten the taste and darken the mixture. Cool before packing in sterilized jars. (DH)

## October 29

### What Homemakers Should Know about Cream

The U.S. Food and Drug Administration has set up standards for many of the different types of cream shipped in interstate commerce. These standards give minimum milkfat requirements for each type.

Light cream, sometimes called coffee or table cream, must have at least 18 percent milkfat under Federal standards and most state standards. For maximum shelf life, do not return unused light cream from a pitcher to its original container. Store it separately in the refrigerator, or better, pour from the container only the amount to be used at one time.

Half-and-half is a mixture of milk and cream, homogenized. Under state requirements, it must have between 10 and 12 percent fat. Half-and-half can be mixed at home, using half homogenized whole milk and half table cream. As with light cream, do not return unused half-and-half to its original container.

Light whipping cream must have at least 30 percent milkfat under Federal standards. To whip this kind of cream, have both the bowl and the cream well chilled.

Heavy whipping cream must have at least 36 percent milkfat. Although heavy whipping cream is more easily whipped than light whipping cream, it is still a good idea to have the cream and the bowl well chilled. Do not overwhip heavy cream, it may get grainy.

Sour cream is made by adding lactic-acid bacteria culture to light cream. It is smooth and thick and contains at least 18 percent milkfat. Sour cream is sometimes called "salad cream" or "cream dressing" in supermarkets.

Sour half-and-half is the same as half-and-half except that a culture has been added. It can replace sour cream if you prefer less fat.

---

**DID GEORGE WASHINGTON eat hot dogs?** He may have. Some researchers think they were developed as long ago as the 13th century. In 1952, the city of Frankfurt, Germany, held a celebration for the dog named after it.

---

**GET FULL FLAVOR from iced coffee** by using ice cubes made from a fresh pot of coffee. Using cubes frozen from plain water dilutes the drink.

---

## Pumpkin Fruit Bowl for Halloween

While you are buying a pumpkin for a Halloween jack-o-lantern, get another for a seasonal fruit bowl, an old custom we think deserves to be revived. Choose a pumpkin that's quite large and squat.

To convert the pumpkin into a bowl, rest it on a table with its bottom end down. Then cut it in half at midpoint, or perhaps a little above, slicing parallel to the table.

Remove seeds and membrane from the lower half. Then, if desired, you may scoop out the pumpkin flesh and put it aside for pie making, but be careful not to cut through the rind of the pumpkin. Finally, with a sharp knife cut jagged points or "teeth" around the top edge of the pumpkin's bottom half.

Line the inside of the pumpkin bowl with corn silk (if available) or stuff in a lining of colorful autumn leaves. Fill the interior with polished apples, pears, and other available fruits and nuts. This makes a beautiful centerpiece.

## October Potpourri for Homemakers

Save money by making your own yogurt. (It will taste better, too.) There are several brands of yogurt makers on the market now. Look in the housewares section of department stores.

Add lemon juice to a nearly empty catsup bottle. Shake well and add to mayonnaise for Russian salad dressing. Or add oil, vinegar, and your favorite seasonings. *Voilà!* You have a dressing for your salad. (HD)

Gift idea: Personalized bottles of wine—the name of the recipient printed on the labels. Write to Hudson Valley Wine Company, Highland, N.Y. 12528, for information.

To keep sprouts from developing when you remove a live tree or bush, use a herbicide such as 2, 4-D or 2, 4, 5-T. Apply it carefully at the line where bark joins wood within a day of cutting.

To avoid loss of silverware, count the pieces when you return them to the drawer or chest.

## Your Own Reminders:

# November 1

## Prepare to Administer First Aid

Every homemaker ought to prepare for the emergency that may never come. You owe it to your loved ones to do so. They each will have a better hold on life if an adult member of the household knows the latest first-aid techniques. Who will it be? In most homes, the homemaker herself is likely to be the person most often available.

Taking a course in first aid is the best answer. In many communities, such a course is given as part of the adult education program. If not, suggest to your local administrators that one be given —and invite a few of your neighbors and friends to accompany you to the class.

Meanwhile, get yourself a book on first aid. In our opinion, you can't beat the *First Aid Textbook*, sponsored by the American National Red Cross and published by Doubleday & Company, Garden City, N.Y. 11530. Copies may be obtained from local offices of the Red Cross and bookstores. Or write directly to Doubleday.

Make sure you understand mouth-to-mouth or mouth-to-nose artificial respiration, the methods now recommended. Learn, too, the recommended procedure to stop bleeding—pressure applied directly to the wound with a clean bandage.

You ought to have a first-aid kit in your house. These are available assembled from drugstores.

As a homemaker, you may also feel a need for guidance in caring for ill members of your family. You can get this advice from a number of books. Two that are good:

*Modern Home Remedies* by Morris Fishbein, M.D. Dr. Fishbein has written a syndicated newspaper column for years. His book is published by Doubleday & Company.

*The Family Handbook of Home Nursing and Medical Care* by I. J. Rossman and Doris R. Schwartz, physician and nurse. Publisher is Random House, New York, N.Y. 10022.

**NYLON FOOTBALL PANTS were introduced on Nov. 1, 1941. The occasion was a scoreless Army-Notre Dame game played in the mud at Yankee Stadium.**

## November 2

### Do You Offer Rodents Winter Homes in Outbuildings?

Make your property less attractive to mice and rats by checking your storage areas and outbuildings at this time of year. A pile of cushions from outdoor furniture makes a very attractive nesting area for rodents. Don't stack them—hang them separately from beams or from hooks along the wall. Try not to accumulate boxes or piles of old rags or papers. These make happy homes for mice. If you store outdoor electrical cords for the winter, hang them out of the reach of rodents. They sometimes gnaw the insulation, a preliminary to future short circuits, shocks, or even a fire. (JOP)

## November 3

### Market Still Needs a GOOD Jar Opener

Screw-on jar caps have long been a problem. The canning jars of yesteryear always seemed to resist efforts to open them—and someone with a strong grip was often called to break the seal. Knocking the cap against the edge of a table or rapping it with a table knife sometimes helped.

About a quarter of a century ago the perfect opener came into the Stevenson kitchen, one that we never have known to fail. It's very simple—a Y-shaped metal casting with serrations on the inner edge of each jaw of the Y. You push the cap against the serrations—hard—and turn the jar. It always works. The opener is mounted solidly on a wall or cabinet. The Y part hinges downward while not in use. The wall mount includes a bottle opener.

Can you get one like it? Apparently not. We remember that when we got ours it was called a "Jam Handy." It remained on the market for several years—but we have not been able to find it of late. We do find many other openers in the housewares departments we have visited for just this purpose. We have tried all of them. But in our opinion none is equal to the one we have, now (unfortunately) a lame duck. Why didn't ours survive in the marketplace? Largely, we suspect, because no advertiser believed in it enough to push it hard.

# November 4

## Buying Meat for a Freezer: Do You Save?

At this time of year, you can often find beef available at a favorable price, particularly young steers raised locally under 4-H or FFA programs. But whether you will save money by stocking a freezer depends on a number of variables.

When you buy a whole carcass or side (half a carcass, including both fore- and hindquarters), you get the entire range of cuts, both high- and low-priced. These will include some you might not normally buy. Most butchers who specialize in preparing meat for the freezer will convert cuts a buyer does not want to use "as is" into ground meat or stew meat.

A carcass, side, or quarter is normally sold by its gross weight. This means the weight before cutting and trimming. The amount of usable meat you take home will be considerably less, of course. For a beef carcass, cutting loss (bone, fat trim, shrink, etc.) could vary from 20 to 30 percent or more. A 25-percent cutting loss (not unusual) means that a 300-pound side of beef will yield 225 pounds.

A rule of thumb for carcass beef is: 25 percent waste, 25 percent ground beef and stew meat, 25 percent steaks, and 25 percent roasts. Not all of the steaks and roasts, however, are from the loin and rib, the most tender portions.

You should be aware of the difference in the kinds of cuts you get from a hindquarter as compared with a forequarter. A hindquarter of beef will yield more steaks and roasts, but will cost more per pound than a forequarter. A forequarter of beef, while containing the delectable rib roast, has more less-tender cuts. The chuck, or shoulder, makes up about one-half of the forequarter's weight. The yield of usable lean meat, however, is greater in the forequarter than in the hindquarter.

If you don't want all of the cuts that come with a side or quarter, of if your freezer space is limited, consider buying wholesale cuts. For example, you might buy a beef short loin, from which you will get porterhouse, T-bone, top loin steaks, plus some ground beef or stew meat; a whole pork loin, for pork loin roasts and chops; or a leg of lamb, for several leg chops or steaks and a roast. Wholesale cuts usually are bought from locker and freezer provisioners and others who sell meat as sides or quarters, although sometimes they can be bought at a supermarket.

A third alternative is buying at retail only the particular cuts you prefer. By watching for advertised "specials" on these cuts, you can often save money. But remember, also, retail cuts usually must be rewrapped for long-term freezer storage —and the cost of this wrapping paper or foil should be taken into account.

In determining whether or not you can save money by buying meat in quantity remember to consider the yield of meat you will get from the carcass, the quality of the meat, and the costs of cutting, wrapping, and quick-freezing. You should find out, when buying carcass meat, whether these costs are included in the price per pound, of if you'll have to pay additional for them. The usual charge is 8 to 10 cents per pound.

---

**PLANNING TO BUY SLEEPWARE for a child for Christmas? Check its flammability. Under U.S. government regulations, pajamas, nightgowns, and robes in sizes O through 6X made after July 29, 1972, either must pass a strict flame test or have a conspicuous "flammable" label.**

---

## Learn Yield Grade in Buying Wholesale Beef

Consumers who buy only retail cuts need not be concerned about yield grades since these grades apply only to carcasses and wholesale cuts. In buying retail cuts, however, check to see that excess fat and bone have been removed.

But if you are buying carcasses or wholesale cuts, you should know about yield grades, and seek to buy beef which has been yield graded. The shield-shaped yield-grade mark can be found stamped once on each quarter or wholesale cut—it is not rolled on the length of the carcass as is the quality-grade shield.

Literally, the yield grades measure the yield of boneless, closely trimmed retail cuts from the high-value parts of the carcass: the round, loin, rib, and chuck. However, they also reflect differences in total yield of retail cuts. The following percentages represent expected yields of retail cuts by yield grade.

Yield Grade 1—the carcass will yield 79.8 percent or more in retail cuts.

Yield Grade 2—75.2 to 79.7 percent.

Yield Grade 3—70.6 to 75.1 percent.

Yield Grade 4—66 to 70.5 percent.

Yield Grade 5—65.9 percent or less.

Obviously you can afford to pay somewhat more for a higher-yielding carcass—or if no price differential is charged, you get more for your money.

---

TIMESAVER: When a recipe calls for two cups of brown sugar firmly packed, you need not measure. Just add an entire one-pound package.

---

# November 6

## How Much Meat Should You Buy?

How much meat you should buy at any one time depends on how much you want to spend at one time, the amount of freezer storage space available, and how much your family consumes. You will need to do some figuring.

Properly wrapped meat cuts, stored at zero degrees Fahrenheit or lower, maintain their quality for a long time. This varies with the kind of meat. The times below represent a range within which you can store the meat with reasonable expectation that it will maintain its quality. Meats can be kept safely frozen for longer periods, but they are apt to lose quality.

Beef, 8 to 12 months; lamb, 8 to 12 months; pork, fresh, 4 to 8 months; ground beef and lamb, 3 to 4 months; and pork sausage, 1 to 3 months.

On the average, one cubic foot of freezer space will accommodate 35 to 40 pounds of cut and wrapped meat, though it will be slightly less if the meat is packaged in odd shapes.

Meat should be initially frozen at $-10$ degrees F. or lower as quickly as possible. If you are freezing it yourself, allow space between packages for air to circulate.

The amount of food frozen at one time should be limited in order to get quick and efficient freezing. Only the amount that will freeze within 24 hours should be put into the freezer. Usually that will be about two or three pounds to each cubic foot of freezer capacity.

For large meat purchases, it is usually best to have the freezing done by a commercial establishment properly equipped to do the job. Quick freezing causes less damage to the meat fibers. Slower freezing causes more of the cells to rupture, due to formation of large ice crystals, so that more meat juices are lost when the meat is thawed.

Proper wrapping of meat for the freezer is as important as proper storage. Use a moistureproof wrap, such as heavy aluminum foil, heavily waxed freezer paper, or specially laminated papers. Wrap the meat closely, eliminating all air if possible. Double thicknesses of waxed paper should be placed between chops and steaks to prevent sticking. Seal the packages well and date them. The rule in using frozen meat should be: first in, first out.

Improperly wrapped packages will allow air to enter and draw moisture from the meat, resulting in "freezer burn," or meat which is dry and less flavorful.

It is perfectly safe to refreeze meat that has been kept refrigerated after thawing. However, refreezing of defrosted meat is not usually recommended because there is some loss of meat quality.

## November 7

### What to Do about a Smoking Fireplace

Even a fireplace that's correctly designed may smoke at times. One of these times is when an exhaust fan is running. The fan may create such a draft that air is drawn down the chimney. The fire, of course, will smoke. Cure: Close the door to the room (kitchen or bath) where the exhaust fan is operating, or open a window near the fan.

A fire may send smoke out into the room just as you are starting it because the chimney is still cold. The cold air inside the chimney settles downward, causing a downdraft. Reverse the draft by holding a burning newspaper up inside the flue as you ignite the fire.

A modern well-built home may be so snug and tight that the hearth fire can't get enough air—and consequently smokes. Provide air—and a draft—by opening a window just a crack.

In some cases the fireplace opening is too high. Raising the fire may be the cure in such cases. Experiment by placing one or two layers of bricks over the section of the hearth that's inside the chimney. If this does it, then install the bricks permanently.

## November 8

### Resilient Tiles Look Like Other Kinds of Flooring

Resilient tiles do not all look like the kind of flooring we have long been accustomed to seeing underfoot. Some tiles have the look of real wood, for instance handcrafted parquet flooring. And you must look twice to be sure some resilient tiles aren't brick or slate. On many tiles, surface embossing heightens the effect of wood or brick textures. All of this will be good to know the next time you are considering putting down new flooring.

---

CALIFORNIANS ARE REMINDED that they can get a lot of expert advice on home and garden subjects in publications developed by the Division of Agricultural Sciences at the University of California. All are listed in an annual catalog. Get it from the local University of California farm adviser or write to Publications, University Hall, University of California, Berkeley, Calif. 94720.

---

## November 9

### Facts about Cooking Meat and Poultry

Always make sure that you cook all meat or poultry products to the proper degree of doneness. You may cook beef to rare, medium, or well done; lamb to medium or well done. Veal is usually preferred well done. Always make sure that pork and poultry are cooked thoroughly and that the center of stuffing cooked inside the bird reaches the proper temperature (165 degrees Fahrenheit).

Cook meat and poultry products at low to moderate temperatures (300 to 350 degrees F.). This provides maximum tenderness and juiciness and results in less shrinkage. It also ensures that the center of the product is fully cooked without the outside being overdone.

Estimate the time it will take to cook the product by type and size of cut and the method to be used. Remember that if you are broiling, you should place a thick cut of meat farther from the source of heat than a thinner cut to assure proper cooking. When cooking meat or poultry in steam or liquid, keep the cooking liquid just below the boiling point to make sure the product will be cooked thoroughly.

To check a steak or other smaller cut, slice into it along the bone or in the center and check interior color. Rare meat will be somewhat pink, but make sure the juice from pork or poultry is not pink.

Test doneness of poultry by pressing the fleshy part with your fingers. Poultry is done if the meat feels soft.

Frozen items take about one and a half times as long to cook as unfrozen cuts of the same weight and size.

---

**CONVERSATIONAL TIDBIT: Early pioneers knew November's full moon as the "Beaver Moon." Reason: Pelts were prime then, and the animals had their pond homes secure for the winter and well supplied with food.**

---

## November 10

### Introducing an Older Cat to a New Kitten

An older cat is not always pleased to have a new kitten brought into the house. The new arrival apparently is considered a threat to the older cat's security. Possessiveness and jealousy are strong emotions, perfectly understandable, and should be acknowledged and respected.

It is sad when an older cat is driven from home by the arrival of a new kitten; it is just as sad if the older cat turns on the youngster and injures it or drives it away. By considering the feelings of the established cat member of your family, harmony can be assured if a few thoughtful days are spent to

make the mistake of holding one while the other is free. There may be some hissing and spitting for a little while, but do not interfere unless it is absolutely essential. After a short time, praise them both and then tuck the kitten back into its refuge. Repeat the meeting in a few hours, or the next day—don't try to hurry things along. These things take time.

How quickly they will accept each other depends entirely on the individual cats. Occasionally an older cat will refuse to accept a rival into the house no matter what you do. If things are not going well after three weeks, chances are they never will. Usually, however, tensions will ease after the first three days and then gradually continue to improve until it is safe to let them stay together all the time. (JSD)

## *November* **11**

### Cooking Vegetables with Spices and Herbs

Discover how spices and herbs can lift humdrum vegetable dishes out of the ordinary. For suggested ways to successfully combine vegetables with spices and herbs see the Appendix.

Spices and herbs must be used sparingly or they overpower, rather than enhance, the natural flavor of vegetables. One-fourth to ½ teaspoon of most dried spices and herbs is enough for 2 cups of a vegetable.

The term "spices," as generally used, includes the herbs as well as true spices. Herbs are leaves and sometimes the flowers of aromatic plants grown in the Temperate Zone; spices come from aromatic plants grown in the Tropics.

ensure the welcome of the new arrival.

Separate the kitten from the cat by putting it in a room by itself. This can be any room where the kitten can be fed, kept warm and safe, and given a litter pan of its own. Keep the door closed and firmly latched.

The older cat will know the kitten is there; he and the kitten can communicate through the door. Do not make the mistake of confining the older cat and letting the kitten run free. This will only serve to make the older cat more jealous and angry. Keep them separated for two or three days.

Then, at some quiet and convenient moment, making as little fuss about it as possible, let the two cats meet in a big room. Stay with them, but do not

Dried herbs are more concentrated than fresh herbs. Use about ¼ teaspoon of a dried herb for 2 cups of vegetable and add it at the beginning of the cooking period. With fresh herbs, increase the amount to ¾ to 1 teaspoon for 2 cups of vegetable. Chop herbs very fine to allow some of the flavoring oils to escape. Chopped herbs may be heated in melted butter and added to the vegetable after it has been cooked.

## November 12

### Salmon: Good Food for Those on a Diet

If being overweight is a problem for some members of your family, keep canned salmon in mind. Salmon provides protein as do meat, poultry, cheese, and eggs. Equal portions of salmon and lamb chops contain about the same amount of protein. But four ounces of salmon contain only 150 calories, while four ounces of lamb contain 450. This word comes to us from the Canned Salmon Institute.

The institute sponsored a full-color recipe booklet that you may want to own. Called "Take a Can of Salmon," the booklet was produced by the Bureau of Commercial Fisheries of the U.S. Department of the Interior. It's available from the Superintendent of Documents in Washington.

---

**QUICK FRUIT SALAD DRESSING:** A little lemon juice added to mayonnaise and sweetened with grenadine syrup.

---

## November 13

### Our Recipe for Quiche

Pronounced "keesh," this is a cheese custard baked in a pie shell. It's commonly made in several European countries. It serves as an excellent brunch or luncheon main dish or, cut into small wedges, a delicious hot hors d'oeuvre. Recipes are available in many cookbooks. Our version:

You may make your own pastry, but prepared shells found in the frozen-food section of a grocery store will do nicely.

Quiche requires last-minute preparation. So it helps to have ready the ingredients which take time to prepare—½ pound grated Swiss cheese, 6 slices bacon cooked to a crisp then crumbled, and 1 medium onion, diced and cooked in the bacon fat until transparent.

Put half of the bacon, onion, and cheese into each of two frozen pie shells in that order. Pour over each, half of a mixture you have made by beating 4 eggs, ½ teaspoon salt, and ¼ teaspoon ground pepper into 2 cups of scalded milk. Set the pie plates on a cookie sheet which will catch any spills. Bake in a 450-degree preheated oven for 10 minutes. Reduce the heat to 300 degrees and continue baking until a knife inserted in the custard comes out clean (about 30 minutes more). Cut into wedges and serve immediately.

## November 14

### 1853 Maxims for Raising Children

Parents have always sought advice on rearing their children, and they still do. Back in 1853, Mrs. Abell had the following to say. (See a reference to her book on April 21.)

"Remember that children are men and women in miniature, and though they should be allowed to act as children, still our dealings with them should be manly, and not morose; recollect, also that every look, word, tone and gesture, nay even your dress makes an impression.

"Never correct a child on suspicion, or without understanding the whole matter, nor trifle with a child's feelings when under discipline.

"Be always mild and cheerful in their presence; communicative but never extravagant, trifling or vulgar in language or gesture. Never trifle with a child, nor speak beseechingly, when it is doing wrong. Always follow commands with a close and careful watch, until the thing is done, allowing no evasion, and no modification, unless the child ask for it, and it be expressly granted.

"Never speak in an impatient, fretful manner, if you have occasion to find fault.

"Never disappoint the confidence a child reposes in you, whether it be a thing placed in your care or a promise.

"Always give prompt attention to a child when he speaks, so as to prevent repeated calls, and that he may learn to give prompt attention when you call him.

"Even in sickness, gentle restraint is better for the child than indulgence.

"Never try to impress a child with religious truth when in anger, or talk to him of God, as it will not have the desired effect. Do it under more favorable circumstances.

"Improve the first ten years of life as the golden opportunity, which may never return. It is the seed time, and your harvest depends upon the seed then sown.

"Selfishness that binds the miser in chains, that chills the heart, must never be allowed a place

255

in the family circle. Teach the child to share his gifts and pleasures with others, to be obliging, kind and benevolent, and the influence of such instruction may come back into your own bosom to bless your latest hour.

"Dread an insubordinate temper. Deal with it as one of the greatest of evils. Let the child feel by your manner, that he is not a safe companion for the rest of the family when in anger. Allow no one to speak to him at such times, not even to answer a question; take from him books, and whatever he may have, and place him where he shall feel that the indulgence of a bad temper shall deprive him of all enjoyment, and he will soon learn to control it himself."

For more, see tomorrow.


## November 15

### 1853 Nursery Maxims for Use in Company

"Never reprove children severely in company, nor hold them up to ridicule, or make light of their failings.

"At the table a child should be taught to sit up and behave in a becoming manner, not to tease when denied, or to leave his chair without asking. A parent's wish at such a time should be a law, from which no appeal should be made.

"There should never be two sets of manners, the one for home and the other for company, but a gentle behaviour should be always required.

"Never say to a child, 'I don't believe what you say,' nor even express doubts. If you have such feelings, keep them to yourself, and wait; truth will eventually be made plain."

### Pointers for Selecting Portable Lamps

Pay close attention to what's under the shade when you buy portable lamps for your home. A lamp must combine function and beauty. Choose those that make seeing comfortable and, at the same time, harmonize with your furnishings, color schemes, and with other lamps and accessories in the room.

Generally, the design of a lamp should be related to the style and decoration of the room, and its scale should be appropriate to the piece of furniture it is used on or over. The light it gives should be suitable for the purpose intended.

If you select a lamp for style or color alone, do not expect to use it for close work. Remember that it's a decorative lamp. Use it to brighten a corner, foyer, or hallway; to display an object of art or accessory; or for limited general lighting.

Lamps controlled by a dimmer switch give you greater flexibility than lamps that use three-way bulbs.

---

FLUORESCENT lights above the kitchen sink and under cabinets normally use less power than do ceiling lights.

---

"A child should always say what's true
And speak when he is spoken to,
And behave mannerly at table;
At least as far as he is able."
—Robert Louis Stevenson

---

"The ripest fruit first falls."
—Shakespeare

---

## November 17

### Taking Care of Cast-Iron Utensils

Cast-iron utensils have been with us for thousands of years. Cast-iron currently is used for a special class of utensils. It includes a variety of skillets, roasters and Dutch ovens, broilers, griddles, and such specialty items as muffin pans. These utensils are excellent for browning foods.

Cast-iron utensils benefit from slightly different handling than those made of other materials. Cast-iron ware usually is preseasoned. It should not be washed with strong detergents or scoured. Instead, hot soapy water may be used, and the utensil rinsed and wiped dry. Frequently after washing, the inside of the utensil should be coated with unsalted shortening. Before using it, wipe with a dry cloth or paper towel.

Never store a cast-iron utensil with the cover on, as this can cause "sweating"; keep these utensils in a dry place.

Cast-iron utensils can be "reseasoned" if necessary. To do this scour the utensil thoroughly, wash it in soap and water and dry it, and then coat the inside surface with unsalted fat, preferably suet, and place the utensil in a moderate oven for about two hours. Remove the utensil from the oven and wipe off excess grease.

## November 18

### Should a Roast Be Seared?

Roasts are often seared in the belief that coagulation of the surface protein forms a coating that prevents the escape of meat juices and thus reduces cooking losses. This belief is now considered "a fallacy."

In a recently revised edition of "Lessons on Meat," a booklet published for the use of teachers by the National Live Stock and Meat Board, you can read that "meat which is seared, whether at the beginning or the end of the roasting period, loses more than meat which has not been seared. This loss is due to fat loss rather than to the loss of juices. The old idea of 'searing to keep in juices' has been discarded. Searing develops aroma and flavor in outside slices and produces drippings of a richer brown color.

"The constant oven temperature has many advantages. For example, the meat is more evenly cooked, less attention is required, there is less spattering of grease, and roasting pans are easier to clean. However, the searing method for roasting meat may be used if the searing period is short and a low constant oven temperature is maintained throughout the cooking period following searing. Roasts cooked at a constant low to moderate oven temperature are similar to roasts cooked by searing (at 450 degrees Fahrenheit and then finished at 250 degrees F.) in cooking losses, cooking time, and palatability.

"When the searing method is used with roasts, the oven is preheated to 450 degrees F. Place roast fat side up in an open roasting pan and brown for 20 to 30 minutes. Then reduce the oven temperature to 250 degrees F., by turning down the regulator and opening the oven door for a few minutes. Continue to cook at this temperature until the thermometer registers the desired degree of doneness."

## *November* **19**

### Timely Tips about Thanksgiving Turkeys

To lift the turkey from roasting pan to platter, wad several paper towels to protect each hand. Place hands under both sides of the bird. This will help to avoid the problem of the wings and legs separating from the body.

When timing the turkey according to poundage, remember to add a pound for the stuffing.

For easier carving, allow the turkey to sit on the serving platter for a half hour after taking it from the oven.

Include in the "fixin's" you serve with the turkey scoops of fruit sherbet. The contrasting tastes complement each other.

Roast turkey in heavy-duty foil on a flat pan if you don't have a roaster. To make a large enough piece of foil to encase the bird, place one piece next to another overlapping them an inch or so, then fold the edges two or three times.

# November 20

**TODAY IN HISTORY:** *Most of us tend to forget that Swedes were among the first colonists in America. On Nov. 20, 1637, two shiploads of settlers sailed from Gothenburg to establish New Sweden. In March of the next year they landed at what is now Wilmington, Delaware. In honor of those pioneers, we present a special recipe for today.*

## Swedish Roast Leg of Lamb

**1 leg of lamb (about 6 to 8 pounds)**
**Salt and pepper**
**3 medium onions, sliced**
**3 medium carrots, sliced**
**1 cup beef bouillon**
**1 Tbs. lemon juice**
**½ tsp. ground cardamom**
**½ tsp. grated lemon peel**
**2 Tbs. instant coffee powder**
**1 Tbs. sugar**
**1 cup boiling water**
**½ cup heavy cream**

Sprinkle the leg of lamb with salt and pepper. Place lamb on a rack in a shallow roasting pan. Place the onion slices in the bottom of pan. Bake at 325 degrees for 30 minutes. Drain off the drippings. Add the carrots to the onions in pan. Mix bouillon, lemon juice, cardamom, and lemon peel, and pour over lamb. Continue cooking 30 minutes, basting lamb with the liquid. Dissolve the instant coffee and sugar in the boiling water. Add the cream and pour over lamb. Roast 1½ hours longer, or until meat thermometer registers 165 to 170 degrees for medium doneness. Baste frequently with the gravy. Remove lamb to platter and keep warm. Strain gravy and reheat. Serve with the lamb. If desired, garnish with onion rings and carrot slices. This serves 12.

**CHILDREN WANT LIMITS and want to know those limits. Tell them what is permitted and what is not.**

# November 21

**TODAY IN HISTORY:** *Abraham Lincoln wrote a touching letter on Nov. 21, 1864, to a Mrs. Bixby, of Boston, Mass., who had paid a dear price to support her country.*

## Lincoln's Letter to Mrs. Bixby:

"Dear Madam: I have been shown in the files of the War Department a statement of the Adjutant-General of Massachusetts that you are the mother of five sons who have died gloriously on the field of battle. I feel how weak and fruitless must be any words of mine which should attempt to beguile you from the grief of a loss so overwhelming. But I cannot refrain from tendering to you the consolation that may be found in the thanks of the Republic they died to save. I pray that our heavenly Father may assuage the anguish of your bereavement, and leave you only the cherished memory of the loved and lost, and the solemn pride that must be yours to have laid so costly a sacrifice upon the altar of freedom.

"Yours very sincerely and respectfully,

Abraham Lincoln"

## For the Gift of Gifts, the Cookbook of Cookbooks

No matter how many cookbooks you own, we're confident you'd also enjoy *Beeton's Book of Household Management* and find it a guide for various house activities as well as a storehouse of recipes. The book was originally published in London in 1861. A facsimile copy of the first edition is now available. We're telling you about it today in case you want to ask your bookseller to order one or more for delivery before Christmas. The publisher is Farrar, Straus & Giroux, 19 Union Square West, New York, N.Y. 10003. The fat 1,112-page volume makes an excellent gift.

Mrs. Isabella Beeton was a bride of 21 when she began compiling the book. In her preface, Mrs. Beeton wrote:

"I have always thought that there is no more fruitful source of family discontent than a housewife's badly-cooked dinners and untidy ways. Men are now so well served out of doors—at their clubs, well-ordered taverns, and dining-houses, that in order to compete with the attractions of these places, a mistress must be thoroughly acquainted with the theory and practice of cookery, as well as be perfectly conversant with all the other arts of making and keeping a comfortable home."

The jacket calls her book "the biggest selling cookery book of all time."

---

**CONSISTENCY IS A MUST in disciplining children. Another must is that parents refrain from contradicting each other at the times discipline is necessary.**

---

## Bottle Up a Winter Garden

Over a hundred years ago a London physician named Nathaniel Ward discovered that he could grow ferns and mosses inside glass cases. His development, called the "Wardian" bottle, can give the whole family hours of gardening enjoyment during the winter months ahead.

Instructions from The American Association of Nurserymen will help you develop your own garden in a bottle.

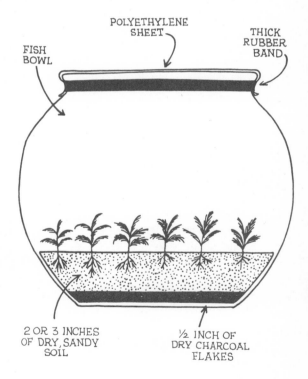

A brandy snifter, a fish bowl, or a large bottle is a suitable container for your terrarium. The size and shape is up to you, but you will need to cover the opening at the top after planting.

Wash, dry, and polish the container until it sparkles. Then pour in a half inch of dry charcoal flakes. On top of that add several inches of dry sandy soil. Some bottle gardeners place moss, green side up, on the charcoal and then add the sandy soil.

Most small house plants that thrive in a moist atmosphere will be happy in a bottle garden. You may want to use wandering Jew (*Zebrina pendula*), pellionia, miniature ivy, and small ferns. Creeping fig plant and the prayer plant are also wise choices. If you need ideas, seek advice at your nursery or garden center.

If you are using a bottle, actual planting may be similar to building a ship inside a bottle. You will need long instruments to place the plants. Handy tools can be created by taping a fork and a spoon to sticks or poles.

After planting, water until the soil is damp. Then cover or cork the container. The plants will give off moisture. This will accumulate on the sides of the container and return to the roots. It will provide sufficient moisture for about a year.

Place the bottle in good light, but not direct sun. Then sit back and watch everything grow.

**SEE YOUR FLORIST** about miniature orange trees that you can grow indoors during the winter.

**DRAPERIES OR FURNITURE** may block the flow of warm air in your home, thus reducing the effectiveness of your heating system. Check the situation now. Be sure the way is clear to the return-air registers in a warm air system.

## Growing an Avocado Plant from Seed

An avocado plant brings a pleasant touch of green indoors during the winter. Why not start your own soon? Each friend you know who has one probably has her own method of getting the seed to germinate. The ways of caring for the plant will undoubtedly differ, too. Don't let this conflicting advice dissuade you from trying to raise an avocado yourself. After all, what can you lose? The seed is free. What you bought was the flesh surrounding it that you used in a salad or your favorite recipe.

Here's the germination method that has worked for us—and we've grown a good many!

Insert three toothpicks around the middle of the seed. They will support the seed when it is placed in a teacup or custard cup so that its bottom is in water. Wait for roots to develop. This may take several weeks, but don't give up. During this period there is nothing to do but add water as needed to keep the bottom of the seed immersed.

## November 25

The top will take a while longer to sprout. Again, patience! Once the seed sprouts, and the sprout attains a height of about three inches, pot the seed in a mixture of rich soil.

When the sprout is about five inches tall, cut off about three inches of the growth. This will encourage branching. You may even be rewarded by having one or more additional sprouts grow from the seed.

Keep the potted plant in a spot out of direct sunshine, and water it well and often. At any time that it develops an ungainly appearance, lop off the branches to encourage bushiness.

**INDOOR CREATIVE ACTIVITY for children: "Painting" with soap flakes or powder (not detergent) to which you've added only enough water to result in a consistency thick enough to stick to a brush. Black art construction paper shows up the results best. Spills are easily cleaned up.**

**TODAY IN HISTORY:** *A patent for an "apparatus" for producing evaporated milk was granted on Nov. 25, 1884, to John B. Meyenberg, of St. Louis, Mo.*

## Facts about Milk in Its Various Forms

Fresh whole milk is usually homogenized and usually fortified with vitamins. Sometimes it is also fortified with minerals. It must meet the requirements for minimum milkfat content set by the state or municipality where it is sold. The milkfat content usually is about 3.25 percent.

All Grade A milk and milk products sold today are pasteurized—heated to kill harmful bacteria. Grade A pasteurized milk must come from healthy cows and be produced, pasteurized, and handled under strict sanitary control enforced by state and local milk sanitation officials. Requirements may

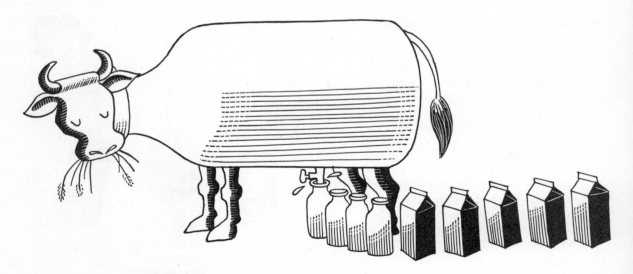

vary in different localities. The Grade A rating designates wholesomeness rather than a level of quality.

Homogenized milk has been treated so as to reduce the size of the milkfat globules. This prevents the cream from separating and keeps the product uniform.

Chocolate-flavored milk is made from pasteurized whole milk with sugar and chocolate syrup or cocoa added. In most states, regulations require that to be labeled chocolate-flavored milk, the product must be made from whole milk; to be labeled chocolate-flavored milk drink, it must be made from skim or partially skimmed milk. Chocolate-flavored milk can be used in cookie or cake recipes that call for both milk and chocolate or cocoa.

Cultured buttermilk is made by adding a lactic-acid-producing bacterial culture to fresh pasteurized skim or partially skimmed milk. The resulting buttermilk is much thicker than skim milk with the same nutritive value. It has an acid flavor and is a good thirst quencher. Most commercially marketed buttermilk is cultured. There is, however, a natural type, a product of buttermaking.

Dry whole milk is pasteurized whole milk with the water removed. It has only limited retail distribution. Where it is distributed, it's used mostly for infant feeding and by persons who don't have access to fresh milk. Because of its fat content, dry whole milk doesn't keep well. It develops an off-flavor if not used soon after being opened.

Nonfat dry milk is made by removing nearly all the fat and water from pasteurized milk. "Instant" nonfat dry milk is made of larger particles, which are more easily dissolved in water. Nonfat dry milk has about half the calories of whole milk and the same nutritive value as fresh skim milk.

Nonfat dry milk needs no refrigeration and

can be stored for several months in a cool dry place. After it is reconstituted, however, it should be refrigerated and handled like fresh milk. It can be used both as a beverage and in cooking. When using nonfat dry milk as a beverage, reconstitute it several hours before serving to allow it time to chill. Use cool water. Nonfat dry milk is very economical. A family of four that has 21 quarts of whole milk delivered each week could save several dollars each week by using nonfat dry milk instead of fresh milk.

Fresh skim (or nonfat) milk usually has less than .5 percent milkfat, the percentage recommended to states under the pasteurized milk ordinance. It is often fortified with vitamins A and D. Skim milk contains all the nutrients of whole milk except the fat. The flavor and food value of skim milk can be improved by adding a teaspoon of instant nonfat dry milk to each glass.

Low-fat milk usually has between .5 and 2 percent milkfat. You may find this milk labeled "2%" or "2-10" in stores. Low-fat milk can be "made" at home by using half whole milk and half skim or reconstituted instant nonfat dry milk.

Evaporated milk is prepared by heating homogenized whole milk under a vacuum to remove half of its water, then sealing it in cans, and sterilizing it. When mixed with an equal amount of water, its nutritive value is about the same as whole milk. Evaporated skim milk is also available. Evaporated milk is convenient to store and is usually less expensive than fresh whole milk. Refrigerate it after opening.

With an equal amount of water added, evaporated milk may replace fresh milk in recipes. (Used full strength, evaporated milk adds extra nutritive value.) It also can be used in coffee or on hot or cold cereal.

Sweetened condensed milk is a concentrated milk with at least 40 percent sugar added to help preserve it. This canned milk is prepared by removing about half the water from whole milk. It is often used in candy and dessert recipes, and, diluted, for infant formulas.

## November 26

### Scalloped Oysters "R" in Season

A dish to accompany roast turkey, or which can stand on its own as a main dish, makes use of oysters, which are in season now.

Put a layer of crushed soda crackers in a 10" x 6" x 2" greased casserole. Top with a layer of 1 pint of oysters. Cover with more crushed crackers and drizzle over them the oyster liquor, 2 tablespoons milk, and ¼ cup melted butter. Grind a little black pepper over the top. Bake at 450 degrees for 30 minutes.

If the recipe is doubled or tripled, use a dish large enough to avoid having more than two layers of oysters; a middle layer will not be done when the others are.

### Select Safe Toys for Your Tot

Injuries from toys account for 700,000 of the 6,000,000 annual injuries related to children's products. As a parent, you can help reduce these figures by looking for and selecting safe toys, supervising small children during playtime, and teaching them safe play habits.

The Bureau of Product Safety, Federal Food and Drug Administration, is charged with the responsibility of preventing unsafe children's articles from reaching the market. They suggest that when choosing toys for a small child, you should be sure that the toy:

Is too large to be swallowed.

Has no detachable parts that can lodge in throat, ears, or nose.

Will not break easily into small pieces or pieces with jagged edges.

Has no sharp edges or points.

Is not put together with easily exposed straight pins, sharp wires, or nails.

Is not made of glass or brittle plastic.

Is labeled "nontoxic." Avoid painted toys for any child who is apt to put playthings into his mouth.

Has no parts which can pinch fingers or catch hair.

Has no long cords or thin plastic bags if selected for a child under two.

Tomorrow's article will discuss the selection of toys for the older child.

---

**HASTEN DRYING OF WET BOOTS** by blowing air into them for a few minutes with the blower attachment of a vacuum cleaner.

---

# November 28

## How to Determine Which Toys Are Safe?

Choose carefully and selectively. Any toy if misused can be dangerous. There is no substitute for parental supervision.

Choose a toy appropriate for the child's age and development. Many toys have age-group labels on the package. Heed warnings such as "Not Intended for Children under 3 Years of Age."

Remember that younger brothers and sisters may have access to toys intended for older children once the toy has been brought into the home. Avoid toys and games with small parts and sharp points.

Check labels on fabric products for a "non-flammable," "flame-retardant," or "flame-resist-ant" notice, as well as "washable" and "hygienic materials" for stuffed toys and dolls.

Check instructions. They should be easy to read and understand. Instruct children in the proper use of toys.

Avoid toys that produce excessive noise. Even toy cap pistols fired too close to a child's ear may cause damage. Avoid shooting games, especially those involving darts and arrows, unless the games are played under parental supervision.

Check toys and games periodically for potential hazards, such as sharp points, jagged edges, and loose small parts. Remember, rusting on outdoor toys leads to structural weakening.

Select chemistry sets and electrically operated toys, especially those which produce heat, for older children only. Do not allow the child to remove or replace electrical components.

# November 29

## Ordered Christmas Dinner? Do So Soon

What will you serve your family for Christmas dinner this year? Roast turkey, as most Americans do? Roast goose, as in Germany? Roast beef? Duck? Why not consider roast suckling pig? If the latter idea interests you, skip a few pages ahead and read what we've written for December 24. Whatever your decision, it's time now to place your order with your butcher. You can sometimes order roast suckling pig by mail. Check magazine and news-paper advertisements.

# *November* **30**

## November Potpourri
## for Homemakers

Fine chopping of hard-cooked egg whites is easily accomplished with a doughnut cutter from which you have removed the center.

Change styles with buttons without sewing more than once. New "Togs" buttons, available in notions departments, snap on nylon discs that you sew to the garment.

Restore luster to marble: Wrap a cut lemon in a soft cloth, dip in water then in borax. Rub the surface. Repeat if necessary.

Try removing stubborn stains from tubs and ceramic tile by soaking a heavy cloth with a mixture (slushy consistency) of turpentine and table salt. Use rubber gloves. Remove the turpentine odor by a final wash with detergent.

## Your Own Reminders:

DECEMBER

# December 1

**TODAY IN HISTORY:** *Soilless crop production, later known as "hydroponics," was the subject of a patent issued on Dec. 1, 1936, to E.W. Brundin and Frank F. Lyon, of Montebello, Calif.*

## Cleaning and Polishing Household Copperware

Copper pots and pans and other copper and brass articles around a home may become tarnished from sulfur in the atmosphere. Periodic cleaning and polishing is required to restore the original appearance.

Copper is sometimes lacquered to prevent tarnishing. For treatment of lacquered items, see tomorrow's article.

Do not use an abrasive to remove tarnish from plain copper and brass surfaces. Rub lightly with a cleaner intended for cleaning copper or brass. Among the good commercial cleaners are Noxon, Samae, and Twinkle. A homemade cleaner can be prepared of equal parts of salt, flour, and vinegar. Wash off cleaning residue, rinse well, and dry. Use clean gloves to avoid leaving fingerprints on the cleaned articles.

If you want a higher polish than you get with the cleaner, make a paste of whiting and denatured alcohol. Allow the paste to dry on the article, then polish with a cloth. Wash, rinse, and dry, being careful to avoid water spots and fingerprints.

Another formula for polish is a paste of rottenstone and boiled linseed oil. (Do not attempt to boil the linseed oil. Buy it boiled.) Olive oil may be used instead of boiled linseed oil. Apply the paste, then wipe off with a cloth moistened with the oil.

Polish with a dry cloth.

Polished copperware can be sprayed with a clear lacquer. Allow to dry and apply a second coat. Clear plastic coatings for home use, which come in aerosol cans, may be used. Use the spray only in a well-ventilated area.

Instead of lacquering, polished articles also may be waxed. Wax coatings should be periodically renewed.

CAUTION: Brass with an antique finish should be cleaned and polished only with boiled linseed oil, olive oil, or lemon oil.

**OUTDOOR PAINTS used indoors may be a hazard to infants. They may contain lead. Chewing or mouthing on articles coated with lead paint may result in lead poisoning.**

# December 2

## Taking Care of Lacquered Copperware

Lacquer that has been applied to copperware to protect its polish may in time become chipped and require renewal.

First all of the old lacquer should be stripped off. To do this, apply a lacquer thinner to the surface with one cloth. Then using a coarse cloth, rub off the lacquer. Wash in warm, sudsy water and dry.

Another method, more effective but requiring more care and skill, involves use of a strong solution of caustic soda (sodium hydroxide), about one pound per gallon of cold water. Add a small amount of soap. Apply the solution with a brush or a cotton rag. IMPORTANT: *Wear rubber gloves while handling the solution.* As soon as the lacquer becomes soft, it should be completely removed by rubbing or peeling. Then rinse thoroughly in cold water and dry.

When the surface is completely dry, use an aerosol can of clear lacquer and apply two coats to the cleaned and polished copper or brass article. Work in a well-ventilated area when you apply the spray.

Lacquered copperware should not be polished as this may damage the lacquer. Dust and, when necessary, wash with lukewarm water and a mild detergent. Rinse with lukewarm water and wipe dry. (Hot water may damage the lacquer coating.) Lacquered finishes may be protected with occasional waxing with any good furniture wax.

---

**NEWLY CLEANED ALUMINUM can be kept tarnish-free by applying a coat of clear lacquer or wax.**

---

# December 3

## Do Skis Clutter Up Your Home?

The amateur builder in your home can easily make a wooden rack to store as many as five pairs of skis. The materials you need are an eight-foot 2″ x 4″ of Ponderosa pine or Douglas fir and a one-inch dowel three feet long.

A section 42 inches long is cut from the 2″ x 4″. To one end of this a pattern derived from the curved end of one ski is transferred. The entire 42-inch piece is then trimmed to this curved line with saw, plane, and sandpaper. Five pairs of blocks, each three inches long, are finally cut from the shaped piece of wood. Placed together in pairs with the curved edges facing, each pair of blocks supports a pair of skis against the uncut 54-inch length of 2″ x 4″. A piece of dowel five inches long on which to hang the poles is glued into a hole between each pair of blocks.

Detailed instructions and sketches giving further information will be sent to you if you send a dime to Ski Storage Plans, Louisiana-Pacific Corporation, 1300 S.W. Fifth Ave., Portland, Ore. 97201.

## *December* 4

### The Case for Plastic Christmas Trees

Despite ancient traditions of bringing in the greens, plastic Christmas trees make a lot of sense for modern families. Since you store the tree from year to year, there is only the original cost, not an expenditure every year. But there's a point even more important than this. Your use of a plastic tree helps conserve living trees.

If you don't now own a plastic tree, you may want to put it on your shopping list for this week. If you do own such a tree, we'd like to pass on some tips from General Electric's lighting experts:

Use string sets, with the new, cooler bulbs. Plastic needles are more sensitive to heat than natural needles and will melt if subjected to excessive heat. String sets with midget bulbs typically are cooler.

Avoid ceramic-coated or translucent bulbs. Although nicely colored, these are warm enough to deform plastic needles. These bulbs were designed for use on natural trees and for general holiday decoration.

You can give a plastic tree an overall color with a colored floodlight. Or use a color wheel for changing colors.

Whatever string set or floodlight fixture you buy, for safety look for a UL (Underwriter's Laboratories) tag before making the purchase.

IT'S SLEDDING TIME again in northern parts of the U.S. If your youngsters plan to go sledding, make sure the hill is free of dangerous obstacles. Impress upon them the dangers of sledding where there's traffic.

# December 5

## Would You Like Your Own Greenhouse?

Are you such a confirmed gardener that you start yearning for spring this early in the season? A greenhouse, however small, can do a lot toward satisfying your yen.

Perhaps you've noticed that it's possible to install a small greenhouse in one of your house windows. If you find this idea appealing, a neighborhood garden shop can probably tell you where to get one.

Otherwise, we suggest you get information from the Superintendent of Documents, U.S. Government Printing Office, Washington, D.C. 20402. Ask for "Building Hobby Greenhouses," Information Bulletin No. 357, published by the Department of Agriculture. At last report it cost a quarter.

# December 6

## Ready to Remove Ice from Your Walks?

Before the worst part of winter sets in, the smart homemaker will see to it that materials are on hand to keep outside steps and walkways safe when treacherous ice hits.

Many of us have been using rock salt for this purpose, but the environmentalists now say that this is not a good idea. The saline runoff damages or kills trees and shrubs and pollutes water supplies. As a result, road crews in many areas are now having second thoughts about using salt on icy highways.

For our homes a bag or pail of coarse sand can substitute for salt. If kept in the garage year-round, it can be used as an extinguisher in case of an oil fire.

Coal ashes, when you can get them, also bring good footing to an icy stretch. Clean kitty litter is another possibility.

Rock salt still has acceptable uses in the home. It's essential if you make ice cream in a hand freezer, and it will speed up cooling if you add it to the ice into which bottled drinks or containers of food have been placed.

# December 7

## Let Stuffed Puppy Precede Live Christmas Gift

The gift of a puppy on Christmas Day is an enchanting idea but one which can lead to disaster. The combination of distracted parents, overexcited children, and a bewildered puppy can, in just one hectic day, destroy all chances of raising it to be a sound and healthy dog.

271

busy. Without constant adult supervision, a puppy can be stepped on, tripped over, or driven into a state of exhaustion. Many holiday decorations and toys can be lethal to a dog if chewed or swallowed.

All of these points are just as applicable, of course, to the gift of a Christmas kitten. (JSD)

---

**VACUUM RADIATORS and registers frequently during the winter. Dust and lint act as insulation and can waste an appreciable amount of heat.**

---

## *December* 8

### Have the Appropriate Fire Extinguishers

Suppose a grease fire flared up in your oven, or an appliance caught fire because of an electrical short? Would you throw water on the flames? Do you have a fire extinguisher recommended for those types of fires?

Water on such fires might cause them to spread and, in the case of an electrical fire, could endanger your life. Kitchen equipment in every home should include one or more dry chemical or all-purpose fire extinguishers.

Fire extinguisher labels indicate by their letters, A, B, or C, what classes of fires they are suited for. The numbers in front of the letters indicate the approximate size of the fire the extinguisher will handle. For example, an extinguisher rated at 10-B:C will extinguish a fire of approximately twice the size as one marked 5-B:C.

Few conscientious breeders will let a puppy go to its new home on a holiday. If you have chosen a specific puppy, it should be easy to arrange for the breeder to keep it with its littermates until after Christmas Day. Announce its coming by putting a stuffed toy puppy in a stocking, with a tag around its neck explaining that it represents a live puppy which you will be bringing home soon. The child will be just as pleased and then can share in the fun of getting things ready for the new arrival—on a day you have chosen which will be free from confusion.

If you unavoidably must have a young puppy in your house at Christmastime, take extra precautions to protect it from holiday hazards. Make sure you have a place of confinement convenient for you and comfortable for the puppy while you are

A multipurpose dry chemical extinguisher with a minimum 2-A: 10-B:C rating will prepare you for just about any fire you would attempt to combat by yourself in your home. At least one on every floor of the house is a wise precaution.

Class A fires are those in ordinary combustible materials—wood, paper, cloth, and many plastics. Water is a suitable extinguisher. Class B fires are those in flammable liquids, gases, and greases. Class C fires are those in electrical equipment. Use only dry chemicals for Class B and C fires.

**TABLE TOO SMALL?** You can entertain many more people than your table seats if you serve buffet style and restrict your menu to "fork foods" that do not require knives, such as Swedish meatballs, beef or ham loaf, and curries.

## December 9

### A Few Facts about Snow

Tramp down deep snow around young trees to keep rodents from chewing the bark. Shake wet snow from trees and shrubs, especially evergreens, before it freezes. The weight of ice may break limbs.

How much snow equals an inch of rain? It varies. When snow is dry, you may need as many as 30 inches of snow to equal one inch of rain.

Snow falls on only one-third of the earth's surface. Consequently, many people never see it.

Every snowflake is a six-sided crystal, but no two flakes ever have been found to be exactly alike.

Snow is not always white. In Arctic regions, microscopic plants may make it appear red or green after it has fallen.

# December 10

**TODAY IN HISTORY:** *Nylon darning and sewing thread was introduced on this date in 1941.*

## 1853 Remedies for Common Ailments

In the *Skillful Housewife's Book,* remedies for common ailments and accidents suggested by Mrs. Abell in 1853 make interesting reading today. We present a sampling, but by no means do we suggest you try them! (For more about her book see April 21.) Her remedies:

Coughs. Take Iceland moss, 2 ounces, 4 poppy heads, 4 tablespoonsful of barley; put in 3 pints of water, boil down to two, and strain it. Add 1 pound of sugar. Dose, a tablespoonful whenever the cough is troublesome. Another, boil down thoroughwort to a thick syrup, and sweeten with molasses. This cures when other remedies fail.

Common Sore Throat. A simple gargle of salt, vinegar, pepper, and water, in proportions to make a pleasant combination, will cure a common soreness of the throat.

Bleeding at the Nose. Grate dried salt beef, and take two or three pinches as snuff. This is said always to cure. Other remedies will often suppress it—such as the following: Raise the left arm, and keep it up some time. Tie a thread very tight around the little finger.

Warts. Wet them with tobacco juice, and rub them with chalk. Another, rub them with fresh beef every day until they begin to disappear.

Cuts. Bind on brown sugar until it ceases bleeding, then apply any common healing salve, with sugar melted in it; this takes out the soreness, better than the salve alone.

To Prevent Bruises from Turning Black. Make a plaster of salt and tallow to cover the wound.

Toothache. Take gum of opium, gum camphor, and spirits of turpentine, equal parts, rub them in a mortar to a paste. Put in the hollow of the tooth. This, it is said, will cure and prevent it from ever aching.

REMEMBER! We're presenting these old-time remedies just for your entertainment in reading, not for your use.

## December 11

### Should You Cook in Plastic Bags?

Two kinds of plastic bags are now in use for cooking: one for roasting meats, one for boiling vegetables. Before a company can market a cooking bag, it must petition the Food and Drug Administration for a permit, giving the type of food to be cooked, the method of cooking, and other conditions of safe use.

When you buy plastic cooking bags, be sure to read the instructions that should come with them. Never use ordinary plastic bags for cooking.

## December 12

### Do Your Winter Breakfasts Include Enough Vitamin C?

Breakfast is the best time to make sure your family gets foods rich in vitamin C. If you don't have vitamin C at this meal, you're likely to fall short of your daily quota.

Citrus fruits are rich in vitamin C. An orange, half a grapefruit, or half a glass (four ounces) of orange or grapefruit juice—fresh, frozen, or canned—goes far toward meeting vitamin C needs for the day.

If you squeeze citrus juice, serve it unstrained—to get the most vitamins and minerals from the pulp.

Tomatoes, fresh or canned, are also good providers of vitamin C, and can be substituted for citrus fruits when tomatoes are easier to get. It takes about three times as much tomato juice as orange juice to give you an equal amount of vitamin C.

Strawberries, cantaloupe, and some other fresh fruits are valuable sources of vitamin C, and can take a turn providing it when they're in season and when variety is wanted.

---

**DUPLICATE CLEANING SUPPLIES** kept upstairs will save a lot of running up and down.

---

## Food Budgeting for Good Nutrition

Family food planning and buying is a challenging job. It takes knowledge, good judgment, and a keen sense of food values in relation to costs. In the Appendix, you will find sample food plans prepared by U.S. Government nutritionists. Each gives the weekly amounts of different groups of foods that together supply an adequate diet. Amounts are compiled for different age, sex, and activity groups within the family.

Small families usually find that they cannot buy and use food as economically as large families can. In the Appendix tables allowance is made for this in estimating the costs of food. From the food groups in the plans, choose the foods that your family enjoys and that also give you good value for the money.

After choosing the food plan you wish to follow, begin planning for your family by writing down the name of each person. Use the blank lines at the bottom of the tables, a name to a line.

Find the line on the food plan that describes each person. Suppose one boy is 11. You will find his food needs on the line: "Children: 10-12 years." If the boy is growing very rapidly, he may need more food than the average 11-year-old. Then use the line: "Boys: 13-15."

The quantities of food for adults are based on the needs of "moderately active" persons. Such persons spend about eight hours daily at light industrial or office work, three to four hours at moderate exercise or housework, and four to five hours in sedentary activities, such as watching TV, sewing, or reading. Or such persons may spend eight hours in such activities as carpentry, light agricultural jobs, laboratory work, store clerking, or housework, one to two hours in light exercise, and six to seven hours in sedentary activities.

If your activities or those of your family are more or less than specified, food quantities may need to be increased or decreased, according to your schedules.

## December 14

### Prevent Static in Garments and Carpets

Sometimes in cold, dry weather, garments of man-made fibers have a tendency to cling to the body. The clinging is caused by what is commonly called static. This tendency can be reduced in washable garments by adding a small amount of liquid detergent, fabric softener, or a special liquid anti-static agent to the final rinse water.

Some suitable products are liquid detergents, Wisk and Joy; fabric softeners, Sta-Puff and Nu-Soft; anti-static agents, Slip Ease. Liquid detergents·and fabric softeners can be purchased at most grocery stores. Liquid anti-static agents can be obtained at notion counters in drug or department stores.

Wash the garments in the usual manner. Rinse them in a solution of the selected product according to instructions given on the container, or adjust the amount of the product used to suit the needs of the individual.

Static electricity from carpets can be a nuisance, too, during periods of low humidity. Nylon carpets have been found to react similarly to wool carpets in this respect.

Static can be reduced by raising the humidity level. In hot-air heating systems, the installation of humidifying equipment often is a healthful and effective solution to a static problem.

If static is a problem, you may want to consider using an anti-static spray. These include: StaticProof Pro, Wade & Wenger Associates, Inc., Downers Grove, Chicago, Ill. 60514; Statikil, J.E. Doyle Company, 1220 West 6th St., Cleveland, Ohio 44113; Carpetstat, Jordan Chemical Company, 1830 Columbia Ave., Folcroft, Pa. 19032; and Stat-Eze 5, Fine Organics, Inc., 205 Main St., Lodi, N.J. 07644.

StaticProof Pro is customarily applied by franchised cleaners of the Servicemaster system. The other materials are available from the individual manufacturers, who can supply directions for proper application.

## December 15

### French Almond Cookies for Christmas

This year when you are baking cookies for Christmas, try this recipe. It was brought to Fayette County, Pennsylvania, many years ago by the mother of Mrs. Emil Tricot when she emigrated from France as a young woman.

**1 cup butter or oleomargarine**
**2 cups white sugar**
**2 cups brown sugar, firmly packed**
**4 eggs, beaten**
**2 tsp. honey**
**2 tsp. almond extract**
**2 tsp. vanilla extract**
**5 cups flour**
**2 tsp. baking soda**
**2 tsp. baking powder**
**2 tsp. cream of tartar**
**1 cup blanched slivered almonds**

Let the butter or oleomargarine stand until it reaches room temperature. Add the white and brown sugars gradually, creaming until light and fluffy. Add the beaten eggs, honey, and the extracts. Gradually add the flour which has been sifted with the baking soda, baking powder, and cream of tartar, and mix well. Stir in the nuts.

Make small balls the size of walnuts, dip one side into granulated sugar, and place sugar side up on a greased cookie sheet. Make a slight depression in the center of each ball with your thumb. Bake 10 minutes at 350 degrees. This recipe makes about 8 dozen.

The cookies spread when baking, so leave room between the balls and at the edges of the cookie sheet to allow for this. (MLR)

# December 16

## Cats versus House Plants

Do not despair if your favorite house plants and favorite cat have not been able to coexist. Most cats eat house plants at one time or another. Some cats even go so far as to chew and tear apart dried or fresh flower arrangements.

This disheartening damage can be stopped by using Grannick's Bitter Apple. Ask your local pet shop to order it (Valhar Chemical Corporation, 277 Greenwich Ave., Greenwich, Conn. 06830). It is a nontoxic bitter liquid, which can be sprayed in a light, fine mist over indoor plants and flower arrangements. An inexpensive plastic hand sprayer is excellent for this. Unused liquid should be returned to its original bottle. A very light application is enough. It should be sprayed on plants away from furniture or wood finishes.

Though there may be some plants and flowers which cannot tolerate this treatment, it has been used by many cat owners for years on common house plants and even on many varieties of orchids in bloom, with no noticeable effect on plant or blossoms.

After one taste of a leaf sprayed with this product, few cats will return for a second try. A second try usually completely convinces even a stubborn cat to leave the plant alone. (JSD)

---

**IF SLIPCOVERS SLIP** out of place, tuck towels between the cushions and the back or sides of the furniture to keep them snug.

---

**MAKE LAUNDRY SOAP** by grating thin leftovers of personal- and bath-size cakes. Then pour boiling water over the gratings.

---

278

# December 17

## How to Draw Two Kinds of Stars

In all Christian lands, the star is a symbol of Christmas. The reason is told in St. Matthew, Chapter 2, verses 1 and 2:

"Now when Jesus was born in Bethlehem of Judea in the days of Herod the king, behold there came three Wise Men from the east to Jerusalem,

"Saying, Where is He that is born King of the Jews? for we have seen his star in the east, and are come to worship him."

Although stars in the sky seem to be round, we customarily represent them as being pointed. Five-pointed stars are widely used in art and literature, and 50 of them fill the blue field of the American flag. The six-pointed star of David has been a symbol of the Jewish faith for thousands of years.

**To draw a Five-Pointed Star,** scribe a circle the size of the star desired. Draw two diameter lines across the circle at right angles to each other. Divide the radius in half at A. With A as the pivot, set a compass from A to B and swing arc BC. Set compass from B to C and swing arc DE. With the same radius, find point G from E and F from D. FG should then be equal to BE, EG, and so forth. Connect alternate points with straight lines to outline the star.

**To draw a Six-Pointed Star,** draw a circle with the diameter AB, equal to the overall size of the desired star, as the vertical axis. With point A as a center, and with a radius equal to that of the circle, swing arc CD. With point B as a center, and with the same radius, swing arc EF. Draw triangles AEF and BCD to complete the Star of David.

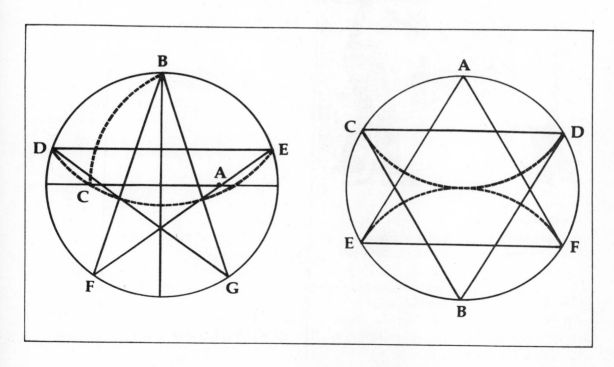

279

# December 18

## Making a Christmas Tree Fire Retardant

A formula from the U.S. Forest Service for a fire-retardant solution for Christmas trees has sodium silicate (water glass) as the main constituent. This is available at drugstores. Mix nine parts by volume of sodium silicate with one part of water to which you already have added a wetting agent (any household detergent) at the rate of one teaspoon per quart of water.

Small batches of cut greens can be dipped into the solution in a large pan, the kitchen sink, or bathtub. For spraying, thin the solution by adding at least an equal amount of water. Apply it with a paint, insecticide, or vacuum-cleaner spray gun. If the tree will fit into a shower stall, that's a fine place for the operation. Spray the tree twice, making sure that you spray all sides of all needles.

# December 19

## What You Should Know about Rayon Products

Rayon was the first of the man-made fibers. It is made from cellulose: The raw materials are converted chemically and then regenerated into cellulose fibers. The two main types of rayon, viscose and cuprammonium, differ in the way the cellulose is processed and regenerated, but their properties are similar. The cuprammonium process is best for yarns of fine diameter, which are used mainly in sheer and semisheer fabrics. In recent years several "new" rayons have been developed to overcome some of the limitations of the regular viscose and cuprammonium rayons. The major distinctive feature of these new fibers is greater strength, particularly when wet.

Rayon is one of the least expensive man-made fibers, and since it combines well with practically all other fibers, it is used extensively in blends. It has advantages of comfort, efficiency, and luster.

Rayon products include apparel, home furnishings, household textile products, linings, and rugs and carpets.

Recommended care: Rayon can be washed by hand with lukewarm water, unless the manufacturer specifies otherwise. Squeeze gently; do not wring or twist. It may be machine washed and tumble dried, and bleached with chlorine bleach, unless it is resin finished. Some resin finishes used on rayon discolor in the presence of chlorine bleach. It may be ironed with a moderate iron. Safe ironing temperatures are 300 to 350 degrees Fahrenheit. Rayon will scorch, but not melt, if the iron is too hot. It may also be dry-cleaned.

Rayon ignites readily and is not self-extinguishing, but it can be made flame resistant.

## December 20

### YOU Shape Your Child's Personality

If the child is to have a well-rounded personality, the home atmosphere must be one which offers the child love, acceptance, and opportunities to achieve success.

Ideally, we all want our children to become adults able to cope with the unknown future. We want them to be able to make wise decisions in that uncertain future world, to enjoy the company of others, but also to possess the self-sufficiency that will enable them to get pleasure from solitary activities. We want them to be cultured individuals, appreciative of literature, art, music, and the other humanities; well-mannered; and able to communicate well. If you agree with this picture of your child's future adulthood, judge the present home atmosphere in which you are attempting to achieve this by asking yourself the following questions today:

Are you treating the child with understanding and with respect for him as an individual?

Are you providing opportunities for him to express himself, verbally and creatively?

Are you providing him with the experiences necessary for individual and social growth— walks, trips, dining out, entertaining at home, quiet periods when he is on his own?

Is the child exposed to religion, the humanities, and to conversations which stimulate his desire to learn?

Does the child have opportunities to make

decisions—to consider the consequences of alternatives? A young child can begin to participate in decision-making by choosing alternatives in the areas of the clothes he wears, the furnishings and décor of his room, making purchases, and taking trips and vacations.

If the atmosphere of your home is conducive to the optimum development of your child's personality, your answers to all of the above questions should be "yes."

## *December* **21**

### Cooking Dried Vegetables

Dried vegetables are often a good choice for the winter months. Dehydrated potatoes take less time to prepare than fresh potatoes. Dehydrated onions may be added, without reconstitution, to dishes that contain a lot of liquid.

Dry beans and whole peas require soaking. Use the amount of water recommended for the vegetable in the Boiling Guide in the Appendix. Boil beans and peas 2 minutes, remove from heat, soak 1 hour, and then cook. Or soak overnight after the 2-minute boil, and then cook.

The long cooking time for beans can be shortened by adding a small amount of baking soda to the water at the beginning of the soaking period. If tap water is of medium hardness, add 1/8 teaspoon soda to the water for each cup of dry beans to reduce cooking time by about one-fourth. Measure the soda exactly. Too much soda affects flavor and the nutritive value of the beans.

To boil, cook in the soaking water to which 1 teaspoon of salt for each cup of the dry vegetable has been added. To reduce foaming during cooking, add 1 tablespoon meat drippings or other fat for each cup of dry beans or whole peas. Boil gently, uncovered, for a few minutes until foaming has decreased. Then cover and boil gently until tender. See Boiling Guide in Appendix for approximate boiling time.

Most dry beans and whole peas can be fully cooked in a pressure cooker in less than 30 minutes after soaking. This length of time allows pressure to rise and fall slowly and cooks these vegetables evenly without breaking the skins.

Follow these directions for soaking and pressure cooking dry beans and whole peas:

Add 2 cups of water for each cup of beans or peas, boil 2 minutes, and soak 1 hour before cooking. Fill pressure cooker no more than one-third full of food and water. If cooker is too full, food may clog the vent tube and cause an explosion. Add 1 tablespoon fat to reduce foaming, and 1 teaspoon salt per cup of dry beans or peas.

Put lid on pressure cooker. Follow manufacturer's directions for exhausting cooker and bringing pressure up to 15 pounds. Cook vegetables at 15 pounds pressure as follows:

Great Northern beans, kidney beans, large lima beans, and whole peas, 3 minutes; black beans and cranberry beans, 5 minutes; navy (pea) beans, 5 to 10 minutes; pinto beans, 10 minutes.

Remove the cooker from heat, and let the pressure drop gradually.

Lentils may be cooked without soaking. Add 1 teaspoon salt to the cooking water for each cup of lentils. Cover and boil gently until done. See Boiling Guide in Appendix.

Soaking split peas helps retain their shape. Follow the Boiling Guide in Appendix for amount of water to use. Boil for 2 minutes. Then soak 30 minutes. Split peas used in soup do not need to be soaked before cooking.

To boil split peas, add ¾ teaspoon salt for each cup of peas, cover, and boil gently without stirring for the time recommended in the guide.

You can also bake split peas after soaking them. Add ¾ teaspoon salt for each cup of peas. Place in a baking dish, cover, and bake at 350 degrees Fahrenheit for 35 minutes.

NOTE: Pressure cooking is not advised for split peas because they may spatter and clog the cooker vent.

Cooked dry beans, peas, and lentils may be seasoned and eaten without further preparation, or they may be baked or combined with other foods. If acid ingredients like tomatoes, catsup, or vinegar are included in the recipe, add them after the vegetables are tender. Acids prevent beans and peas from softening.

---

**DIVIDE LARGE electric skillets with aluminum-foil inserts and prepare several small dishes at one time. It will reduce your power bills.**

---

**FROZEN WATER PIPES can be thawed out by using a hair dryer with a can (or paper cup) cut to fit the nozzle. Flatten the open end of the can to concentrate heat along the pipe.**

---

# December 22

## Cooking Dried Fruits

Dried fruits no longer need soaking before cooking. Cooked dried fruits are plumper and more flavorful if they are refrigerated for several hours before serving.

Wash the fruit, place in a saucepan, add water, and bring to a boil. Simmer fruit until plump and tender. (See guide in Appendix.) Check the label; some processed fruits take less cooking time.

If more sweetening is needed, add sugar at the end of the cooking period. Adding sugar at the beginning inhibits the absorption of moisture which tenderizes the fruit.

For extra flavor in cooked dried fruits, add:

A stick of cinnamon and a few cloves at the beginning of cooking.

One teaspoon of grated lemon or orange rind at the beginning of cooking, or ¼ cup of frozen orange-juice concentrate near the end of the cooking period.

One-half cup raisins to dried apples, apricots, or mixed fruits before cooking.

# December 23

## Tips about Cooking on Top of the Range

Gas and electric range manufacturers tell us that medium-weight aluminum cookware is efficient for rangetop cooking. Fit the size of the pan to the size of the burner or heating unit. A lot of heat is wasted if the pan is smaller than the source of heat. Straight-sided pans also avoid heat loss. Poor quality cookware will dent and warp, leading to hot spots that scorch food. This wastes heat, as well as food and the cook's time.

On temperature-controlled burners, aluminum pans conduct heat evenly and efficiently. Materials that do not conduct heat well often develop hot spots. This means that thickened mixtures, such as sauces and puddings, may scorch. Good cooks know that pans should be nearly full for efficient use of heat, as well as for good results. Too large a pan causes excessive evaporation; one that's too small may boil over or cook unevenly.

Close contact between the cover and rim of a pan will retain steam, preventing excessive evaporation. The temperature inside a covered pan may be as much as 20 degrees higher than that of an open pan. The recommended procedure for top-of-the-stove cooking is to place the covered saucepan over medium heat. When the cover is hot to touch, or the first wisp of steam escapes around the cover, reduce heat to very low. Don't remove the cover during cooking except to test for doneness near the end of the cooking time. Utensils made of heavy-gauge aluminum, designed with tight-fitting covers, keep heat and vapor losses to a minimum, allowing cooking to be done over low heat with a very small amount of water. This preserves the flavor and nutritive value of food, as well as energy.

Frying pans are used directly over heat and usually without liquid. Oil and fat reach higher temperatures than water, so the pan should be made of medium or heavy aluminum to withstand heat without warping. Frying is done in an uncovered pan; however, a tight-fitting domed cover allows for cooking of thicker cuts of meat and some top-of-range baking. Heavy utensils, including aluminum, do heat more slowly, but they hold heat very well.

# December 24

## A Tall Tale about Roast Suckling Pig

Will you heed an old English tradition and have roast suckling pig for your holiday dinner tomorrow? You can, you know. Roasting a piglet is no more difficult than roasting a turkey. All standard cookbooks tell you how.

Whatever you'll feed your family, we thought you might relax for a few moments today and enjoy reading our condensation of one of the finest tall tales in the English language—Charles Lamb's *Dissertation upon Roast Pig.*

"Mankind, says a Chinese manuscript . . . for the first seventy thousand years ate meat raw . . . the art of roasting was accidentally discovered. The swineherd, Ho-ti, having gone to collect mast for his hogs, left his cottage in the care of his eldest son Bo-bo who being fond of playing with fire let some sparks escape into a bundle of straw. Together with the cottage a fine litter of new-farrowed pigs perished. Bo-bo was in the utmost consternation. He stooped down to feel the pig. He burnt his

fingers, and to cool them he applied them in his booby fashion in his mouth. Some of the crumbs of the scorched skin had come away with his fingers, and for the first time in the world's life he tasted *crackling*. Again he felt and fumbled at the pig. It did not burn him so much now, still he licked his fingers. The truth at last broke into his slow understanding . . . he fell to tearing up whole handfuls of the scorched skin with the flesh next to it, and was cramming it down his throat when his sire entered amid the smoking rafters. 'Oh father, the pig, the pig, do come and taste how nice the burnt pig eats.' Ho-ti trembled in every joint while he grasped the abominable thing . . . the crackling scorched his fingers . . . and he in his turn tasted some of its flavor. In conclusion both father and son never left off until they had despatched all that remained of the litter.

"Bo-bo was strictly enjoined not to let the secret escape. Nevertheless it was observed that Ho-ti's cottage was burned down more frequently than ever. Nothing but fires from this time forward. Some would break out in broad day, others in the night time. As often as the sow farrowed, so sure was the house of Ho-ti to be in a blaze. At length the terrible mystery (was) discovered and father and son summoned to trial. Evidence was given, the obnoxious food itself produced in court . . . the foreman of the jury begged that some might be handed into the box . . . they all handled it, burning their fingers . . . they brought in a verdict of Not Guilty.

"The judge when the court was dismissed, went privily, and bought up all the pigs. In a few days his lordship's town house was observed to be on fire. The thing took wing, and now there was nothing but fires in every direction. Insurance offices one and all shut up shop. People built slighter and slighter until it was feared that architecture would be lost to the world. Thus this custom of firing houses continued, till a sage arose who made a discovery that the flesh of any animal might be cooked (burnt, as they called it) without the necessity of consuming a whole house. Then first began the rude form of a grid-iron. Roasting by the string or spit came in a century or two later. . . ."

## Christmas Quiz

Why do we decorate our homes with evergreens at Christmastime? The origin of the custom is lost in the mists of pagan times. "Deck the halls with boughs of holly," are words of a carol so ancient that it may have been sung even before the first Christians reached Britain.

"Holly and ivy, box and bay, put in the church on Christmas Day" is an old English rhyme. Some early peoples associated evergreens with eternal life. Others thought they brought good luck. Druid priests believed the parasitic mistletoe was the soul of their sacred tree, the oak, and they passed out sprigs of mistletoe as charms to ward off evil spirits.

When were Christmas trees first used? It is a simple step from decorating with cut boughs to decorating with the entire tree. So our ancestors probably began bringing in evergreen trees thousands of years ago. A fir tree, according to legend, was the Saint Boniface miracle tree. Saint Boniface, born in England and christened Winifrid, was assigned by the Pope to carry Christianity to the pagan tribes of northern Germany. One day in about A.D. 750 he found a group of heathens about to offer the young Prince Asulf to the god Thor under an oak, their sacred tree. The missionary saved the prince from death and then had the oak chopped down. As the oak fell, a small fir was observed nearby. Saint Boniface told the heathens the fir represented Christ.

What was the origin of the yule log? Early Anglo-Saxons and Scandinavians venerated the oak tree. Once a year they built a bonfire around a huge oak log as a religious ceremony associated with Thor, the god of thunder. This was called burning the juul (pronounced "yule"). As years passed, the ceremony was moved indoors to huge fireplaces. When these peoples became Christians, they carried over this happy custom.

**TODAY IN HISTORY:** *A coffee percolator was patented on Dec. 26, 1865, by James H. Nason, of Franklin, Mass.*

## Word Games for Winter Days

On small squares of heavy paper or cardboard (1½" x 2") print the letters of the alphabet, plus several extra sets of vowels, one letter to a card. Have the children help prepare these materials.

Two or more can play. Mix up the letter cards and place them face down on a table. Each player in turn draws a square and calls a word that begins with that letter, within five to ten seconds, or the card is returned to the pile. When all cards have been drawn, each player spreads his letters out and uses them to spell as many words as he can. The consonant letters may be used in only one word, but the vowel cards may be reused. Children may need help with spelling. To score, allow one point for each letter card won during drawing, and one for each word completed and correctly spelled. The player with the most points wins.

Variations of this game, as well as other games, are described in a pamphlet "Word Games" prepared by the National Reading Center and obtainable from the Superintendent of Documents for 20 cents.

The games are especially designed to increase reading ability. They were planned for use with children who are just beginning to read—first to third graders—but can be useful to older children, even at the secondary-school level, who have reading difficulties, as well.

The games follow good learning psychology

—they involve the learner in that he helps to prepare the simple materials needed, and they use a multisensory approach (sight, sound, speech, and the small muscles are all brought into play).

Part of the fun of these games is that both parents and children may suggest changes or improvements. How long you play depends upon the length of the child's attention span. Enjoy the games yourself—or at least appear to—and the child will too.

## December 27

### Freeze Your Own "TV Dinners" and Save Money

There's no doubt about it—the so-called TV dinners that you buy in the supermarket are a great convenience. But they are expensive. You can achieve the same convenience, and reduce the cost, by preparing and freezing a variety of combination main dishes during slack periods when you have time to devote to such matters.

Does your family like such main dishes as chicken à la king, beef loaf, beans and sausage, lasagna, baked frankfurters and rice, and curried ham and turkey? You can get the information you need to prepare these and other dishes from "Freezing Combination Main Dishes," Home and Garden Bulletin No. 40 available from the Superintendent of Documents, Washington, D.C.

All recipes in the bulletin are for 24 servings. Directions are given for dividing the prepared food into four parts of six servings each. One part may be completely cooked and served at the time of preparation. The remaining parts may be frozen for use at a later time.

## December 28

### How Chewing Gum Began

Guess what! Chewing gum was patented on December 28, 1869. William F. Semple, of Mount Vernon, Ohio, got the patent on his claim of a "combination of rubber with other articles, in any proportions adapted to the formation of an acceptable chewing gum."

Chewing gum had been made before this, however. The Curtis brothers made what they called "State of Maine Pure Spruce Gum" in Bangor, Maine, in 1848.

## December 29

### How to Plan a Family Budget

Family budgeting must be done if we are to live within our means and make a start toward achieving such long-range goals as educating our children and providing for old age. Many people shy away from this financial task because they visualize the budget as the proverbial pie sliced into neat wedges representing percentages of income which should be allotted for housing, food, clothing, etc. And they know that the pie doesn't slice that way anymore.

We suggest that you forget the "pie" and plan your budget this way:

First, estimate your annual income and average it to arrive at a monthly income. Then, keep a record for a few months of your actual expenses: rent or mortgage payments, insurance, taxes, transportation, time payments, food, utilities, laundry and dry cleaning, clothing, cleaning supplies, medical and dental care, drugs and medicines, contributions, and recreation (including magazines and newspapers). Determine a monthly average for each of these categories.

Think ahead to the months that you have not included in your record of expenses—will taxes, an insurance premium, or some other payment come due? If so, add this to your list of expenses and revise the monthly average.

Add the averages for each category of expenses and subtract from your monthly income. The remainder is what you have to apportion for contingencies, vacations, and saving for long-range goals. At this point, it might be well to examine what expenses could be reduced in order to increase this remainder.

Discuss the final figures with the entire family. An important part of sharing family responsibility is helping to make the budget work.

Periodic revisions will probably be necessary if the budget is to be a viable one. Discuss these with the family, too.

## Life Insurance for Homemakers?

As the year draws to a close, one tends to plan for the year ahead, including the family budget (see yesterday's article). One big budgeting item is insurance. Fire, theft, accident, car, medical, and life insurance. At times it seems we can't afford to pay all the premiums, yet we definitely can't afford not to have protection.

When you review your insurance for the coming year—and today is a good time to do just that—consider the advisability of insuring the life of the homemaker, a prime asset in any home. As stated in the introduction to this Almanac, the services provided by the homemaker might cost more than $10,000 a year, and that figure is rising along with everything else. Should the homemaker die before her husband, the amount of money he would have to pay each year for child care and household maintenance would not only represent a large yearly cash liability, but would decrease the value of his estate, as well.

Consider whether you can afford *not* to insure the homemaker's life.

## December **31**

### December Potpourri for Homemakers

Make Christmas gift enclosure cards for next year by cutting suitable portions from the cards you received this year. Use a hole punch to make a hole in one corner.

Strings of cranberries used to decorate a Christmas tree in the old-fashioned way may be hung on an outdoor tree for the birds.

As you are dismantling the tree and other Christmas decorations, make a list of things you need for next year: another string of lights, bulb replacements, more tinsel.

Revise your Christmas card list for next year before discarding the cards you received. Note replies you wish to make to personal messages included with the cards.

Ring out the old, ring in the new
Ring happy bells, across the snow;
The year is going, let him go;
Ring out the false, ring in the true.

Ring out false pride in place and blood,
The civic slander and the spite;
Ring in the love of truth and right,
Ring in the common love of good.
—Alfred, Lord Tennyson

### Your Own Reminders:

# Appendix

The tables and charts that follow may be used to supplement specific items in the Almanac, or as a convenient reference source to household matters. The appendix includes information on fiber and apparel care, charts on cooking fruits and vegetables, facts about storing frozen foods, family food plans, charts showing retail cuts of meat, and weight, measure, and metric equivalents.

# How to Remove Stains from Resilient Flooring

To use this table, first locate the type of stain in the alphabetical listing. Then determine the removal method by referring to the appropriate steps in the removal key that follows the table.

| Type of Stain | Removal Method | Type of Stain | Removal Method |
|---|---|---|---|
| Alkali | ACJ | Ice cream | AEJ |
| Asphalt adhesive | ADGHJ | Ink | BEJ or BGHJ |
| Alcoholic beverages | ACJ | Iodine | BEJ or BGHJ |
| Blood | AGHJ | Lacquer | BEJ or DGHJ |
| Butter | DEJ | Medicine | BEJ or BGHJ |
| Candle wax | DGHJ | Mercurochrome | BFJ or BGHJ |
| Catsup | AEJ or AGHJ | Mildew | GHJ |
| Cement (household) | DGHJ | Milk | AEJ |
| Chewing gum | DGHJ | Mucilage | BDEGHJ |
| Cigarette burns | GHJ | Mustard | AEJ |
| Cleansers | ACJ or GJ | Nail polish | BEJ or DGHJ |
| Coffee | ACJ | Nail-polish remover | BEJ |
| Cosmetics | ADGHJ | Oil (petroleum) | AEJ |
| Detergents | ACJ or GJ | Oil (vegetable) | AEJ |
| Drain cleaners | ACJ or GJ | Paint | BEJ or DGHJ |
| Dry-cleaning fluids | BEJ | Rubber-heel marks | GHJ |
| Dye | BGHJ | Rust stains | GHJ or A |
| Eggs | ACJ | Shellac | BGJ or FJ |
| Fats | ADGHJ | Shoe polish | AGHJ |
| Foodstuffs | ADGHJ | Soft drinks | ACJ |
| Fruit juice | AEJ | Solvents | BEJ |
| Furniture polish | ADGHJ | Strong soaps | ACJ |
| Grass stains | GHJ | Tar | ADGHJ |
| Grease (petroleum) | ADGHJ | Tea | ACJ |
| Grease (vegetable) | ADGHJ | Varnish | BEJ or DGHJ |

## Key to Removal Method

A. Remove or wipe from floor.

B. If freshly spilled, take up immediately by blotting —do not rub. Then allow to dry.

C. Wash with rag dipped in water.

D. If dry, remove with putty knife.

E. Wash with cloth dipped in liquid cleaner, rinse.

F. Rub lightly with cloth dipped in alcohol, rinse.

G. Rub with No. 00 steel wool dipped in liquid cleaner, rinse.

H. If step G fails, dust with mild household cleanser, rub with No. 00 steel wool dipped in liquid cleaner. Rinse thoroughly.

J. Polish when dry.

*(The table and key above were developed by the management of Azrock Floor Products.)*

## Understanding Apparel Care Labels

This guide is designed to help you understand the brief care instructions found on permanent labels on garments you buy. Be sure to read the care instructions completely.

### Machine Washable

| when label reads: | it means: |
|---|---|
| Machine wash | Wash, bleach, dry, and press by any customary method including commercial laundering and dry cleaning. |
| Home launder only | Same as above, but do not use commercial laundering. |
| No chlorine bleach | Do not use chlorine bleach. Oxygen bleach may be used. |
| No bleach | Do not use any type of bleach. |
| Cold wash Cold rinse | Use cold water from tap or cold washing machine setting. |
| Warm wash Warm rinse | Use warm water or warm washing machine setting. |
| Hot wash | Use hot water or hot washing machine setting. |
| No spin | Remove wash load before final machine spin cycle. |
| Delicate cycle Gentle cycle | Use appropriate machine setting; otherwise wash by hand. |
| Durable-press cycle Permanent-press cycle | Use appropriate machine setting; otherwise use warm wash, cold rinse, and short spin cycle. |
| Hand wash separately | Hand wash alone or with like colors. |

### Not Machine Washable

| when label reads: | it means: |
|---|---|
| Hand wash | Launder only by hand in lukewarm (hand comfortable) water. May be bleached. May be dry-cleaned. |
| Hand wash only | Same as above, but do not dry-clean. |
| Hand wash separately | Hand wash alone or with like colors. |
| No bleach | Do not use bleach. |
| Damp wipe | Surface clean with damp cloth or sponge. |

### Home Drying

| when label reads: | it means: |
|---|---|
| Tumble dry | Dry in tumble dryer at specified setting—high, medium, low, or no heat. |
| Tumble dry Remove promptly | Same as above, but in absence of cool-down cycle remove at once when tumbling stops. |
| Drip dry | Hang wet and allow to dry with hand shaping only. |
| Line dry | Hang damp and allow to dry. |
| No wring No twist | Hang dry, drip dry, or dry flat only. Handle to prevent wrinkles and distortion. |
| Dry flat | Lay garment on flat surface. |
| Block to dry | Maintain original size and shape while drying. |

### Ironing or Pressing

| Cool iron | Set iron at lowest setting. |
|---|---|
| Warm iron | Set iron at medium setting. |
| Hot iron | Set iron at hot setting. |
| Do not iron | Do not iron or press with heat. |
| Steam iron | Iron or press with steam. |
| Iron damp | Dampen garment before ironing. |

### Miscellaneous

| Dry-clean only | Garment should be dry-cleaned only, including self-service. |
|---|---|
| Professionally dry-clean only | Do not use self-service dry cleaning. |
| No dry-clean | Use recommended care instructions. No dry-cleaning materials to be used. |

*This care Guide was produced by the Consumer Affairs Committee, American Apparel Manufacturers Association and is based on the Voluntary Guide of the Textile Industry Advisory Committee for Consumer Interests.*

# Alphabetical Guide to Fiber and Fabric Trademarks

| Trademark is followed by generic name | | |
|---|---|---|
| Acele—*acetate* | Cupioni—*rayon* | Nylmet—*metallic* |
| Acrilan—*acrylic* | Dacron—*polyester* | Nyloft—*nylon* |
| ANIM/8—*anidex* | Dan-Press— | Orlon—*acrylic* |
| Antron—*nylon* |    *durable-press* | Penn Prest—*durable-press* |
| Arnel—*triacetate* | DLP—*olefin* | PPG—*glass* |
| Avisco—*acetate* | Durastran—*metallic* | Qiana—*nylon* |
| Avisco—*rayon* | Dynel—*modacrylic* | Rayflex—*rayon* |
| Avlin—*polyester* | Enkalon—*nylon* | Sanforized Plus— |
| Avril—*rayon* | Estron—*acetate* |    *wash-and-wear* |
| Avron—*rayon* | Fiberglas—*glass* | Saran 25S—*saran* |
| Belfast—*wash-and-wear* | Fibro—*rayon* | Spandelle—*spandex* |
| Bemberg—*rayon* | Fortisan—*rayon* | Strawn—*rayon* |
| Beta Glass—*glass* | Fortrel—*polyester* | Suprenka—*rayon* |
| Cantrece—*nylon* | Glospan—*spandex* | Tebilized—*wash-and-wear* |
| Caprolan—*nylon* | Herculon—*olefin* | Trevira—*polyester* |
| Celanese—*acetate* | Jetspun—*rayon* | Unel—*spandex* |
| Celanese—*rayon* | Kodel—*polyester* | Vectra—*olefin* |
| Celaperm—*acetate* | Koratron—*durable-press* | Velon—*saran* |
| Celara—*acetate* | Lactron—*rubber* | Verel—*modacrylic* |
| Chromeflex—*metallic* | Lamé—*metallic* | Vincel 64—*rayon* |
| Chromspun—*acetate* | Lastex—*rubber* | Vitron—*glass* |
| Coloray—*rayon* | Lus-Trus—*saran* | Vycron—*polyester* |
| Coneprest—*durable-press* | Lurex—*metallic* | Wrinkl-Shed—*wash-and-wear* |
| Creslan—*acrylic* | Lycra—*spandex* | Zantrel—*rayon* |
| Cumuloft—*nylon* | Nupron—*rayon* | Zefran—*acrylic* |

## Cotton

Cotton products include apparel, carpets and rugs, home furnishings, and household textile products.

**Recommended care.** Cotton can be sterilized, machine washed and tumble dried, dry-cleaned. It can be bleached with chlorine or peroxide bleaches, but excessive or prolonged use of bleach may weaken the fabric. Some cotton finishes may cause the fabric to yellow when exposed to chlorine bleach. Cotton can be ironed, but "easy care" finishes may not require it. A safe ironing temperature is 400 degrees F. Cotton fabrics should be pre-shrunk for home sewing.

Cotton ignites readily and is not self-extinguishing, but it can be treated and made flame resistant to some extent, with some loss of durability and aesthetics. Effect of heat: yellows slowly at 245 degrees F.

## Linen

Linen products include apparel, handkerchiefs, home furnishings, table linens, and towels.

**Recommended care.** Linen can be machine washed and tumble dried, dry-cleaned, bleached if white (although bleaching tends to weaken linen fibers), ironed (dampen for best results). A safe ironing temperature is 400 degrees F. Sheen can be increased by ironing on the right side of the fabric when damp. Creases should not be pressed in. Table linens should be rolled on cardboard rollers rather than folded, since sharp angles may cause linen fibers to break.

Linen ignites readily and is not self-extinguishing, but it can be treated to make it flame resistant to some extent with some loss of durability. Linen does not lint.

## Silk

Silk products include apparel, home furnishings.

**Recommended care.** Silk can be hand laundered, though certain dyes "bleed" color when washed. It can be dry-cleaned, ironed with a warm iron. A safe ironing temperature is 250 to 275 degrees F. White silk can be bleached with hydrogen peroxide or sodium perborate bleaches, but chlorine should not be used.

Silk does not ignite readily, but materials added to silk to change its color or other properties may in some instances create a flammability hazard. Silk is weakened by sunlight and perspiration; yellowed by strong soap, age, and sunlight.

## Wool

Wool products include apparel, blankets, carpets.

**Recommended care.** Wool can be laundered, but only with extreme care. Use cool water, mild detergent, and gentle action. Never rub. Felting occurs when wool is subjected to heat, moisture, and mechanical action. Laundered garments should be dried on a flat surface, or spread over two or three lines to distribute weight. Wool products should be handled carefully when they are damp or wet. Wool can be dry-cleaned, pressed with a cool iron and steam. Hanging garments over a bathtub filled with hot water will sometimes remove wrinkles. Garments should be brushed after wearing, and allowed to rest 24 hours before they are worn again. Mothproof wool before storage.

Wool is not readily ignited in some constructions, and is self-extinguishing. Effect of heat: becomes harsh at 212 degrees F., scorches at 400 degrees F., and chars at about 572 degrees F.

## Acetate

Although acetate is made from cellulose, it is considered a man-made fiber because in production the cellulose is altered by chemical means. It is closely related to rayon; in fact, it was called acetate-rayon until a 1952 Federal Trade Commission ruling separated the two fiber groups into "acetate" and "rayon." Acetate combines well with other fibers. Its luster, silkiness, body, good draping qualities, and crispness have made fashion fabrics such as bengaline, taffeta, satin, faille, crepe, brocade, double knit, and tricot the major uses of acetate. Solution-dyed or spun-dyed acetate has excellent color fastness to light, perspiration, atmospheric contaminants, and washing.

**Recommended care.** Acetate can be hand laundered, in some constructions, if you use warm water and gentle agitation. Garments should not be soaked, wrung out, or twisted. Acetate can be dry-cleaned. It can be ironed with a cool iron. Acetate fibers melt at high temperatures. A safe ironing temperature is 250-300 degrees F. Garments made of acetate should be protected from nail polish, paint remover, and some perfumes that dissolve the fibers.

Acetate ignites readily and is not self-extinguishing, but it can be made flame resistant with some loss of other properties.

## Triacetate

Chemically, triacetate is quite similar to, and has many properties in common with, acetate; low strength when wet and low resistance to abrasion, but excellent appearance, drapability and resistance to moths and mildew. Triacetate's chief difference and most valuable characteristic is resistance to damage by heat. This property permits the heat-setting treatments which are responsible for the fabric's outstanding features of durable crease and pleat retention, dimensional stability, and resistance to glazing during ironing. Because triacetate is comparatively insensitive to high temperature, it can be made into products which launder easily, dry quickly, and require little special care.

**Recommended care.** Triacetate can be machine washed and tumble dried. It can be ironed, if necessary, with a hot iron. Safe ironing temperature is 450 degrees F.

Triacetate ignites readily and is not self-extinguishing. It can be made flame resistant, with some loss of other properties.

## Acrylic

Wool-like qualities and easy care are acrylic's major contributions to textiles. Although the fibers can be made into crisp fabrics, they are associated mainly with the soft, high bulk, textured yarns used in sweaters and furlike fabrics. In comparison to wool, acrylic fabrics are stronger, easier to care for, softer, do not felt, and provide more warmth for less weight. The versatility of this fiber is illustrated by the fact that while it is more durable than rayon or acetate, it can be made to perform more like wool than can nylon or polyester. Acrylic is not harmed by common solvents and is resistant to weathering, bleaches, and dilute acids and alkalis. Because of these qualities, its use—alone or in blends—ranges from fine fabrics to work clothing and fabrics which are chemical resistant.

**Recommended care:** Acrylic can be machine washed and tumble dried at low temperatures. It can be dry-cleaned. A safe ironing temperature is 300-325 degrees F. It can be bleached with either chlorine or peroxide bleaches.

Acrylic ignites and burns readily. Acrylic is subject to static build-up.

## Anidex

A new elastic fiber, anidex has exceptional resistance to chemicals, sunlight, and heat. Ease-of-care properties make it possible to combine anidex in blends with both natural and man-made fibers. Wool, cotton, linen, nylon, and silk may be blended with anidex without changing the natural look and feel of the basic material. A major application of these blends is in woven and knit fabrics where anidex contributes properties of stretch and recovery. In apparel, the blend fabric permits freedom of body movement while reducing or eliminating sagging or bagging. When used in upholstered furniture, anidex blends provide greater freedom of design because the fabric can stretch to conform to the furniture contours.

**Recommended care.** Anidex can be machine washed and tumble dried at "normal" settings. To bleach, use chlorine bleaches recommended by the fiber manufacturer. It can be pressed at temperatures up to 320 degrees F. if in the core-spun form (that is, composed of a central fiber with others wound around it).

Anidex does not ignite readily, but it will burn. Since anidex is usually 5 to 10 percent by weight of the fabric being considered, its flammability and reaction to heat are largely dependent on the fibers with which it is combined.

## Glass

Glass fibers have many properties which make them particularly suitable for industrial and home-furnishing products (especially curtains and draperies). Because of their weight, low abrasion resistance, and poor bending strength they are not suitable for apparel. The most important recent advance in the glass-fiber industry has been the development of ultrafine, continuous filament "Beta" yarns. These are stronger than previous glass yarns.

**Recommended care.** Glass-fiber fabrics can be machine washed if agitated gently, but hand washing is safer. They should not be spin-dried, twisted, or wrung out. No ironing is necessary. If machine washed, rinse out washer thoroughly before loading with apparel. Glass fabrics can be drip dried until almost dry, then hung on rods to complete the drying. Dry cleaning is not recommended. Hang draperies so they do not touch the floor or window sill.

Glass fibers are nonflammable except when treated with flammable resinous finishing materials.

## Metallic

As defined by the Federal Trade Commission, "metallic" is any manufactured fiber composed of metal, plastic-coated metal, metal-coated plastic, or a core completely covered by metal. The history of pure metal yarns goes back for thousands of years, but their uses were restricted because they were heavy, brittle, expensive, and easily tarnished. New processes have been developed to overcome these problems. The resulting lustrous yarns are finding increasing use in many types of apparel and household furnishings.

**Recommended care.** Metallic fabrics can be washed if the basic fibers with which they are combined are washable. They usually can be ironed with a cool iron. But consult hang tags and labels for specific care instructions.

Metallic yarns are extremely sensitive to heat because their plastic components soften and shrink.

## Modacrylic

As its name implies, modacrylic is modified acrylic fiber. It possesses many properties in common with acrylic. The heat sensitivity of modacrylic fibers permits them to be stretched, embossed, and embossed into special shapes, and to be used in fabrics or fabric blends that require no ironing. Dense furlike fabrics are possible. Products include blankets, carpets, dolls' hair, draperies, furlike pile fabrics, knitwear, and wigs.

**Recommended care.** Modacrylics can be machine washed in warm water and tumble dried at low temperatures. Remove the article from the machine as soon as the tumble cycle stops. They can be ironed, if necessary, a safe ironing temperature is 200-250 degrees F. They also can be dry-cleaned. A fur cleaning process is recommended for deep pile.

Modacrylics are flame resistant and generally self-extinguishing. They soften at comparatively low temperatures.

## Nylon

For facts about nylon see February 16.

## Olefin

The olefin fibers, polyethylene and polypropylene, are petroleum products. They have the lightest weight of all fibers. Nonabsorbent, they are difficult to dye, but recent modification of the fiber structure has made it possible to dye them by standard procedures. It is doubtful that you will find polyethylene in apparel products, but polypropylene is used in a variety of textile products, including apparel. Other uses are blankets, floor coverings (indoor-outdoor carpets), upholstery.

**Recommended care.** Olefins can be machine washed in lukewarm water. Some can be tumble

dried at low temperatures. Caution: If the fiber is used as the batting or filler in quilted pads and other items and is not treated with a wash-resistant anti-oxidant by the manufacturer, heat from the dryer may build up in the fiber filling until it reaches the kindling point, RESULTING IN FIRE. Articles of 100 percent olefin cannot be ironed, but blends may be ironed at low temperatures (250 degrees F. or lower). Olefins can be dry-cleaned. They can be bleached at low water temperatures (below 150 degrees F.).

Olefins which have been given a wash-resistant, anti-oxidant treatment do not ignite readily, but once ignited they burn, melt, and drip.

## Polyester

With the advent of the polyester fiber, the old dream of "wash-and-wear" or "easy-care" clothing became a reality. Polyester does not shrink or stretch appreciably during normal use. Heat-set pleats and creases stand up extremely well under everyday wear, even when the wearer is young and active. Waterborne stains may be quickly and easily removed. Because of polyester's outstanding wrinkle resistance and dimensional stability, it is used extensively in blends with other fibers, notably with cotton, rayon, and wool. A major use of polyester is in cotton blends used in durable-press textiles.

**Recommended care.** Polyester can be machine washed and tumble dried. Articles containing fiberfill may also be machine washed and dried, depending on the cover fabric. It can be bleached with chlorine bleaches, ironed, and dry-cleaned. A safe ironing temperature is 300-350 degrees F.

Polyester does not ignite readily, but when ignited it burns, melts, and drips. In blends, particularly with cellulosic fibers, it burns readily.

**Rayon**

For facts about rayon see December 19.

**Saran**

Saran has many desirable characteristics, but because it melts at low temperatures its use in apparel is limited. Saran is virtually impervious to weathering and is highly resistant to chemicals in the atmosphere. Uses include awnings, indoor-outdoor carpets, garden furniture, handbags and luggage, and screening.

**Recommended care.** Saran can be washed with soap or detergent. It can be bleached with chlorine bleach, but the water must be at a temperature of 100 degrees F. or below.

Saran does not support combustion. When combined with flammable fibers, saran acts as a retardant. It softens at temperatures about 212 degrees F. and melts at 340 degrees.

**Spandex**

Spandex is a man-made fiber with great elasticity. Garments containing spandex core-spun yarns retain their holding power better than other garments of similar weight made with covered natural rubber yarns. Foundation garments containing spandex are usually soft, and provide great freedom of movement. Currently, however, few garments are made of 100 percent spandex, since only a small amount is needed to provide the desired holding power. In home sewing on spandex fabrics, there is little danger of damage from needles.

**Recommended care.** Spandex can be machine washed and tumble dried at low temperatures. It can be ironed if necessary. Safe ironing temperature is below 300 degrees F. But it is necessary to iron quickly and not leave the iron in the same position too long. It can be dry-cleaned. Use only nonchlorine bleaches.

Spandex does not ignite readily, but when ignited it melts and burns.

## What Size Stocking Do You Wear?

Your shoe size—length and width—is usually a good guide to the size
of stocking that will fit you best. Use this chart.

| Shoe Size | | Stocking Size Needed | Shoe Size | | Stocking Size Needed |
|---|---|---|---|---|---|
| Length | Width | | Length | Width | |
| 2½ | AAA to B | 8 | 6½ | AAA to B | 9½ |
| | | | 7 | AAA or AA | |
| 2½ | C to EE | 8½ | 6 | E or EE | 10 |
| 3 | AAA to EEE | | 6½ | C to EE | |
| 3½ | AAA to EE | | 7 | A to D | |
| 4 | AAA to B | | 7½ | AAA to B | |
| 4½ | AAA or AA | | 8 | AAA or AA | |
| 4 | C to EE | 9 | 7 | E or EE | 10½ |
| 4½ | A to D | | 7½ | C to EE | |
| 5 | AAA to D | | 8 | A to EE | |
| 5½ | AAA to AA | | 8½ | AAA to D | |
| | | | 9 | AAA or AA | |
| 4½ | E or EE | 9½ | 8½ | E or EE | 11 |
| 5 | E or EE | | 9 | A to EE | |
| 5½ | A to E | | 9½ | AAA to EE | |
| 6 | AAA to D | | | | |

## Equivalents of Capacity Units Used in Kitchen

| Units | Fluid drams | Tea-spoon-fuls | Table-spoon-fuls | Fluid ounces | ¼ cup-fuls | Gills (½ cup-fuls) | Cup-fuls | Liquid pints | Liquid quarts | Cubic centi-meters | Liters |
|---|---|---|---|---|---|---|---|---|---|---|---|
| 1 fluid dram equals | 1 | ¾ | ¼ | ⅛ | 1/16 | 1/32 | 1/64 | 1/128 | 1/256 | 3.7 | 0.004 |
| 1 teaspoonful equals | 1⅓ | 1 | ⅓ | ⅙ | 1/12 | 1/24 | 1/48 | 1/96 | 1/192 | 4.9 | 0.005 |
| 1 tablespoonful equals | 4 | 3 | 1 | ½ | ¼ | ⅛ | 1/16 | 1/32 | 1/64 | 15 | 0.015 |
| 1 fluid ounce equals | 8 | 6 | 2 | 1 | ½ | ¼ | ⅛ | 1/16 | 1/32 | 30 | 0.030 |
| ¼ cupful equals | 16 | 12 | 4 | 2 | 1 | ½ | ¼ | ⅛ | 1/16 | 59 | 0.059 |
| 1 gill (½ cupful) equals | 32 | 24 | 8 | 4 | 2 | 1 | ½ | ¼ | ⅛ | 118 | 0.118 |
| 1 cupful equals | 64 | 48 | 16 | 8 | 4 | 2 | 1 | ½ | ¼ | 237 | 0.237 |
| 1 liquid pint equals | 128 | 96 | 32 | 16 | 8 | 4 | 2 | 1 | ½ | 473 | 0.473 |
| 1 liquid quart equals | 256 | 192 | 64 | 32 | 16 | 8 | 4 | 2 | 1 | 946 | 0.946 |
| 1 cubic centimeter equals | 0.27 | 0.20 | 0.068 | 0.034 | 0.017 | 0.0084 | 0.0042 | 0.0021 | 0.0011 | 1 | 1/1000 |
| 1 liter equals | 270 | 203 | 67.6 | 33.8 | 16.9 | 8.45 | 4.23 | 2.11 | 1.06 | 1000 | 1 |

## Appropriate Spices and Herbs for Cooking Vegetables

| Vegetable | Spice or herb | Vegetable | Spice or herb |
|---|---|---|---|
| Asparagus | Mustard seed, sesame seed, or tarragon. | Cucumbers | Basil, dill, mint, or tarragon. |
| Beans, lima | Marjoram, oregano, sage, savory, tarragon, or thyme. | Eggplant | Marjoram or oregano. |
| Beans, snap | Basil, dill, marjoram, mint, mustard seed, oregano, savory, tarragon, or thyme. | Onions | Caraway seed, mustard seed, nutmeg, oregano, sage, or thyme. |
| Beets | Allspice, bay leaves, caraway seed, cloves, dill, ginger, mustard seed, savory, or thyme. | Peas | Basil, dill, marjoram, mint, oregano, poppy seed, rosemary, sage, or savory. |
| Broccoli | Caraway seed, dill, mustard seed, or tarragon. | Potatoes | Basil, bay leaves, caraway seed, celery seed, dill, chives, mustard seed, oregano, poppy seed, or thyme. |
| Brussels sprouts | Basil, caraway seed, dill, mustard seed, sage, or thyme. | Salad greens | Basil, chives, dill, or tarragon. |
| Cabbage | Caraway seed, celery seed, dill, mint, mustard seed, nutmeg, savory, or tarragon. | Spinach | Basil, mace, marjoram, nutmeg, or oregano. |
| Carrots | Allspice, bay leaves, caraway seed, dill, fennel, ginger, mace, marjoram, mint, nutmeg, or thyme. | Squash | Allspice, basil, cinnamon, cloves, fennel, ginger, mustard seed, nutmeg, or rosemary. |
| Cauliflower | Caraway seed, celery salt, dill, mace, or tarragon. | Sweet potatoes | Allspice, cardamom, cinnamon, cloves, or nutmeg. |
|  |  | Tomatoes | Basil, bay leaves, celery seed, oregano, sage, sesame seed, tarragon, or thyme. |

*Note: Pepper and parsley may be added to any of the above vegetables. Curry powder is good with creamed vegetables.*

300

## How Long Can You Keep Frozen Foods and Expect to Have Top Quality?

| | Approximate holding period at 0° F. | | Approximate holding period at 0° F. |
|---|---|---|---|
| Fruits: | Months | Cooked meat: | Months |
| Cherries | 12 | Meat dinners | 3 |
| Peaches | 12 | Meat pie | 3 |
| Raspberries | 12 | Swiss steak | 3 |
| Strawberries | 12 | | |
| Fruit juice concentrates: | | Chicken: | |
| Apple | 12 | Cut-up | 9 |
| Grape | 12 | Livers | 3 |
| Orange | 12 | Whole | 12 |
| | | Duck, whole | 6 |
| | | Goose, whole | 6 |
| Vegetables: | | Turkey: | |
| Asparagus | 8 | Cut-up | 6 |
| Beans | 8 | Whole | 12 |
| Cauliflower | 8 | Cooked chicken and turkey: | |
| Corn | 8 | Chicken or turkey dinners | |
| Peas | 8 | (sliced meat and gravy) | 6 |
| Spinach | 8 | Chicken or turkey pies | 6 |
| | | Fried chicken | 4 |
| Bread and yeast rolls: | | Fried chicken dinners | 4 |
| White bread | 3 | | |
| Cinnamon rolls | 2 | Fish: | |
| Plain rolls | 3 | Fillets: | |
| Cakes: | | Cod, flounder, haddock, | |
| Angel | 2 | halibut, pollack | 6 |
| Chiffon | 2 | Mullet, ocean perch, sea | |
| Chocolate layer | 4 | trout, striped bass | 3 |
| Fruit | 12 | Pacific Ocean perch | 2 |
| Pound | 6 | Salmon steaks | 2 |
| Yellow | 6 | Sea trout, dressed | 3 |
| Danish pastry | 3 | Striped bass, dressed | 3 |
| Doughnuts: | | Whiting, drawn | 4 |
| Cake type | 3 | Shellfish: | |
| Yeast raised | 3 | Clams, shucked | 3 |
| Pies (unbaked): | | Crabmeat: | |
| Apple | 8 | Dungeness | 3 |
| Boysenberry | 8 | King | 10 |
| Cherry | 8 | Oysters, shucked | 4 |
| Peach | 8 | Shrimp | 12 |
| | | Cooked fish and shellfish: | |
| Beef: | | Fish with cheese sauce | 3 |
| Hamburger or chipped | | Fish with lemon butter | |
| (thin) steaks | 4 | sauce | 3 |
| Roasts | 12 | Fried fish dinner | 3 |
| Steaks | 12 | Fried fish sticks, scallops, | |
| Lamb: | | or shrimp | 3 |
| Patties (ground meat) | 4 | Shrimp creole | 3 |
| Roasts | 9 | Tuna pie | 3 |
| Pork, cured | 2 | | |
| Pork, fresh: | | Ice cream | 1 |
| Chops | 4 | Sherbet | 1 |
| Roasts | 8 | | |
| Sausage | 2 | | |
| Veal: | | | |
| Cutlets, chops | 9 | | |
| Roasts | 9 | | |

## Boiling Guide for Fresh Vegetables

| Vegetable | Cooking time after water returns to boil | Approximate amount as purchased for six servings (about ½ cup each) |
|---|---|---|
| | Minutes | Pounds |
| Asparagus | 5 to 10 (whole spears)<br>5 to 10 (cuts and tips) | 2½ for spears<br>1¾ for cuts and tips |
| Beans, lima<br>Beans, snap (green or wax) | 25 to 30<br>12 to 16 (1-inch pieces) | 2¾ in pods<br>1 |
| Beets | 30 to 45 (young, whole)<br>45 to 90 (older, whole)<br>15 to 25 (sliced or diced) } | 2½ with tops or<br>1½ without tops |
| Broccoli | 10 to 15 (heavy stalk split) | 2 |
| Brussels sprouts | 15 to 20 | 1½ |
| Cabbage | 3 to 10 (shredded)<br>10 to 15 (wedges) | 1¼<br>1½ |
| Carrots | 15 to 20 (young, whole)<br>20 to 30 (older, whole)<br>10 to 20 (sliced or diced) } | 1½ without tops |
| Cauliflower | 8 to 15 (separated)<br>15 to 25 (whole) } | 2. |
| Celery | 15 to 18 (cut-up) | 1½ |
| Corn | 5 to 15 (on cob) | 3 in husks |
| Kale | 10 to 15 | 1¼ untrimmed |
| Okra | 10 to 15 | 1¼ |
| Onions, mature | 15 to 30 | 1¾ |
| Parsnips | 20 to 40 (whole)<br>8 to 15 (quartered) } | 1½ |
| Peas | 12 to 16 | 3 in pods |
| Potatoes | 25 to 40 (whole, medium)<br>20 to 25 (quartered)<br>10 to 15 (diced) } | 1½<br>1¼ |
| Spinach | 3 to 10 | 1½ prepackaged |
| Squash, summer | 8 to 15 (sliced) | 1½ |
| Squash, winter | 15 to 20 (cut-up) | 2½ |
| Sweet potatoes | 35 to 55 (whole) | 2 |
| Tomatoes | 7 to 15 (cut-up) | 1¼ |
| Turnip greens | 10 to 30 | 2¾ prepackaged |
| Turnips | 20 to 30 (whole)<br>10 to 20 (cut-up) } | 1¾ without tops |

## Boiling Guide for Frozen Vegetables

| Vegetable | Cooking time after water returns to boil | Approximate amount as purchased for 6 servings (½ cup each) |
|---|---|---|
| | Minutes | Ounces |
| Asparagus, whole | 5 to 10 | 24 |
| Beans, lima | 10 to 18 | 18 |
| Beans, snap (green or wax), cut | 12 to 20 | 16 |
| Broccoli spears | 8 to 15 | 22 |
| Brussels sprouts | 10 to 15 | 20 |
| Carrots, sliced or diced | 5 to 10 | 18 |
| Cauliflower | 5 to 8 | 20 |
| Corn: | | |
| Whole kernel | 3 to 6 | 20 |
| On cob | 3 to 5 | 32 |
| Kale | 8 to 12 | 25 |
| Peas | 3 to 5 | 18 |
| Potatoes, small, whole | 10 to 12 | 21 |
| Spinach | 5 to 14 | 25 |
| Squash, summer, sliced | 10 to 12 | 22 |
| Turnip greens | 15 to 20 | 27 |

## Boiling Guide for Dry Beans, Peas, and Lentils

| Vegetable (1 cup) | Amount of water | Approximate boiling time | Yield |
|---|---|---|---|
| | Cups | Hours | Cups |
| Black beans | 3 | 2 | 2 |
| Blackeye beans (blackeye peas, cowpeas) | 2½ | ½ | 2½ |
| Cranberry beans | 3 | 2 | 2 |
| Great Northern beans | 2½ | 1 to 1½ | 2½ |
| Kidney beans | 3 | 2 | 2¾ |
| Lentils | 2 | ½ | 2½ |
| Lima beans, large | 2½ | 1 | 2½ |
| Lima beans, small | 2½ | 1 | 2 |
| Navy (pea) beans | 3 | 1½ to 2 | 2½ |
| Peas, whole | 2½ | 1 | 2½ |
| Pinto beans | 3 | 2 | 2½ |
| Soybeans | 3 | 2½ | 2½ |
| Split peas | 2 | ⅓ | 2½ |

## Guide for Cooking Canned Vegetables

(6 servings of ½ cup each)

| Vegetable | Vegetable Quarts | Fat Tablespoons | Salt Teaspoons | Water | Cooking time Minutes |
|---|---|---|---|---|---|
| Beans, snap, (green or wax) sliced in 1-inch pieces | 1 | 1½ | ½ | ⅔ cup | 20 to 25 |
| Cabbage, finely shredded | 1½ | 1½ | ¾ | 3 Tbs | 6 to 8 |
| Carrots, thinly sliced | 1 | 2 | ½ | 3 Tbs | 10 |
| Corn, cut | 1 | 1½ | ½ | ⅓ cup | 15 to 18 |
| Spinach, finely shredded | 3 | 2 | ½ | | 6 to 8 |
| Summer squash, thinly sliced | 1 | 1½ | ½ | 3 Tbs | 12 to 15 |

## Guide to Simmering Dried Fruits

| Kind of fruit | Amount of fruit Ounces | Amount of water Cups | Amount of sugar Cup | Cooking time Minutes | Approximate number of ½-cup servings |
|---|---|---|---|---|---|
| Apples | 8 | 3½ | ⅓ | 10 | 8 |
| Apricots | 8 | 2¼ | ⅓ | 10 | 6 |
| | 11 | 3 | ½ | 10 | 8 |
| Mixed fruits | 8 | 2¼ | ⅓ | 20 | 6 |
| | 11 | 3 | ½ | 20 | 8 |
| Peaches | 8 | 3 | ⅓ | 25 | 7 |
| | 11 | 4 | ½ | 25 | 9 or 10 |
| Pears | 8 | 2 | ⅛ | 25 | 4 |
| | 11 | 3 | ¼ | 25 | 6 |
| Prunes | 16 | 4 | ¼ to ½, if desired | 25 | 8 or 9 |

## Guide to Simmering Fresh Fruit

| Kind of fruit | Amount of fruit, as purchased Pounds | Amount of water Cup | Amount of sugar Cup | Cooking time after adding fruit Minutes | Approximate number of ½-cup servings |
|---|---|---|---|---|---|
| Apples | 2 | ½ | ¼ | 8-10 | 6 |
| Apricots | 1½ | ½ | ¾ | 5 | 6 |
| Peaches | 1½ | ¾ | ¾ | 5 | 6 |
| Pears: Soft varieties | 2 | ⅔ | ⅓ | 10 | 6 |
| Firm varieties | 2 | ⅔ | ⅓ | 20-25 | 6 |
| Plums | 1 | ½ | ⅔ | 5 | 6 |

## Guide to Making Fresh Fruit Sauces

| Kind of fruit | Amount of fruit, as purchased Pounds | Amount of water Cups | Amount of sugar Cups | Cooking time after adding fruit Minutes | Approximate yield Cups |
|---|---|---|---|---|---|
| Apples | 2 | ⅓ | ¼ | 12-15 | 3 |
| Cherries | 1 | ⅔ | ½ | 5 | 2 |
| Cranberries | 1 | 2 | 2 | 15 | 4 (whole) 3 (strained) |
| Peaches | 1 | ⅔ | ½ | 5-8 | 2 |
| Rhubarb | 1½ | ¾ | ⅔ | 2-5 | 3 |

## Basic Low-Cost Family Food Plan

Weekly quantities of food[1] for each member of family

| Sex-age group | Milk, cheese, ice cream[2] (Qt.) | Meat, poultry, fish[3] Lb. | Oz. | Eggs (No.) | Dry beans, peas, nuts Lb. | Oz. | Flour, cereals, baked goods[4] Lb. | Oz. | Citrus fruit, tomatoes Lb. | Oz. | Dark-green and deep-yellow vegetables Lb. | Oz. | Potatoes Lb. | Oz. | Other vegetables and fruits Lb. | Oz. | Fats, oils Lb. | Oz. | Sugars, sweets Lb. | Oz. |
|---|---|---|---|---|---|---|---|---|---|---|---|---|---|---|---|---|---|---|---|---|
| **Children:** | | | | | | | | | | | | | | | | | | | | |
| 7 months to 1 year | 5½ | 1 | 0 | 5 | 0 | 0 | 0 | 12 | 1 | 8 | 0 | 2 | 0 | 8 | 1 | 0 | 0 | 1 | 0 | 2 |
| 1-3 years | 5½ | 1 | 4 | 5 | 0 | 1 | 1 | 4 | 1 | 8 | 0 | 4 | 0 | 12 | 2 | 4 | 0 | 4 | 0 | 4 |
| 4-6 years | 5½ | 1 | 8 | 5 | 0 | 2 | 2 | 0 | 1 | 12 | 0 | 4 | 1 | 4 | 3 | 4 | 0 | 6 | 0 | 6 |
| 7-9 years | 5½ | 2 | 0 | 6 | 0 | 4 | 2 | 4 | 2 | 0 | 0 | 8 | 2 | 0 | 4 | 4 | 0 | 8 | 0 | 10 |
| 10-12 years | 6½ | 2 | 4 | 6 | 0 | 6 | 3 | 0 | 2 | 4 | 0 | 8 | 2 | 8 | 5 | 0 | 0 | 8 | 0 | 12 |
| **Girls:** | | | | | | | | | | | | | | | | | | | | |
| 13-15 years | 7 | 2 | 8 | 6 | 0 | 4 | 3 | 0 | 2 | 4 | 0 | 12 | 2 | 8 | 5 | 0 | 0 | 10 | 0 | 12 |
| 16-19 years | 7 | 2 | 8 | 6 | 0 | 4 | 2 | 12 | 2 | 4 | 0 | 12 | 2 | 4 | 4 | 12 | 0 | 6 | 0 | 10 |
| **Boys:** | | | | | | | | | | | | | | | | | | | | |
| 13-15 years | 7 | 2 | 8 | 6 | 0 | 6 | 4 | 4 | 2 | 8 | 0 | 12 | 3 | 4 | 5 | 4 | 0 | 12 | 0 | 12 |
| 16-19 years | 7 | 3 | 4 | 6 | 0 | 8 | 5 | 4 | 2 | 8 | 0 | 12 | 4 | 12 | 5 | 8 | 0 | 14 | 0 | 14 |
| **Women:** | | | | | | | | | | | | | | | | | | | | |
| 20-34 years | 3½ | 2 | 8 | 5 | 0 | 4 | 2 | 8 | 2 | 0 | 0 | 12 | 2 | 0 | 5 | 8 | 0 | 6 | 0 | 10 |
| 35-54 years | 3½ | 2 | 8 | 5 | 0 | 4 | 2 | 8 | 2 | 0 | 0 | 12 | 1 | 8 | 4 | 8 | 0 | 4 | 0 | 10. |
| 55-74 years | 3½ | 2 | 8 | 5 | 0 | 4 | 2 | 4 | 2 | 0 | 0 | 12 | 1 | 4 | 3 | 8 | 0 | 4 | 0 | 6 |
| 75 years and over | 3½ | 2 | 8 | 5 | 0 | 4 | 2 | 0 | 2 | 0 | 0 | 12 | 2 | 4 | 3 | 0 | 0 | 6 | 0 | 8 |
| Pregnant | 7 | 2 | 8 | 7 | 0 | 4 | 2 | 8 | 3 | 8 | 1 | 8 | 2 | 0 | 5 | 8 | 0 | 6 | 0 | 8 |
| Nursing | 10 | 3 | 4 | 7 | 0 | 4 | 3 | 0 | 4 | 8 | 0 | 8 | 3 | 4 | 5 | 8 | 0 | 8 | 0 | 10 |
| **Men:** | | | | | | | | | | | | | | | | | | | | |
| 20-34 years | 3½ | 3 | 12 | 6 | 0 | 6 | 4 | 4 | 2 | 4 | 0 | 12 | 3 | 4 | 5 | 8 | 0 | 12 | 1 | 0 |
| 35-54 years | 3½ | 3 | 8 | 6 | 0 | 6 | 3 | 12 | 2 | 4 | 0 | 12 | 3 | 0 | 5 | 0 | 0 | 10 | 0 | 12 |
| 55-74 years | 3½ | 3 | 4 | 6 | 0 | 4 | 3 | 8 | 2 | 4 | 0 | 12 | 2 | 8 | 4 | 12 | 0 | 10 | 0 | 10 |
| 75 years and over | 3½ | 3 | 4 | 6 | 0 | 4 | 3 | 4 | 2 | 0 | 0 | 12 | 2 | 4 | 4 | 8 | 0 | 8 | 0 | 10 |
| **Total** | | | | | | | | | | | | | | | | | | | | |

[1] Food as purchased or brought into the kitchen from garden or farm.
[2] Fluid, whole, or its calcium equivalent in cheese, evaporated milk, dry milk, ice cream.
[3] Bacon and salt pork should not exceed ⅓ pound for each 5 pounds of meat group.
[4] Weight in terms of flour and cereal. Count 1½ pounds bread as 1 pound flour.

## Moderate-Cost Family Food Plan

Weekly quantities of food[1] for each member of family

| Sex-age group | Milk, cheese, ice cream[2] (Qt.) | Meat, poultry, fish[3] (Lb. / Oz.) | | Eggs (No.) | Dry beans, peas, nuts (Lb. / Oz.) | | Flour, cereals, baked goods[4] (Lb. / Oz.) | | Citrus fruit, tomatoes (Lb. / Oz.) | | Dark-green and deep-yellow vegetables (Lb. / Oz.) | | Potatoes (Lb. / Oz.) | | Other vegetables and fruits (Lb. / Oz.) | | Fats, oils (Lb. / Oz.) | | Sugars, sweets (Lb. / Oz.) | |
|---|---|---|---|---|---|---|---|---|---|---|---|---|---|---|---|---|---|---|---|---|---|
| **Children:** | | | | | | | | | | | | | | | | | | | | | |
| 7 months to 1 year | 6 | 1 | 4 | 6 | 0 | 0 | 0 | 12 | 1 | 8 | 0 | 2 | 0 | 8 | 1 | 8 | 0 | 1 | 0 | 2 |
| 1-3 years | 6 | 1 | 12 | 6 | 0 | 0 | 1 | 0 | 1 | 8 | 0 | 4 | 0 | 12 | 2 | 12 | 0 | 4 | 0 | 4 |
| 4-6 years | 6 | 2 | 4 | 6 | 0 | 1 | 1 | 12 | 2 | 0 | 0 | 4 | 1 | 0 | 4 | 0 | 0 | 6 | 0 | 10 |
| 7-9 years | 6 | 3 | 0 | 6 | 0 | 2 | 2 | 0 | 2 | 4 | 0 | 8 | 1 | 12 | 4 | 12 | 0 | 10 | 0 | 14 |
| 10-12 years | 6½ | 4 | 0 | 7 | 0 | 4 | 2 | 12 | 2 | 8 | 0 | 12 | 2 | 4 | 5 | 8 | 0 | 10 | 0 | 14 |
| **Girls:** | | | | | | | | | | | | | | | | | | | | | |
| 13-15 years | 7 | 4 | 8 | 7 | 0 | 2 | 2 | 12 | 2 | 8 | 0 | 12 | 2 | 4 | 5 | 12 | 0 | 12 | 0 | 14 |
| 16-19 years | 7 | 4 | 4 | 7 | 0 | 2 | 2 | 8 | 2 | 8 | 0 | 12 | 2 | 0 | 5 | 8 | 0 | 10 | 0 | 12 |
| **Boys:** | | | | | | | | | | | | | | | | | | | | | |
| 13-15 years | 7 | 4 | 12 | 7 | 0 | 4 | 4 | 0 | 2 | 12 | 0 | 12 | 3 | 0 | 6 | 0 | 0 | 14 | 1 | 0 |
| 16-19 years | 7 | 5 | 8 | 7 | 0 | 6 | 5 | 0 | 3 | 0 | 0 | 12 | 4 | 4 | 6 | 4 | 1 | 2 | 1 | 2 |
| **Women:** | | | | | | | | | | | | | | | | | | | | | |
| 20-34 years | 3½ | 4 | 4 | 6 | 0 | 2 | 2 | 4 | 2 | 8 | 0 | 12 | 1 | 8 | 5 | 12 | 0 | 8 | 0 | 14 |
| 35-54 years | 3½ | 4 | 4 | 6 | 0 | 2 | 2 | 0 | 2 | 8 | 0 | 12 | 1 | 4 | 5 | 4 | 0 | 8 | 0 | 12 |
| 55-74 years | 3½ | 4 | 4 | 6 | 0 | 2 | 1 | 12 | 2 | 4 | 0 | 12 | 1 | 4 | 4 | 4 | 0 | 6 | 0 | 8 |
| 75 years and over | 3½ | 3 | 12 | 6 | 0 | 2 | 1 | 12 | 3 | 8 | 1 | 8 | 1 | 0 | 3 | 12 | 0 | 6 | 0 | 8 |
| Pregnant | 7 | 4 | 4 | 7 | 0 | 2 | 2 | 4 | 3 | 8 | 1 | 8 | 1 | 8 | 5 | 12 | 0 | 8 | 0 | 12 |
| Nursing | 10 | 5 | 0 | 7 | 0 | 2 | 2 | 12 | 5 | 0 | 1 | 8 | 2 | 12 | 6 | 4 | 0 | 12 | 0 | 12 |
| **Men:** | | | | | | | | | | | | | | | | | | | | | |
| 20-34 years | 3½ | 5 | 8 | 7 | 0 | 4 | 4 | 0 | 2 | 12 | 0 | 12 | 3 | 0 | 6 | 8 | 1 | 0 | 1 | 4 |
| 35-54 years | 3½ | 5 | 4 | 7 | 0 | 4 | 3 | 8 | 2 | 12 | 0 | 12 | 2 | 8 | 5 | 12 | 0 | 14 | 1 | 0 |
| 55-74 years | 3½ | 5 | 0 | 7 | 0 | 2 | 3 | 4 | 2 | 12 | 0 | 12 | 2 | 4 | 5 | 8 | 0 | 12 | 0 | 14 |
| 75 years and over | 3½ | 5 | 0 | 7 | 0 | 2 | 2 | 12 | 2 | 8 | 0 | 12 | 2 | 0 | 5 | 4 | 0 | 10 | 0 | 12 |
| **Total** | | | | | | | | | | | | | | | | | | | | | |

[1] Food as purchased or brought into the kitchen from garden or farm.

[2] Fluid, whole, or its calcium equivalent in cheese, evaporated milk, dry milk, ice cream.

[3] Bacon and salt pork should not exceed ⅓ pound for each 5 pounds of meat group.

[4] Weight in terms of flour and cereal. Count 1½ pounds bread as 1 pound flour.

## Liberal Family Food Plan

Weekly quantities of food[1] for each member of family

| Sex-age group | Milk, cheese, ice cream[2] (Qt.) | Meat, poultry, fish[3] (Lb.) | (Oz.) | Eggs (No.) | Dry beans, peas, nuts (Lb.) | (Oz.) | Flour, cereals, baked goods[4] (Lb.) | (Oz.) | Citrus fruit, tomatoes (Lb.) | (Oz.) | Dark-green and deep-yellow vegetables (Lb.) | (Oz.) | Potatoes (Lb.) | (Oz.) | Other vegetables and fruits (Lb.) | (Oz.) | Fats, oils (Lb.) | (Oz.) | Sugars, sweets (Lb.) | (Oz.) |
|---|---|---|---|---|---|---|---|---|---|---|---|---|---|---|---|---|---|---|---|---|
| **Children:** | | | | | | | | | | | | | | | | | | | | |
| 7 months to 1 year | 6 | 1 | 4 | 7 | 0 | 0 | 0 | 12 | 1 | 12 | 0 | 2 | 0 | 8 | 1 | 8 | 0 | 2 | 0 | 2 |
| 1-3 years | 6 | 2 | 4 | 7 | 0 | 1 | 1 | 0 | 1 | 12 | 0 | 4 | 0 | 12 | 2 | 12 | 0 | 4 | 0 | 4 |
| 4-6 years | 6 | 3 | 0 | 7 | 0 | 1 | 1 | 8 | 2 | 4 | 0 | 8 | 0 | 12 | 4 | 8 | 0 | 8 | 0 | 12 |
| 7-9 years | 6 | 3 | 12 | 7 | 0 | 2 | 1 | 12 | 2 | 12 | 0 | 8 | 1 | 8 | 5 | 4 | 0 | 10 | 1 | 0 |
| 10-12 years | 6½ | 4 | 12 | 7 | 0 | 4 | 2 | 12 | 3 | 0 | 0 | 12 | 2 | 4 | 6 | 0 | 0 | 10 | 1 | 0 |
| **Girls:** | | | | | | | | | | | | | | | | | | | | |
| 13-15 years | 7 | 5 | 8 | 7 | 0 | 2 | 2 | 8 | 3 | 0 | 0 | 12 | 2 | 4 | 6 | 0 | 0 | 12 | 1 | 2 |
| 16-19 years | 7 | 5 | 4 | 7 | 0 | 2 | 2 | 4 | 3 | 0 | 0 | 12 | 1 | 12 | 5 | 12 | 0 | 10 | 1 | 0 |
| **Boys:** | | | | | | | | | | | | | | | | | | | | |
| 13-15 years | 7 | 5 | 8 | 7 | 0 | 4 | 4 | 0 | 3 | 4 | 0 | 12 | 3 | 0 | 6 | 8 | 1 | 14 | 1 | 4 |
| 16-19 years | 7 | 6 | 4 | 7 | 0 | 6 | 5 | 0 | 3 | 8 | 0 | 12 | 4 | 4 | 7 | 4 | 1 | 4 | 1 | 2 |
| **Women:** | | | | | | | | | | | | | | | | | | | | |
| 20-34 years | 4 | 4 | 12 | 6 | 0 | 1 | 2 | 0 | 3 | 0 | 0 | 12 | 1 | 4 | 6 | 4 | 0 | 8 | 1 | 2 |
| 35-54 years | 4 | 4 | 12 | 6 | 0 | 1 | 1 | 12 | 3 | 0 | 0 | 12 | 1 | 0 | 6 | 0 | 0 | 8 | 1 | 0 |
| 55-74 years | 4 | 4 | 12 | 6 | 0 | 1 | 1 | 8 | 3 | 0 | 0 | 12 | 1 | 0 | 4 | 8 | 0 | 6 | 0 | 12 |
| 75 years and over | 4 | 4 | 4 | 6 | 0 | 1 | 1 | 0 | 3 | 0 | 0 | 12 | 1 | 12 | 4 | 0 | 0 | 6 | 0 | 10 |
| Pregnant | 7 | 4 | 12 | 7 | 0 | 1 | 2 | 0 | 4 | 8 | 1 | 8 | 1 | 4 | 6 | 4 | 0 | 8 | 0 | 10 |
| Nursing | 10 | 5 | 12 | 7 | 0 | 2 | 2 | 12 | 5 | 8 | 1 | 8 | 2 | 8 | 6 | 4 | 0 | 12 | 1 | 2 |
| **Men:** | | | | | | | | | | | | | | | | | | | | |
| 20-34 years | 4 | 6 | 0 | 7 | 0 | 4 | 3 | 12 | 3 | 0 | 0 | 12 | 2 | 12 | 7 | 12 | 1 | 0 | 1 | 8 |
| 35-54 years | 4 | 5 | 8 | 7 | 0 | 4 | 3 | 8 | 3 | 0 | 0 | 12 | 2 | 4 | 6 | 8 | 1 | 14 | 1 | 4 |
| 55-74 years | 4 | 5 | 4 | 7 | 0 | 2 | 3 | 4 | 3 | 0 | 0 | 12 | 2 | 0 | 6 | 0 | 0 | 12 | 1 | 2 |
| 75 years and over | 4 | 5 | 4 | 7 | 0 | 2 | 2 | 12 | 2 | 12 | 0 | 12 | 1 | 12 | 5 | 12 | 0 | 10 | 1 | 0 |
| **Total** | | | | | | | | | | | | | | | | | | | | |

[1] Food as purchased or brought into the kitchen from garden or farm.
[2] Fluid, whole, or its calcium equivalent in cheese, evaporated milk, dry milk, ice cream.
[3] Bacon and salt pork should not exceed ⅓ pound for each 5 pounds of meat group.
[4] Weight in terms of flour and cereal. Count 1½ pounds bread as 1 pound flour.

# Retail Cuts of Beef and How to Cook Them

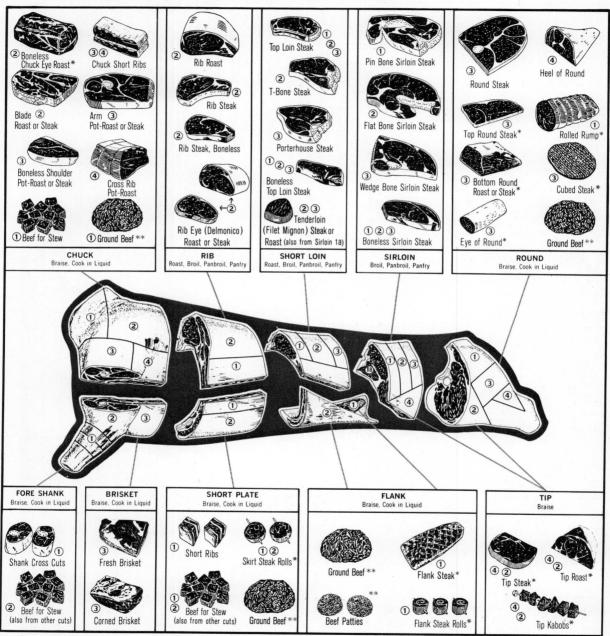

**CHUCK**
Braise, Cook in Liquid

② Boneless Chuck Eye Roast*
③④ Chuck Short Ribs
Blade ② Roast or Steak
Arm ③ Pot-Roast or Steak
③ Boneless Shoulder Pot-Roast or Steak
Cross Rib Pot-Roast
① Beef for Stew
① Ground Beef **

**RIB**
Roast, Broil, Panbroil, Panfry

② Rib Roast
② Rib Steak
② Rib Steak, Boneless
②← Rib Eye (Delmonico) Roast or Steak

**SHORT LOIN**
Roast, Broil, Panbroil, Panfry

① ② Top Loin Steak ③
② T-Bone Steak ③
③ Porterhouse Steak
① ② ③ Boneless Top Loin Steak
② ③ Tenderloin (Filet Mignon) Steak or Roast (also from Sirloin 1a)

**SIRLOIN**
Broil, Panbroil, Panfry

① Pin Bone Sirloin Steak ③
Flat Bone Sirloin Steak
Wedge Bone Sirloin Steak
① ② ③ Boneless Sirloin Steak

**ROUND**
Braise, Cook in Liquid

③ Round Steak
④ Heel of Round
③ Top Round Steak*
① Rolled Rump*
③ Bottom Round Roast or Steak*
③ Cubed Steak*
Eye of Round*
Ground Beef **

**FORE SHANK**
Braise, Cook in Liquid

① Shank Cross Cuts
② Beef for Stew (also from other cuts)

**BRISKET**
Braise, Cook in Liquid

③ Fresh Brisket
③ Corned Brisket

**SHORT PLATE**
Braise, Cook in Liquid

① Short Ribs
① ② Skirt Steak Rolls*
① ② Beef for Stew (also from other cuts)
Ground Beef **

**FLANK**
Braise, Cook in Liquid

Ground Beef **
① Flank Steak*
Beef Patties **
① Flank Steak Rolls*

**TIP**
Braise

④ ② Tip Steak*
④ ② Tip Roast*
④ ② Tip Kabobs*

*May be Roasted, Broiled, Panbroiled or Panfried from high quality beef.    **May be Roasted, (Baked), Broiled, Panbroiled or Panfried.

# Retail Cuts of Veal and How to Cook Them

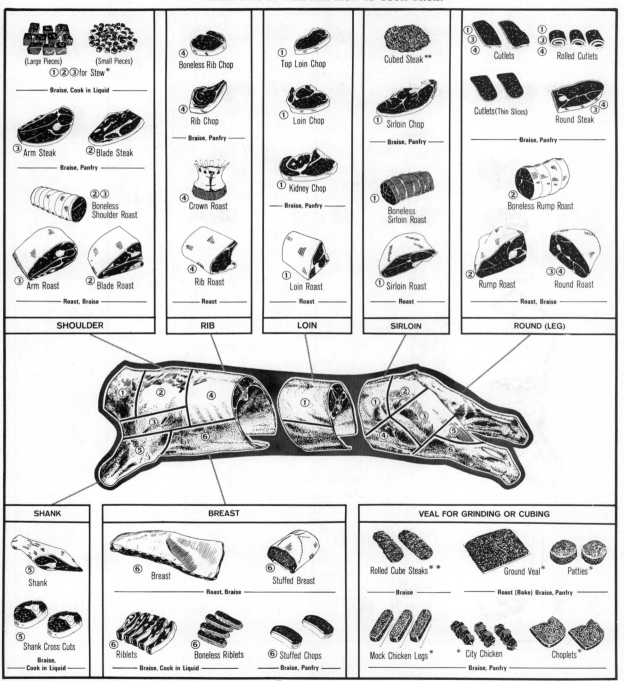

**SHOULDER**

(Large Pieces)    (Small Pieces)
①②③for Stew*
— Braise, Cook in Liquid —
③ Arm Steak    ② Blade Steak
— Braise, Panfry —
②③ Boneless Shoulder Roast
③ Arm Roast    ② Blade Roast
— Roast, Braise —

**RIB**

④ Boneless Rib Chop
④ Rib Chop
— Braise, Panfry —
④ Crown Roast
④ Rib Roast
— Roast —

**LOIN**

① Top Loin Chop
① Loin Chop
① Kidney Chop
— Braise, Panfry —
① Loin Roast
— Roast —

**SIRLOIN**

Cubed Steak**
① Sirloin Chop
— Braise, Panfry —
① Boneless Sirloin Roast
① Sirloin Roast
— Roast —

**ROUND (LEG)**

①③④ Cutlets    ①③④ Rolled Cutlets
Cutlets (Thin Slices)    ③④ Round Steak
— Braise, Panfry —
② Boneless Rump Roast
② Rump Roast    ③④ Round Roast
— Roast, Braise —

**SHANK**

⑤ Shank
⑤ Shank Cross Cuts
— Braise, Cook in Liquid —

**BREAST**

⑥ Breast    ⑥ Stuffed Breast
— Roast, Braise —
⑥ Riblets    ⑥ Boneless Riblets    ⑥ Stuffed Chops
— Braise, Cook in Liquid —    — Braise, Panfry —

**VEAL FOR GRINDING OR CUBING**

Rolled Cube Steaks**    Ground Veal*    Patties*
— Braise —    — Roast (Bake) Braise, Panfry —
Mock Chicken Legs*    * City Chicken    Choplets*
— Braise, Panfry —

*Veal for stew or grinding may be made from any cut.    **Cube steaks may be made from any thick solid piece of boneless veal.

309

# Retail Cuts of Pork and How to Cook Them

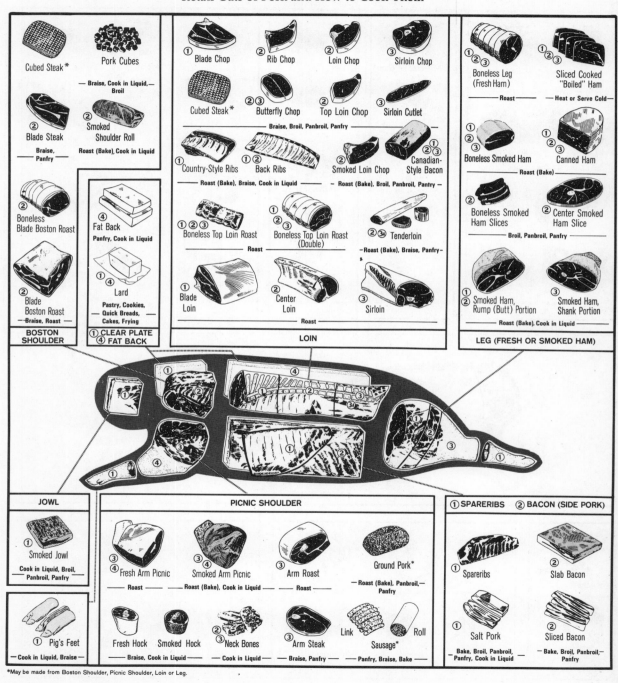

**BOSTON SHOULDER**

Cubed Steak*

Pork Cubes
— Braise, Cook in Liquid, —
Broil

② Blade Steak
**Braise,
Panfry**

② Smoked
Shoulder Roll
**Roast (Bake), Cook in Liquid**

② Boneless
Blade Boston Roast

② Blade
Boston Roast
— **Braise, Roast** —

① CLEAR PLATE
④ FAT BACK

④ Fat Back
**Panfry, Cook in Liquid**

① ④ Lard
**Pastry, Cookies,
Quick Breads,
Cakes, Frying**

**LOIN**

① Blade Chop

② Rib Chop

② Loin Chop

③ Sirloin Chop

② ③ Cubed Steak*

② ③ Butterfly Chop

② ③ Top Loin Chop

③ Sirloin Cutlet

— **Braise, Broil, Panbroil, Panfry** —

① Country-Style Ribs

① ② Back Ribs

② Smoked Loin Chop

① ③ Canadian-Style Bacon

— **Roast (Bake), Braise, Cook in Liquid** —   — **Roast (Bake), Broil, Panbroil, Pantry** —

① ② Boneless Top Loin Roast

① ② ③ Boneless Top Loin Roast (Double)

② ③④ Tenderloin

— **Roast** —   — **Roast (Bake), Braise, Panfry** —

① Blade Loin

② Center Loin

③ Sirloin

— **Roast** —

**LEG (FRESH OR SMOKED HAM)**

① ② ③ Boneless Leg (Fresh Ham)

① ② ③ Sliced Cooked "Boiled" Ham

— **Roast** —   — **Heat or Serve Cold** —

① ② ③ Boneless Smoked Ham

① ② ③ Canned Ham

— **Roast (Bake)** —

① ② Boneless Smoked Ham Slices

② Center Smoked Ham Slice

— **Broil, Panbroil, Panfry** —

① ② Smoked Ham, Rump (Butt) Portion

③ Smoked Ham, Shank Portion

— **Roast (Bake), Cook in Liquid** —

**JOWL**

① Smoked Jowl
**Cook in Liquid, Broil,
Panbroil, Panfry**

① Pig's Feet
— **Cook in Liquid, Braise** —

**PICNIC SHOULDER**

③ ④ Fresh Arm Picnic

③ ④ Smoked Arm Picnic

③ Arm Roast

Ground Pork*

— **Roast** —   — **Roast (Bake), Cook in Liquid** —   — **Roast** —   — **Roast (Bake), Panbroil,** —
**Panfry**

Fresh Hock   Smoked Hock

② ③ Neck Bones

③ Arm Steak

Link   Roll
Sausage*

— **Braise, Cook in Liquid** —   — **Cook in Liquid** —   — **Braise, Panfry** —   — **Panfry, Braise, Bake** —

① SPARERIBS   ② BACON (SIDE PORK)

① Spareribs

Slab Bacon

① Salt Pork

② Sliced Bacon

— **Bake, Broil, Panbroil,**
**Panfry, Cook in Liquid** —   — **Bake, Broil, Panbroil,**
**Panfry** —

*May be made from Boston Shoulder, Picnic Shoulder, Loin or Leg.

# Retail Cuts of Lamb and How to Cook Them

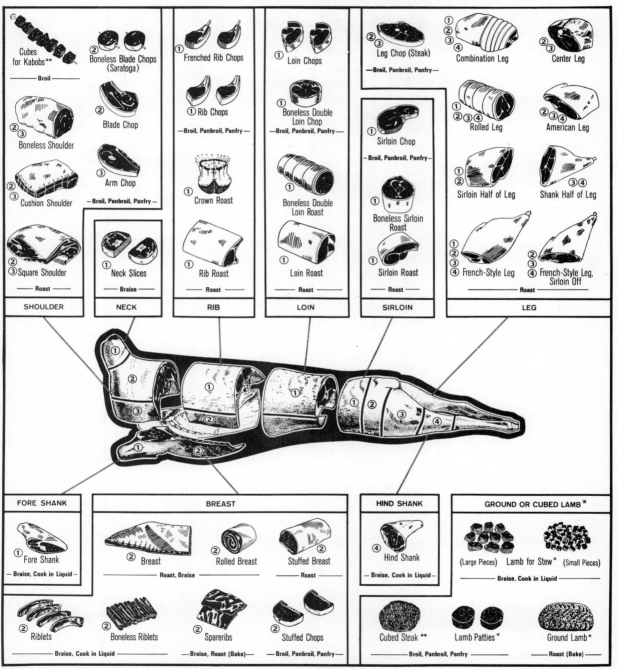

**SHOULDER**

Cubes for Kabobs**
— Broil —

② Boneless Blade Chops (Saratoga)

② Blade Chop

③ Arm Chop
— Broil, Panbroil, Panfry —

② Boneless Shoulder

②③ Cushion Shoulder

②③ Square Shoulder
— Roast —

**NECK**

① Neck Slices
— Braise —

**RIB**

① Frenched Rib Chops

① Rib Chops
— Broil, Panbroil, Panfry —

① Crown Roast

① Rib Roast
— Roast —

**LOIN**

① Loin Chops

① Boneless Double Loin Chop
— Broil, Panbroil, Panfry —

① Boneless Double Loin Roast

① Loin Roast
— Roast —

**SIRLOIN**

②③ Leg Chop (Steak)
— Broil, Panbroil, Panfry —

① Sirloin Chop
— Broil, Panbroil, Panfry —

① Boneless Sirloin Roast

① Sirloin Roast
— Roast —

**LEG**

②③ Combination Leg

②③ Center Leg

①②③④ Rolled Leg

②③④ American Leg

①② Sirloin Half of Leg

③④ Shank Half of Leg

①②③④ French-Style Leg

①②③④ French-Style Leg, Sirloin Off
— Roast —

**FORE SHANK**

① Fore Shank
— Braise, Cook in Liquid —

② Riblets
— Braise, Cook in Liquid —

**BREAST**

② Breast

② Rolled Breast

② Stuffed Breast
— Roast, Braise —     — Roast —

② Boneless Riblets

② Spareribs
— Braise, Roast (Bake) —

② Stuffed Chops
— Broil, Panbroil, Panfry —

**HIND SHANK**

④ Hind Shank
— Braise, Cook in Liquid —

Cubed Steak **
— Broil, Panbroil, Panfry —

Lamb Patties *

**GROUND OR CUBED LAMB***

(Large Pieces) Lamb for Stew* (Small Pieces)
— Braise, Cook in Liquid —

Ground Lamb *
— Roast (Bake) —

* Lamb for stew or grinding may be made from any cut.    **Kabobs or cube steaks may be made from any thick solid piece of boneless Lamb.

# Weights and Measures

### Linear Measure

| | |
|---|---|
| 12 inches | = 1 foot |
| 3 feet | = 1 yard = 36 inches |
| 5½ yards | = 1 rod = 16½ feet |
| 40 rods | = 1 furlong = 660 feet |
| 8 furlongs | = 1 mile = 5,280 feet |
| 3 miles | = 1 league = 15,840 feet |
| 6,080.20 feet | = 1 nautical, or sea mile |

### Area Measure

| | |
|---|---|
| 144 square inches | = 1 square foot |
| 9 square feet | = 1 square yard |
| 30¼ square yards | = 1 square rod |
| 160 square rods | = 1 acre |
| 640 acres | = 1 square mile |
| 1 mile square | = 1 section |
| 6 miles square | = 1 township |

### Cubic Measure

| | |
|---|---|
| 1,728 cubic inches | = 1 cubic foot |
| 27 cubic feet | = 1 cubic yard |

### Apothecaries' Measure

| | |
|---|---|
| 60 minims | = 1 fluid dram |
| 8 fluid drams | = 1 fluid ounce |
| 16 fluid ounces | = 1 pint |
| 2 pints | = 1 quart |
| 4 quarts | = 1 gallon |

### Surveyors' Measure

| | |
|---|---|
| 7.92 inches | = 1 link |
| 100 links | = 1 chain = 4 rods = 66 feet |
| 80 chains | = 1 statute mile = 320 rods = 5,280 feet |

### Avoirdupois Weight

| | |
|---|---|
| 27¹¹/₃₂ grains | = 1 dram |
| 16 drams | = 1 ounce |
| 16 ounces | = 1 pound |
| 100 pounds | = 1 short hundredweight |
| 20 hundredweights | = 1 short ton = 2,000 pounds |
| 112 pounds | = 1 long hundredweight |
| 20 long hundredweights | = 1 long ton = 2,240 pounds |

### Liquid Measure

| | |
|---|---|
| 4 gills | = 1 pint |
| 2 pints | = 1 quart |
| 4 quarts | = 1 gallon |

### Dry Measure

| | |
|---|---|
| 2 pints | = 1 quart |
| 8 quarts | = 1 peck |
| 4 pecks | = 1 bushel |

## Metric System

### Linear Measure

| | |
|---|---|
| 10 millimeters | = 1 centimeter |
| 10 centimeters | = 1 decimeter |
| 10 decimeters | = 1 meter |
| 10 meters | = 1 dekameter |
| 10 dekameters | = 1 hectometer |
| 10 hectometers | = 1 kilometer |

### Weight

| | | | |
|---|---|---|---|
| 10 milligrams | = 1 centigram | 10 grams | = 1 dekagram |
| 10 centigrams | = 1 decigram | 10 dekagrams | = 1 hectogram |
| 10 decigrams | = 1 gram | 10 hectograms | = 1 kilogram |
| | | 1,000 kilograms | = 1 metric ton |

### Cubic Measure

| | |
|---|---|
| 1,000 cubic millimeters | = 1 cubic centimeter |
| 1,000 cubic centimeters | = 1 cubic decimeter |
| 1,000 cubic decimeters | = 1 cubic meter |

### Volume Measure

| | |
|---|---|
| 10 milliliters | = 1 centiliter |
| 10 centiliters | = 1 deciliter |
| 10 deciliters | = 1 liter |
| 10 liters | = 1 dekaliter |
| 10 dekaliters | = 1 hectoliter |
| 10 hectoliters | = 1 kiloliter |

### Equivalents

| | |
|---|---|
| 1 centimeter | = 0.3937 inch |
| 1 fathom | = 1.829 meters |
| 1 foot | = 0.305 meter |
| 1 hand | = 4 inches |
| 1 inch | = 2.540 centimeters |
| 1 kilometer | = 0.621 mile |
| 1 meter | = 39.37 inches |
| 1 mile (land) | = 1.609 kilometers |
| 1 mile (sea) | = 1.853 kilometers |
| 1 acre | = 4,840 square yards |
| 1 cord (firewood) | = 128 cubic feet |
| 1 liter | = 1.057 liquid quarts |
| 1 pint, dry | = 0.551 liter |
| 1 pint, liquid | = 0.473 liter |
| 1 gram | = 0.035 ounce, avoirdupois |
| 1 kilogram | = 2.205 pounds |
| 1 ounce | = 28.350 grams |
| 1 pound, avoirdupois | = 453.592 grams |

# Index